Velázquez in Seville

SPONSORED BY

DAVID DAVIES · ENRIQUETA HARRIS

EDITED BY MICHAEL CLARKE

WITH CONTRIBUTIONS FROM

PETER CHERRY · RONALD CUETO

JOHN H. ELLIOTT · GABRIELE FINALDI

VICENTE LLEÓ CAÑAL · ENRIQUE PAREJA LÓPEZ

JUAN MIGUEL SERRERA · MARJORIE TRUSTED

ENRIQUE VALDIVIESO · ZAHIRA VELIZ

AIDAN WESTON-LEWIS

JAMES YORKE

VELÁZQUEZ
IN SEVILLE

NATIONAL GALLERY OF SCOTLAND
MCMXCVI

Published by the Trustees of the
National Galleries of Scotland for the exhibition at the
National Gallery of Scotland, Edinburgh · 8 August – 20 October 1996
Text © the Trustees of the National Galleries of Scotland

Library of Congress Catalogue Card Number 96–60915
A catalogue record for this book is available from the British Library
HARDBACK ISBN 0 300 06949 9
Hardback edition distributed by Yale University Press
PAPERBACK ISBN 0 903598 62 0

Front cover:
The Waterseller of Seville
[cat 31]

Back cover:
An Old Woman Cooking Eggs
[cat 16]

Designed and typeset by Dalrymple
Printed by BAS Printers Limited, Over Wallop

This book is set in Monotype Columbus, a typeface designed by Patricia Saunders in 1992,
based on sixteenth-century Spanish models. The roman type is adapted from the edition of Virgil's
Opera Omnia printed by Jorge Coci in Saragossa in 1513; the italic and the ornaments derive from
Recopilacion subtilissima intitulada Orthographica practica printed by Bartolomé de Najéra
in Saragossa in 1548. The display typeface is Enschedé Trinité,
designed by Bram de Does in 1982.

Lenders

Barcelona
Museu Nacional d'Art de Catalunya
Art Hispania, s.a. (Carlos Ferrer)

Boston
Museum of Fine Arts

Budapest
Szépmüvészeti Múzeum

Chicago
The Art Institute

Dublin
National Gallery of Ireland

Durham
Ushaw College

Edinburgh
National Gallery of Scotland

Granada
Museo de Bellas Artes

London

The British Library
Trustees of The British Museum
Trustees of The National Gallery
Trustees of the Victoria and Albert Museum

Madrid
Biblioteca Nacional
Museo del Prado
Patrimonio Nacional, Biblioteca del Palacio Real

Orléans
Musée des Beaux-Arts

Oxford
Christ Church Picture Gallery

St Petersburg
The Hermitage Museum

Seville
Arzobispado de Sevilla
Church of the Annunciation, Seville University
Museo de Bellas Artes
Excmo. Ayuntamiento de Sevilla

Strasbourg
Musée des Beaux-Arts

Valladolid
English College

Private Collections
Juan Abello
Teresa Heinz
Viscount Windsor
and lenders who wish to remain anonymous

Foreword

IT IS AXIOMATIC of an enterprise such as *Velázquez in Seville* that the National Gallery of Scotland is indebted to many individuals and institutions. First of all, we thank and acknowledge David Davies, University College, London, who, in collaboration with Enriqueta Harris Frankfort, Honorary Fellow of the Warburg Institute, and Michael Clarke, the Keeper of the Gallery, has curated this exhibition. It is based on the Gallery's own celebrated Velázquez – *An Old Woman Cooking Eggs*. That we have been able to develop our project so fully testifies to the respect in which Enriqueta Harris, *doyenne* of Velázquez scholars, is held by those who love and admire Spanish art. We are also delighted that so many other distinguished scholars and curators have contributed essays and entries to the catalogue. Translations from Spanish into English have kindly been undertaken by María Inés Finaldi.

Given the relatively small size of Velázquez's Sevillian oeuvre, it was imperative that we secured wholehearted co-operation from owners, both public and private. This, almost without exception, we have done, and we are particularly grateful to the authorities in London, Madrid, and Seville who, as the list of lenders reveals, have been especially generous.

We are most indebted to Soledad Becerril Bustamante, Mayoress of Seville, for her unswerving support. Enrique Pareja López, Director of the Museo de Bellas Artes, Seville, was unfailingly helpful and offered much sound advice. At Seville University the Vicerectora, Piedad Bolaños Donoso, generously agreed to lend the University's sculpture by Martínez Montañés and Professors Vicente Lleó Cañal, Juan Miguel Serrera and Enrique Valdivieso all offered expert assistance and made important contributions to the catalogue. We especially wish to acknowledge the sympathetic hearing we received from the Vicar-general of the Cathedral, Rev. F. Antonio Domínguez Valverde. In Madrid, our primary debt of gratitude is, of course, to the Prado Museum which has most generously lent all its Sevillian paintings by Velázquez. We acknowledge the support of the Director, Fernando Checa, and the untiring efforts of Manuela Mena Marqués, who has assisted our exhibition in countless ways. Our negotiations in Seville and Madrid were aided immeasurably by the participation and presence of Enriqueta Harris and Ronald Cueto. Requests for loans elsewhere in Spain have also met with success and we thank:

Juan Abello, Emilia Aglio Mayor, His Grace Carlos Amigo Vallejo, Alejandro Fernández de Araoz y Marañón, Carmen Araoz de Urquijo, István Barkóczi, Santiago Alcoba Blanch, Dolores de Araoz y Marañón, Paz Cabello, Eduard Carbonell i Esteller, José Contreras Rodríguez-Jurado, María Margharita Cuyás, Antonio Fernández Estévez, Carlos Ferrer, Concepción García Saiz, José Luis García García, F. Juan Manuel García Junco, Ludmila Kagané, Felipe Vicente Garín Llombart, Carlos Gollonet Carnicero, Manuel Garrido Orta, Román Ledesma Rodríguez, Maria Luisa López-Vidriero, José Maria Luzón Nogué, Juan Carlos de la Mata González, Juan Ramón Medina Precioso,

Monsignor Francisco Navarro, Francisco Ortiz Ortega, Elena Páez Ríos, Antonio Ruiz Bassols, Araceli Sánchez Piñol, Elena Santiago, and Enriqueta Vila Vilar.

The Cultural Counsellor of the Spanish Embassy in London, Dámaso de Lario, was unfailingly helpful, and we are also grateful to His Excellency Alberto Aza, the Spanish Ambassador to the Court of St James, and His Excellency A. D. Brighty, British Ambassador in Spain, for their assistance.

In London we are especially indebted to the National Gallery and its Director, Neil MacGregor, and its Curator of Spanish Painting, Gabriele Finaldi. The Wellington Museum, under the care of the Victoria and Albert Museum, has been equally generous and we thank Alan Borg, Director, and John Murdoch, formerly Assistant Director and now Director of the Courtauld Institute Galleries.

In respect of loans from other collections we particularly acknowledge: Giacomo Algranti, Robert Anderson, Peter Barber, James Hunter Blair, Patrick Hunter Blair, Hilary Bracegirdle, Tony Campbell, Douglas Druick, David Ekserdjian, Ildikó Ember, Jean-Louis Faure, Larry Feinberg, Carlos Gollonet, Antony Griffiths, Teresa Heinz, Raymond Keaveney, Eric Moinet, Miklós Mojzer, Lady Elisabeth Moyne, Tessa Murdoch, Nicholas Penny, Mikhail Piotrovsky, Rodolphe Rapetti, Janice Reading, Sue W. Reed, Malcolm Rogers, R. B. Rutherford, Peter Seed, George Shackelford, Mgr. Paul F. Smith, Peter Sutton, Lucy Whitaker, Viscount Windsor, Martha Wolff, James Wood, Eric M. Zafran.

At the National Galleries of Scotland the exhibition benefited greatly, during its later stages, from the participation of Aidan Weston-Lewis, Assistant Keeper at the National Gallery. Janis Adams oversaw the difficult task of seeing the catalogue to press, and was ably assisted by Victoria Keller. Sheila Scott, Secretary to the Keeper, cheerfully coped with the vast amounts of typing and the challenging manner in which the project developed. Kathryn O'Dowd of the Education Department kindly assisted with translations. Margaret Mackay, Assistant Registrar ensured with her customary efficiency and ingenuity that all the loans arrived in Edinburgh. We would particularly like to acknowledge the assistance of the Spanish firm SIT Transportes Internacionales, S.A. Both the Registrar's and Conservation Departments have worked hard on the installation of the exhibition and the Keeper of Conservation, John Dick, has overseen remedial treatment for the Roelas altarpiece borrowed from Ushaw. The catalogue has been designed by Robert Dalrymple. Installation work has been overseen by Jim Wheeler of the Building Department.

Finally, and most importantly, we pay tribute to our sponsors, the Banco Santander and The Royal Bank of Scotland, without whose enlightened patronage the exhibition would have been impossible. Appropriately, this is a Spanish-Scottish alliance, mirroring the whole spirit of the exhibition. We record our particular thanks to the respective Chairmen, Emilio Botín and Lord Younger of Prestwick. The initial approach to the sponsors came about through the good offices of the Chairman of the Trustees of the National Galleries of Scotland, Angus Grossart.

TIMOTHY CLIFFORD
Director, National Galleries of Scotland

8

Sponsors' Foreword

VELÁZQUEZ: PORTRAIT OF THE GENIUS
AS A YOUNG MAN

WE AT The Royal Bank of Scotland and Banco Santander are delighted to help bring together in Edinburgh this fascinating array of paintings. It is one of the many and varied fruits of our seven-year alliance and will, we are sure, provide an unforgettable experience for many thousands of visitors. Banco Santander's support is naturally concentrated in Spain but it has been keen to sponsor Spanish events in London and in Edinburgh, notably combining with the Royal Bank to introduce *zarzuela*, that uniquely Spanish musical experience, to the Edinburgh International Festival in 1989.

Both banks are enthusiastic and long-standing supporters of the arts. We have, however, never been able to decide which is the more effective – the immediacy of a performance or the more thoughtful response created by a well assembled exhibition.

Our answer is to support both equally. If the opera house, theatre and concert hall have provided us with many memorable evenings, the galleries have been no less effective in linking our name with enjoyment, enlightenment and excellence.

The Royal Bank, for example, has supported a wide range of exhibitions over the years, focusing on individual artists such as Camille Pissarro, Alfred Munnings, René Lalique and L. S. Lowry, or exploring themes such as Impressionist drawings, the link between patrons and painters in seventeenth- and eighteenth-century Scotland, Children and Childhood in British art and the Japanese craft art of Mingei.

None can be more exciting and magnificent than this exhibition of the youthful works of one of the world's great artists. We are given this unique opportunity to see the genius of Velázquez in his late teens and early twenties, before he moved to Madrid, before he met and talked with Rubens, before he travelled to Rome to study the works of the great masters, and before he became royal painter at the court of one of the great world powers of the day.

LORD YOUNGER OF PRESTWICK
Chairman, The Royal Bank of Scotland

DON EMILIO BOTÍN RIOS
Chairman, Banco Santander

Acknowledgements

THE IDEA FOR an exhibition centred on Velázquez's *An Old Woman Cooking Eggs* was first proposed by Timothy Clifford, the Director of the National Galleries of Scotland, at the opening of the exhibition *Palaces of Art* in Dulwich Picture Gallery in November 1991. It was immensely gratifying to be invited to curate the exhibition.

To ensure its success, Michael Clarke, the Keeper of the National Gallery of Scotland, has given unstinted support. He has shouldered the responsibility for the organisation of the exhibition. Furthermore, he has always responded positively to my desire to examine Velázquez's oeuvre in context in order to appreciate its function, estimate its meaning for a seventeenth-century Sevillian audience, and assess the painter's achievement. To this end, Michael Clarke's open-mindedness, acumen and enthusiasm have been invaluable. It has been a pleasure to work with him.

In curating the exhibition, the collaboration of Enriqueta Harris has been of inestimable benefit. To have worked with a scholar of her standing – the internationally acclaimed authority on Velázquez – has been a rare privilege. Her scrupulous treatment of evidence, her wise judgements, and her incisive and pithy comments have served as an exemplary model. Neither fact nor sentiment are compromised or fudged – her passion for Velázquez is plain to understand. Indeed, it is due to her reputation and participation that there are more early paintings by Velázquez on show here than have ever been assembled since he left Seville in 1623. To negotiate important loans she valiantly accompanied Michael Clarke and me to Madrid and Seville in 1993. The support of Manuela Mena Marqués of the Prado was crucial to our success. To secure the Sevillian loans, especially the polychrome sculptures of Martínez Montañés that were in churches, the mediation of Dámaso de Lario was of signal importance. In this connection, the eminent historian Ronald Cueto accompanied us on a second visit to Seville in 1996. With indefatigable zeal and unrivalled knowledge of convents, cloisters and chapters, he enabled us to conclude successfully the complex negotiations for these loans.

To complement the exhibition of Velázquez's paintings in relation to these other images, the other essayists and compilers were invited to examine the related political, social, religious, cultural, artistic and technical contexts of Velázquez's work. I am delighted that such distinguished scholars as Peter Cherry, Ronald Cueto, Sir John Elliott, Gabriele Finaldi, Enriqueta Harris, Vicente Lleó Cañal, Enrique Pareja López, Juan Miguel Serrera, Marjorie Trusted, Enrique Valdivieso, Zahira Veliz, Aidan Weston-Lewis and James Yorke have responded so enthusiastically and thereby enabled the reader to gain a fuller understanding of Velázquez's Sevillian oeuvre.

For the inspiring classes on Velázquez given by Philip Troutman, my teacher of long ago, and the critical observations of my clever students, I am also deeply grateful. It has been of benefit, too, to have been released from administrative duties during this academic year, for which I thank Professor David Bindman.

Finally, both Enriqueta Harris and I wish to express our gratitude to the following for their invaluable help: Santiago Alcolea Blanch, Peter Barber, István Barkóczi, Jeannine Baticle, José Buces Aguado, Ronald Cueto, Gabriele Finaldi, Charles Ford, Ángel García Gómez, Carmen Garrido Pérez, Matilde Gladstone, Nigel Glendinning, Marianna Haraszti-Takács, Paula Jojima, Ludmila Kagané, Vicente Lleó Cañal, Rosemarie Mulcahy, Sor Beatriz Navarro, Pilar de Navascués, Enrique Pareja López, Ann Rees, Paloma Renard, Claudie Ressort, Martin Royalton-Kisch, Sheila Scott, Juan Miguel Serrera, John Sunderland, Enrique Valdivieso, Jesusa Vega, Juliet Wilson-Bareau, Enriqueta Vila Vilar, F. Michael Williams, Martha Wolff, Michael Woods, Martin Wyld and Frank Zuccari.

DAVID DAVIES
University College, London

INTRODUCTION

IEGO VELÁZQUEZ (1599–1660) was one of the most subtle and visually intelligent of all painters. The silvery, shimmering light, the deceptively fluid brushwork, and the optical and psychological complexities of his great masterpiece *Las Meninas* (completed in 1656 and now in the Prado) can at first sight appear worlds away from the stark realism of the early works he produced in Seville. Yet before he left his native city in 1623 for Madrid, where he would be appointed painter to King Philip IV of Spain, Velázquez had already produced a body of work that dramatically revealed his prodigious talent.

Nearly all of his Sevillian paintings are included in this exhibition, together with relevant works by his contemporaries. The beginnings of a great artist are not always easy to examine, but fortunately with Velázquez there are sufficient examples surviving for the task to be feasible. There are some problems of attribution, of course, and many more of meaning. Just as *Las Meninas* has still not given up all its secrets, so there remain fascinating questions to be asked of Velázquez's formative years in Seville.

We have divided the introductory section into two parts. The first deals primarily with Seville and its political, social, cultural and religious history. The second is centred on Velázquez himself and begins with an examination of the paintings of his immediate predecessors and contemporaries. Then follow essays on his religious paintings and his kitchen-scenes (*bodegones*); on studio practice and artistic training in Seville; on the question of Velázquez's possible use of studio assistants; and finally aspects of his early painting technique are analysed.

The essays, by a number of distinguished scholars, inevitably overlap on some points. They also contain differing interpretations of certain subjects. Their variety, however, seems wholly appropriate, given the richness of the terrain they are covering. Velázquez and Seville.individually merit exhibitions, let alone together!

Our point of departure is Velázquez's *An Old Woman Cooking Eggs* [cat 16] of 1618. It has been in the National Gallery of Scotland since 1955 and it has provided the impetus for us to reunite it with other masterpieces of that period. But Scotland can lay further claim to providing a justifiable venue for such a prestigious exhibition, because Scots have played a major role in the history of the 'rediscovery' of Spanish painting.

For political and geographical reasons, Spain was somewhat isolated from the main body of Europe from the latter part of the seventeenth century until the later years of the eighteenth. Indeed, Voltaire wrote in 1760 that it was 'a country we know no better than the wildest parts of Africa and which does not merit being better known.' The enlightened attitude of Charles III (reigned 1759–88) helped to bring Spain back into the European mainstream, and in the years following the Peninsular War collectors rapidly began to acquire, often at very modest prices, masterpieces by Zurbarán, Velázquez and Murillo. A grateful Spanish government allowed the victorious Duke of Wellington to keep *The Waterseller* [cat 31], captured from Joseph Bonaparte

at the Battle of Vitoria in 1813. It is salutary to note, however, that the early catalogues of the Louvre listed Velázquez as 'Italian School', such was the paucity of knowledge of Spanish painting at that time.

By the early years of the nineteenth century many masterpieces by Velázquez, particularly those of his Sevillian years, had already left Spain. When the Scottish painter David Wilkie (1785–1841) visited Seville in 1828 he wrote back to his friend Prince Dolgorouki, who was attached to the Russian legation at Madrid:

Of the former [Velázquez] I am disappointed to find here scarce any example; the reputation of being the city of his nativity is all that remains of him at Seville.

Early departures had included the *Tavern Scene with Two Men and a Boy* [cat 26] and the *Head of a Young Man* [cat 27] which were in the Hermitage, St Petersburg by 1797 and 1814 respectively; *An Old Woman Cooking Eggs*, possibly imported from Spain by the dealer Lebrun and recorded in the John Woollett sale in London in May 1813; and *The Virgin of the Immaculate Conception* and the *St John the Evangelist on Patmos* [cats 33 and 34] which were sold from the Seville collection of Manuel López Cepero in 1809 and by 1813 belonged to Bartholomew Frere, who had been British Plenipotentiary Minister *ad interim* in Seville in 1809–10.

In spite of such absences, the Scottish landscape painter David Roberts (1796–1864), who spent the summer of 1833 in Seville, reported that 'the churches abound with the finest specimens of Murillo and Velázquez, and the works of other glorious masters whose productions are almost unknown in England'. But, whereas there certainly were many works by the prolific Murillo still *in situ*, Roberts's enumeration of Velázquez must have been based on ignorance and enthusiasm as opposed to hard fact. A more accurate assessment came from the pen of Richard Ford (1796–1858), author of the definitive early guide-book to Spain *A Hand-Book for Travellers in Spain and Readers at Home*, first published in 1845. He had spent three winters in Seville in the early 1830s on account of his wife's delicate health. However, in his evaluation of the contents of the 'Museo' (the Prado) in Madrid he makes it very clear that the capital is the only place in which to see Velázquez: 'The grand masters to observe are Raphael, Titian, Murillo and still more Velazquez, as the three former may be comprehended equally well at Rome, Hampton Court, Venice and Seville; but Madrid is the only home of the mighty Andalucian, for here is almost his entire work.' Ford makes only the briefest of mentions of Velázquez's 'hard early style, before he was emancipated from the prevalent Ribera peculiarities'.

Ford's friend and art-historical counterpart was the Scot, Sir William Stirling-Maxwell of Keir Bt. (1818–1878), whose *Annals of the Artists of Spain* first appeared in 1848. His chapter on Velázquez was separately re-written and published in 1855, with German and French translations following in 1856 and 1865 respectively. Stirling-Maxwell's discussion of Velázquez's early career is relatively brief, and his understandable reliance on earlier published sources such as Palomino and Pacheco led to his account being more informative on Velázquez's intellectual and artistic education rather than a discussion of the early work.

The next English-language study of Velázquez was also written by a Scot, R. A. M. ('Bob') Stevenson (1847–1900), cousin and friend of the novelist Robert Louis Stevenson. His book, *Velázquez*, was published in 1895 and was more a critical appraisal than a factual biography. As such it was inevitably coloured by Stevenson's own predilections. A former pupil in Paris of Carolus-Duran, an enthusiastic advocate of Corot and the Barbizon School, Stevenson was an admirer of the 'apparent artlessness' of Velázquez's technique which he claimed justified him being considered the first 'Impressionist'. Of the 'realistic' early works, which he significantly referred to as 'pre-Italian' rather than 'Sevillian', Stevenson wrote:

His [Velázquez's] early pictures cannot be attached to any school; they are of doubtful parentage, though, with some truth, one might affiliate them to Caravaggio and the Italian naturalists. From the first he shows sensitiveness to form, and a taste for solid and direct painting. He quickly learnt to model with surprising justness, but for a long time he continued to treat a head in a group as he would if he saw it alone.

Stevenson's actual experience of Velázquez was limited to a relatively brief visit to the Prado. It was the mature work he admired above all. However, from the point of view of form rather than content, his remarks on the early paintings are not without merit. Yet for many Victorians, Seville was both 'picturesque', as evidenced in the watercolours and prints of David Roberts and the English artist John Frederick Lewis, and 'operatic' as portrayed through the productions of Mozart, Rossini and Bizet. This entertaining and anecdotal approach underlies pictures such as the Scottish artist John Phillip's *La Gloria, A Spanish Wake*, commenced in Seville in 1860 and exhibited at the Royal Academy in 1864. Acquired by the National Gallery of Scotland in 1897 for 5000 guineas, it was one of its most expensive early purchases. Technically, it is a most assured piece of work and indulges the popular taste for 'pictures with stories'. As an image, of course, it does not possess the enigmatic profundity achieved by the young Velázquez, the many-layered complexities of which are examined in our exhibition.

MICHAEL CLARKE
Keeper, National Gallery of Scotland

John Phillip 1817–1867 *La Gloria, A Spanish Wake* (National Gallery of Scotland, Edinburgh)

Velázquez in Seville · I
SEVILLE

John H. Elliott

THE SEVILLE OF VELÁZQUEZ

I N 1599, the year of Velázquez's birth, Seville was one of the largest and most cosmopolitan cities of contemporary Europe [fig 1.1]. With a population approaching 150,000, at least before it was struck by the plague which descended from northern Spain during the summer of that same year, it was more populous than London, Lisbon or Rome. Madrid, the effective capital of Spain since 1561, was only then approaching the 100,000 mark. Of all the cities of late sixteenth-century Europe, only Paris and Naples, each with a population of around 200,000, were significantly larger.[1]

This great metropolis, still encircled in the sixteenth century by its Moorish walls, was situated on the left bank of the River Guadalquivir, fifty-four miles inland from the sea. The Guadalquivir could be treacherous – it overflowed its banks in 1604 and again in 1608 and there was to be a devastating flood in 1626. Navigation, too, was difficult, and the notorious sand bar at San Lúcar de Barrameda prevented large galleons from sailing any further upstream. This barrier effectively turned San Lúcar, the administrative centre of the vast estates of the Dukes of Medina Sidonia, into the city's ocean-going port. But Seville combined relatively easy access to the sea with the role of marketing and regional centre for the agricultural products – wine, olive oil and grain – of the fertile plain of Andalusia. This combination gave it the edge over its rival, Cadiz, in the competition to become the commercial capital of the sixteenth-century Atlantic world.

It was Columbus's successful navigation of the Atlantic, and Spain's subsequent acquisition of its 'empire of the Indies', which gave Seville, a city already steeped in history, its spectacular new role on the world stage. The Roman colony of Hispalis – founded, it was said, by Hercules himself – soon outpaced the nearby settle-

ment of Itálica, whose archaeological remains were to excite the curiosity, and enhance the local pride, of sixteenth-century Sevillian antiquaries. The coming of Christianity gave Seville a cluster of saints: two early bishops, Leander and his learned brother Isidore, the Visigothic prince Hermenegild, and the virgin martyrs Justa and Rufina, who were to be depicted by Murillo and other seventeenth-century artists holding aloft between them the famous tower of the Giralda [fig 1.2], which their intervention allegedly saved from collapse in the earthquake of 1504.

It was during the centuries of Moorish occupation, ending with the Christian reconquest in 1248 by the forces of Ferdinand III of Castile ('El Santo') that Seville acquired so many of the physical features that would be familiar to Velázquez as a child – the narrow, irregular streets, like the street of La Gorgoja in which he and his family lived, leading out onto the little plaza of the Buen Suceso; the whitewashed houses looking inwards onto their central patios; the Alcázar or castle with its shaded gardens; and, not least, the Giralda, a minaret now Christianised by the addition of two storeys in the Renaissance style [fig 1.3], which had been transformed into the bell-tower of the vast and cavernous Gothic cathedral [fig 1.4].

Under Christian rule, the Seville of the later Middle Ages was a lively port city and a major point of interchange between the Mediterranean, North Africa, and the ports of the Atlantic seaboard and of northern Europe. The city acquired an important colony of Genoese merchants, attracted both by Seville's commercial link with the north and by hopes of breaking into the gold trade of the Sahara. Between 1450 and 1500 the size of this Genoese colony doubled. Genoese merchants and financiers were active participants in the Iberian colonisation and economic de-

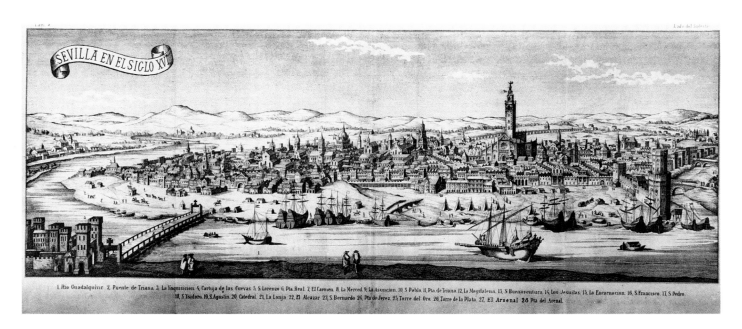

fig 1.1 View of Seville *c.*1600

velopment of Madeira, the Azores and the Canaries; and when Columbus, probing still further into the Atlantic, reported that he had reached 'the Indies', they were quick to respond to the dramatic new prospects for the acquisition of spices and gold. But they were not alone in this. Merchants from northern Spain, from Burgos and the Basque country, had long been established in Seville. Here, as new markets opened up, they were joined by a growing number of foreigners – English, French, Flemings, Germans and Italians – many of whom struck roots in the city, intermarried with Sevillian families, and acquired naturalisation papers in order to participate in the Indies trade.

Seville's North European trade remained buoyant over the course of the sixteenth and seventeenth centuries, but it was the Indies trade which gave sixteenth-century Seville its new and dazzling allure. The establishment in 1503 of the famous House of Trade (*Casa de Contratación*) marked the beginnings of Seville's monopoly of the transatlantic trade. In 1509 the officials of the House of Trade were ordered to keep a register of all passengers to the Indies, and henceforth Seville would be the starting-point for the many emigrants – some 200,000 by the end of the century – who hoped for a new and better life in America.

The conquest of Mexico in the 1520s and of Peru in the 1530s revealed to astonished European eyes new lands, new peoples and new riches on a scarcely imagined scale. In the following two decades vast silver deposits were discovered in Mexico and the high Andes, and systematic exploitation of the mineral resources of America began. As growing quantities of silver had to be shipped back across the Atlantic, it became essential to provide adequate protection for the galleons and a regular organisation for the fleets. In the early 1560s the transatlantic trade – the so-called *Carrera de Indias* – assumed its definitive form. Each year two fleets would set sail from San Lúcar, one leaving in the spring for the Gulf of Mexico, and the other in August for the isthmus of Panama. The two fleets, both of them carrying European commodities for the growing American market, would winter at Vera Cruz and Cartagena respectively and, after joining up in Havana in the following March, would aim to head back for Seville before the start of the hurricane season, laden with American produce – pearls, hides, cochineal, precious woods and dyestuffs and, above all, the silver, along with lesser quantities

of gold, produced by the Viceroyalties of New Spain and Peru.

The precious metals would be unloaded at the wharves beside Seville's famous Golden Tower, the *Torre de Oro*, the most important of the towers forming part of the defence system of the old city walls [fig 1.5]. After registration by officials of the House of Trade, the bullion that was not to be retained in bars was sent to the Casa de Moneda for minting. Of the silver remittances from the Indies some 25% was the property of the Spanish crown, which was entitled to one-fifth of the mineral wealth extracted from the mines. The first call on the crown's annual American windfall was to meet the demands of the German and Genoese bankers from whom it had received loans on the strength of the anticipated arrival of the next treasure fleet. It was in this way that the crown paid for the maintenance of Spain's armies in Italy and the Netherlands, and met the financial requirements of its ambassadors and viceroys. But the larger share of the silver in every fleet was sent back on private account by colonists to their friends and relatives in Spain, or was remitted as payment for consumer goods that had been despatched to the Indies in the outgoing fleets. A substantial part of these remittances was either used by Seville merchants to pay their European agents, or was ploughed back into the Indies trade.

All these transactions placed Seville at the heart of a European network of commerce and credit. Each year, news of the safe arrival of the treasure fleets and their precious cargoes was anxiously awaited not only by the court in Madrid but by the great financial centres in Italy, France, Germany and the Netherlands. On the not infrequent occasions when the fleets were seriously delayed or galleons were lost at sea, there was consternation on the foreign exchanges. When Seville sneezed, all Europe tended to catch cold.

In view of the quantities of bullion arriving at the Golden Tower, it is not surprising that sixteenth-century Seville became known as a city whose streets were paved with gold and silver. Migrants poured in from central and northern Castile, attracted by the lure of easy money, or by hopes of a passage to the Indies. Since there was no way in which this growing population could be contained within the old city walls, it overflowed across the Guadalquivir and filled to overcrowding the tenement houses in the suburb of Triana, the quarter that traditionally accommo-

fig 1.2 (far left)
Bartolemé Murillo
Sts Justa and Rufina
(Museo de Bellas Artes, Seville)

fig 1.3 (left)
The north side of the Giralda, Seville

fig 1.4 (right)
Seville Cathedral

fig 1.5 (far right)
View of the River Guadalquivir and the Golden Tower

dated many of the city's artisans, along with its dockworkers and its seafaring population [fig 1.6]. Although small boats plied continuously to and fro across the river, Triana was also linked to the city by a famous wooden pontoon bridge. It was only towards the end of the sixteenth century that this was supplemented by a new bridge of stone to ease the growing congestion of traffic. Over the bridge trundled wagons laden with fruit and vegetables from the Sevillian hinterland, along with the industrial products of Triana – pottery and tiles, soap, gunpowder and all kinds of cloths.

The cosmopolitanism and the dynamism of this great port city, with its fluid population and its feverish expectations of easy wealth, made it unique among the cities of the Crown of Castile. With its large foreign communities and its close ties to Italy, the Netherlands and the Indies, it was probably the most open among them to influences from abroad. Along with standard commodities like cloths, silks and tapestries, there was a lively trade in books, engravings and works of art from Italy and Flanders. It is not, therefore, surprising that Velázquez, in the years of his apprenticeship, should have had access to engravings of the works of northern artists like Pieter Aertsen [cats 17–20].

Seville, for its part, was an internationally important publishing centre during the sixteenth century and at least the first half of the seventeenth. For some years the German house of Cromberger was the city's leading publishing house, but in the later decades of the sixteenth century a constellation of printers and publishers was producing books for the domestic, the European and – increasingly – the expanding American market. In spite of the shadow cast over Spanish publishing by the tightening of censorship regulations under Philip II, books, broadsheets and newsletters continued to pour from the city's presses, with production at a high point during the years when Velázquez was in his teens.[2]

The city's openness was reflected, too, in the relatively relaxed attitude displayed by Sevillians to trade, and to wealth made in trade, in contrast to the attitude to be found in many other parts of the peninsula. Seville's nobility was essentially an urban nobility, which had infiltrated city offices, monopolised the city council, and was notoriously connected with families which had made their money in trade. A handful of great noble families were linked to the city or its region – in particular the house of Guzmán, headed by the Duke of Medina Sidonia, and the Ribera family of the Dukes of Alcalá – but the bulk of the nobility were lesser nobles and *caballeros*, many of whom were not averse to engaging, if only by proxy, in the occasional trading venture. There were advantageous marriages to be made, too, and not least to the daughters of wealthy Genoese merchant families settled in Seville, or of the notorious *indianos* or *peruleros*, who had returned home after making their fortunes in the Indies, and were at once mocked and envied for their lavish life-styles and for their capacity to spend.

It has been estimated that Seville in Velázquez's day was a city dominated and controlled by fewer than two hundred families.[3] These families, which had made their wealth in land, trade and municipal and public office, constituted a loosely articulated but nonetheless powerful oligarchy. Their members were to be found not only among the recognised members of the urban nobility, but also in the merchant exchange (*Lonja*), in the high court (*Audiencia*), and in the forty lucrative canonries of Seville cathedral. In spite of the close ties of relationship that linked many of these families, there were also deep divisions within the city's élite. The city council was divided into factions based on family affiliation, and the city was perennially riven by bitter disputes over questions of precedence and jurisdiction between corporate bodies which were hyper-sensitive to their rights and privileges: city council versus *Audiencia*; *Audiencia* versus Inquisition; the archbishop versus the cathedral chapter. In 1598, the year preceding the birth of Velázquez, a violent controversy over precedence between officials of the *Audiencia* and the Inquisition brought to an abrupt and embarrassing halt the solemn proceedings surrounding the dedication of the vast catafalque erected in Seville cathedral for the exequies of Philip II.

The crown's representative in the city (*asistente*), was therefore kept busy maintaining the peace and cooling the passions excited by alleged or real slights. But, for all the factional and personal animosities, the élite was united in its conviction of the city's superiority to every other town in Spain. Sixteenth-century Seville liked to call itself the 'New Rome',[4] and during the course of that century great efforts were made to beautify the city and make it worthy of its name. In 1574 the Count of Barajas con-

verted one of the most dank and evil-smelling areas of the city into a public park and promenade, the famous Alameda of Hercules, planted with poplars and graced with two columns bearing statues of Hercules and Caesar respectively [fig 1.7 and cat 3]. The water supply was improved, and more public fountains were built, although in a hot and thirsty city the waterseller with his large earthenware jar at his side, as depicted by Velázquez, was a familiar and essential figure [cat 31].

The sixteenth century, a period of urban renewal, was the century in which Moorish Seville was transformed into a city of the European Renaissance. Palaces and town houses with monumental doorways were constructed in the new Renaissance style, the most famous of them the so-called Casa de Pilatos of the Marquises of Tarifa, later the Dukes of Alcalá. The urban élite also built suburban villas on the outskirts of the city and along the river banks, where its members could pass the hot summer evenings in the shade of their gardens (*huertas*). By the end of the century a green belt surrounded Seville, punctuated by country villas and the occasional monastery.[5]

But the city in which Velázquez grew to maturity was, above all, a city of convents and churches. His parish of San Vicente was one of the twenty-nine into which the city was divided,[6] and the Seville skyline, while dominated by the cathedral and the Giralda, was broken by the bell-towers of its parish churches [cat 2 and fig 1.8]. The silver altar-frontals of these churches were glittering reminders of the riches of the Indies. So, also, were the family chapels for which returning *indianos* and members of the urban patriciate commissioned altarpieces (*retablos*) and images from the studios of local artists, craftsmen and sculptors.

The élite used its money, too, to found, endow and adorn the numerous monasteries and convents that testified to the religious devotion of which Sevillians were so inordinately proud. Following the great period of Counter-Reformation foundations, seventeenth-century Seville contained some thirty-six convents for male members of the religious orders, including six Jesuit houses, and twenty-eight for nuns.[7] Competition among the orders was fierce, and patrons rivalled each other in the lavishness of their gifts and endowments. The largest monastery in Seville, that of San Francisco [fig 1.9], housed 200 Franciscans, but there were also impressive Dominican and Mercedarian establishments and a host of smaller houses, many of them heavily dependent for their income on the generosity of pious members of the Seville patriciate.

These churches and convents provided an impressive backdrop for the spectacular manifestations of religious theatre which constituted such an important part of Seville's public life. Holy Week and Corpus Christi were the great occasions when all Seville took to the streets in fervent displays of collective piety. Religious processions wound their way through the streets, with penitents and flagellants following in the wake of a venerated image borne aloft and flanked by members of the various confraternities that played such an important part in the charitable and devotional life of the city – the Confraternity of the Most Holy Virgin of Solitude, or of the Sweet Name of Jesus, or of Jesus Tied to the Cross, and many others.

In a city so devoted to theatre, it was not surprising that the theatre itself flourished. Around the time of Velázquez's birth, the city boasted four active theatres (*corrales de comedias*). In 1601

fig 1.6 (above left) Anonymous, seventeenth-century *Shipbuilding at Seville* (Hispanic Society of America, New York)

fig 1.7 (left) Anonymous, seventeenth-century *The Alameda, Seville* (Hispanic Society of America, New York)

fig 1.8 (above) The west tower of the parish church of San Pedro, Seville, the church where Velázquez was baptised

the city council, in an attempt to improve its precarious financial position, decided to go into the business of theatrical promotion itself, and obtained a royal licence to construct a new municipal theatre, the *Coliseo*, which opened to the public in 1607. Between 1611 and 1614 it presented 526 plays (*comedias*), and proved so successful that it was replaced over the next two years by an impressive new three-storey structure, built to a circular plan at the enormous cost of 250,000 ducats. The new building lasted only four years before being destroyed by a fire in 1620.[8]

The theatricality of life in Seville was a constant source of admiration and wonder to observers. It was a theatricality which was not confined to religious ceremonial, but was carried over into every form of public life, and – as the seventeenth century advanced – increasingly into the city's architecture, as churches, convents and other public buildings were constructed or embellished in the new and fashionable style of the baroque. This was a city on permanent display, which prided itself on doing everything better and on a more lavish scale than any other city in Spain. Cervantes who, like many others, had stood in awe before the vast catafalque erected inside the cathedral in honour of Philip II, gently mocked this passion for grandeur in his famous sonnet on Philip II's catafalque in Seville [fig 1.10]:

I vow to God that the grandeur of its terrifies me and I would give a doubloon to be able to describe it. for who does this celebrated construction, this splendor, not astonish and amaze? By the body of the living Christ each piece of it is worth a million or more, and what a shame it is that all this will not last a century, oh great Seville, a Rome triumphant in your spirit and nobility ... All this a braggart overheard, who said: 'All you say is right, Sir Soldier, and whoso'er denies it lies.' And then, without more ado, he jammed on his hat, adjusted his sword, gave a sideways glance, departed – and then there was nothing.[9]

'And then there was nothing.' There was much that was febrile, and inevitably ephemeral, about this city in which fortunes were made and lost overnight, and in which enormous sacrifices were made for the sake of outward display – a display that manifested itself in the rich clothing of the élite and its great retinues of servants and in the 2,000 carriages with which it allegedly congested the city's streets in the years around 1600.[10] Beneath the surface glitter of this city in which enormous wealth and abject poverty were violently juxtaposed, there were growing strains and fissures, which were becoming increasingly apparent precisely in the years of Velázquez's childhood and apprenticeship.

In 1601, three years after the accession of Philip III, the banking house run by the Espinosa family collapsed after some unwise speculations in the Indies trade. It carried with it in its sensational downfall some of the leading city merchants, and the city was never again to have a public bank. The Indies trade itself was still producing enormous returns, but from 1610 there were worrying signs that the American market for Spanish and European commodities was reaching saturation. Accompanying this incipient crisis in the transatlantic trade was a falling-off in remittances of silver from the American mines, and particularly in remittances for the Spanish crown which, in 1615 and 1616, received no more than a million ducats a year in contrast to the two million that were arriving annually at the start of the reign.[11]

With confidence and credit shaken, the vulnerability of Seville to the fluctuating fortunes of the Atlantic trade was alarmingly exposed. But the habit of spending remained deeply engrained. If the economic basis of Seville's traditional prosperity was looking increasingly precarious during the first two decades of the seventeenth century, these were nonetheless years of lavish public and private expenditure, with Seville, like the court in Madrid, making the most of Europe's return to a fragile peace as the long wars of the later sixteenth century were brought to a close. The native Sevillian writer, Mateo Alemán, wrote in the second part of his picaresque novel, *Guzmán de Alfarache* (1604), that in Seville, which, unlike Madrid, had the 'smell of a city', 'silver ran in people's daily transactions like copper in other places, and was so little esteemed that it was liberally spent ...'.[12]

The silver trickled down, however capriciously, to the lower orders of society – in the first instance to the large service population of artisans and craftsmen, silversmiths, carpenters and the like, meticulously grouped into some sixty well-regulated guilds;[13] and ultimately to those who lived on the fringes of society, making such living as they could through street-selling, peddling and more nefarious activities. For this was a city with a large sub-world of pimps and prostitutes, scoundrels (*pícaros*), and professional criminals, a sub-world with its own argot, and its own rules and regulations, which Alemán immortalised in his *Guzmán de Alfarache* and Cervantes in his *Exemplary Novels*. Its presence was felt everywhere, but its favoured habitat was the swampy terrain between the river-bank and the city walls, known as the Arenal, where cheap inns, boarding-houses and brothels abounded [fig 1.11].[14]

Any child growing up in this city would have been conscious

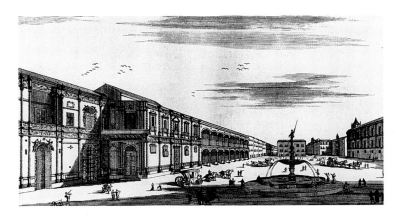

fig 1.9 (above) The Monastery of San Francisco, Seville

fig 1.10 (right) Philip II's catafalque in Seville Cathedral

of its pulsating life, of the violent contrasts of affluence and hunger, and of the extraordinarily varied and often exotic character of the people who thronged its streets. Every nationality and ethnic group was represented here – Cypriots and Armenians, Corsicans and Bretons. Velázquez's own family, the de Silvas, were of Portuguese origin, and large numbers of Portuguese, and especially Portuguese of Jewish origin, had moved into the city following the union of the crowns of Castile and Portugal in 1580.

Until 1609–10, when the government of Philip III ordered its expulsion from Spain, there was also a Morisco population of 7,000 or more, which – since it was excluded from guild organisation – earned its living by such activities as shop-keeping, horticulture, and small-scale trade and transport. Velázquez who, in 1627, would win the competition at court for a painting depicting the *Expulsion of the Moriscos*,[15] would have seen at the age of eleven their enforced departure from his city – an event which moved the people of Seville to expressions of pity, in spite of their traditional wariness of this unassimilated Moorish minority in their midst.[16] He would have been conscious too of the chequerboard effect created by the presence in the city of a slave population, over 6,000 strong, consisting mostly of blacks and North African Moors, along with a sprinkling of Moriscos.[17] In Seville, which had the largest slave community in the peninsula outside Lisbon, male and female slaves were kept for domestic service and Velázquez, in later life, was only following the custom of his native city in owning a Moorish slave, Juan de Pareja, to whom he eventually granted freedom in 1650 while resident in Rome.[18]

As long as the civic élite and the church had money to spend – and there were still large accumulated reserves of wealth in the opening decades of the seventeenth century, even if the foundations of Seville's prosperity were beginning to be eroded – the combination of prodigality and generosity contrived to blunt the sharper edges of extreme social contrast, and to give the city a cohesiveness which it would otherwise have lacked. Members of the élite were generous in establishing hospitals, orphanages and charitable foundations which helped to mitigate some of the worst suffering in years like 1605, when the price of bread was inordinately high.[19]

It was an élite, too, which believed in education. The city's university was an institution of no great distinction, and many families chose to send their sons to Salamanca or elsewhere, while clerics preferred the Dominican University of Santo Tomás.[20] But there were other educational centres of high repute, especially the Jesuit college of San Hermenegildo, which may have been the largest school of its kind in Spain. Here, and in other city schools and colleges, the sons of the city's élite received a grounding in Latin and the humanities; and if Seville's educational system produced more than its share of rich and idle Andalusian young gentlemen (*señoritos*), it also helped create an informed interest in culture and the arts that did much to stimulate artistic and intellectual patronage.

Members of the élite provided generous audiences for the Latin and vernacular plays performed by the students of St Gregory's College, founded in 1592 by Robert Persons for the education of English Catholics.[21] They participated in the literary and poetical competitions which the Jesuits had popularised; and they met in the long summer evenings in the gardens of the Alcázar or some *huerta* on the outskirts of the city, to talk about the local Roman antiquities, or to debate literary questions and points of classical learning. Clerics and members of the Cathedral Chapter were prominent in these discussion groups, some of which evolved into more or less formal academies of poets, scholars and artists.[22] At meetings of the academy at one time run by Canon Pacheco, and then after his death by his nephew, the artist Francisco Pacheco, Velázquez may well have picked up during his years of apprenticeship to Pacheco some of the classical and humanist culture which helped to shape his vision of the world.

A prominent member and patron of this academy was Don Fernando Enríquez Afán de Ribera, 3rd Duke of Alcalá, who had inherited the humanist traditions of his family. In the Casa de Pilatos [fig 1.12], where the family's great collection of Roman antiquities was housed, he built up a splendid library, and himself became a notable patron of the arts.[23] But Alcalá, as a leading member of the Seville nobility [fig 1.13], did not have the field to himself. He was soon engaged in friendly competition with Gaspar de Guzmán, the Count of Olivares [fig 1.14], who lived in his native city of Seville while in his twenties, from 1607–15, while keeping a watchful eye on developments at court.[24] Olivares became a close friend of some of the leading figures in the literary and intellectual world of early seventeenth-century Seville, and especially of the poet and man of letters Fran-

fig 1.11 Anonymous, seventeenth-century *The Arenal, Seville* (Hispanic Society of America, New York)

fig 1.12 The Courtyard of the Casa de Pilatos, Seville

cisco de Rioja, who helped him create a library which eventually eclipsed that of Alcalá. He may well have come across Velázquez for the first time when his portrait, now lost, was painted by Pacheco.

In their lavish patronage of poets, scholars and artists, Alcalá and Olivares, as the two most prominent and cultivated members of the high Sevillian nobility in the early seventeenth century, were behaving in perfect accordance with the traditions of their native city. They spent, and spent to excess, in their competition to prove their credentials as true 'sons' of Seville.[25] But their pride in their city was not misplaced. Still basking in the glow of the silver of the Indies, it remained an open, generous, cosmopolitan city, which combined passionate religious devotion, not least to the doctrine of the Immaculate Conception, with a sense of the visual and the theatrical which created, for a few decades, an ideal environment for the cultivation of the arts.

Having himself been formed in this environment, it is not surprising that Olivares, on becoming the favourite and first minister of the new King Philip IV, should have sought to recreate it

at the court of his royal master. In 1621, when he assumed the reins of power, Seville came to Madrid. Two years later the twenty-four-year-old Velázquez took the most important decision of his life. Encouraged by Olivares and his circle of Sevillian friends at court, he chose to follow them in pursuit of fame and fortune.

fig 1.14 Velázquez *Gaspar de Guzmán, Count of Olivares*
(Museu de Arte de São Paulo)

fig 1.13 Sevillian School, seventeenth-century
Don Fernando Enríquez Afán de Ribera, 3rd Duke of Alcalá
(Biblioteca Capitular y Colombina, Seville)

Vicente Lleó Cañal

The Cultivated Elite of Velázquez's Seville

HISTORIOGRAPHICAL conventions, like that of dividing history into discrete periods – centuries or decades, for example – can sometimes distort our understanding of the past, suggesting links or breaks that are not necessarily there. This is particularly the case with the history of Spain where there is a tendency to contrast the vigour of the sixteenth century with the profound decadence of the seventeenth (to contrast the 'greater' Habsburgs with the 'lesser'), as though from one day to the next a great disaster had overtaken the country and its people. The same applies to Seville [fig 2.1], which is sometimes seen as having transformed itself from one century to the next, as if by magic, from a 'New Rome' into a 'New Babylon', from a vital, cultivated and well-ordered city into a chaotic morass of corruption and misery; in short, into the land of the *pícaro* and the idle *hidalgo*.[1]

The truth is, of course, more complex for, although the seventeenth century was, generally speaking, a period of decline for Spain, this decline was relatively slow, becoming more marked during the reign of Philip IV. As regards Seville, the decline became particularly apparent after the terrible plague of 1649 which decimated the city's population. The period when trade with the Indies, the basis of the city's prosperity, was at its height was between 1592 and 1622.[2] In the first quarter of the seventeenth century the history of the city, rather like painting in the period, juxtaposes brilliantly illuminated passages with darker areas: it is a city of contrasts and contradictions composed of a complex, multi-faceted society. It is the darker areas that up to now have received the greatest attention. This is at least partly due to the universal renown of picaresque literature which has traditionally been taken by certain commentators as an accurate portrayal of Sevillian society.[3] A similar situation has obtained with regard to the paintings known as *bodegones* (see David Davies's essay pp.51–65), a term which in the seventeenth century signified low-

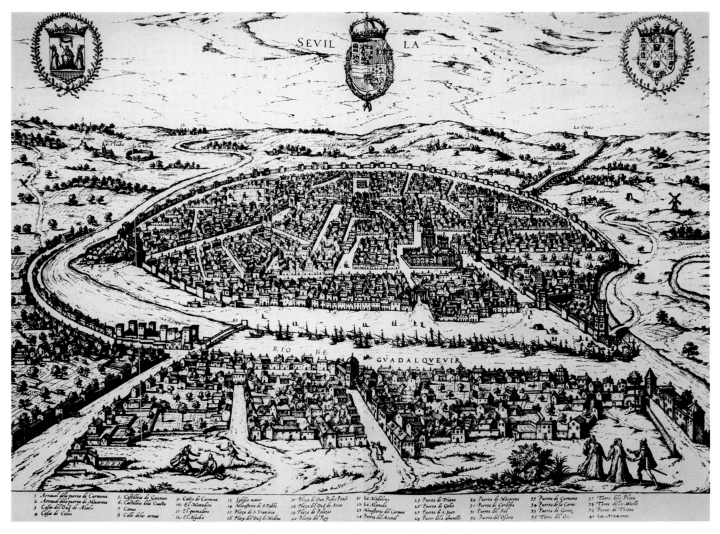

fig 2.1 Braun, *Civitatis orbis terrarum,* View of Seville

life scenes, which have been seen by some almost as photographic documents.[4] Today it would seem more prudent to see these phenomena, both literary and pictorial, as artistic genres each governed by its own rules and conventions, and to be duly wary of the dangers of using them as a form of primary historical documentation.

In any event, there can be little doubt that Seville achieved unprecedented levels of immorality and corruption in the first quarter of the seventeenth century:[5] illegal activity abounded not only in the many taverns and bordellos of the city – in 1630 there were as many as thirty so-called *casas de gula* (literally 'houses of gluttony')[6] and the municipal authorities felt obliged to introduce measures to curb prostitution[7] – but even in convents, like that of the *Arrepentidas* (repentant women) which was the setting for scandalous bacchanals,[8] and in the Archbishop's Palace itself among the Archbishop's familiars.[9] Furthermore, popular piety infected by *Alumbradismo* (pseudo-mysticism) was prey to numerous deceptions and frauds. There was the notorious case of Padre Méndez, a religious of Portuguese origin, who claimed that the hour of his own death had been revealed to him by divine favour and who held extravagant masses lasting several hours which drew large numbers of people.[10] Beginning in the last years of the sixteenth century there was also a popular reaction against the humanism and classical culture which had predominated in the preceding period.[11]

To focus only upon these negative features is to distort severely the truth of the complex panorama of Sevillian life at this time. There are other positive aspects which are habitually ignored by historians and which are of the greatest importance in understanding the context in which Sevillian art develops and helps to explain some of its peculiarities.

Sevillian art of this period has always been perceived as distinctive from that of other Spanish schools on account of a certain classicism which is generally attributed to the idiosyncratic character of the Sevillian environment.[12] In fact, although a hostile attitude towards all forms of classicism in Seville may be detected in this period, for a select group of men classical studies and the cult of antiquity became almost an obsession to which they devoted much of their lives. What is more significant in the present context is that they were members of the circle of the painter Francisco Pacheco, Velázquez's teacher and father-in-law. Without doubt the most prominent figure in this group is Rodrigo Caro (1573–1647) through whose writings and correspondence[13] we can identify a veritable network of amateurs who exchanged information on the discovery of statues, coins and inscriptions.[14]

Already in the closing years of the sixteenth century, in the generation that preceded Caro's, there was an active group of antiquarians in Andalusia. A manuscript in the Biblioteca Capitular in Seville lists the principal members: Ambrosio de Morales, Benito Ariás Montano [fig 2.2], Francisco de Padilla (treasurer of Málaga Cathedral), Canon Francisco Pacheco (the uncle of the painter) Fray Alonso de Chacón, Fray Agustín de Salucio and Juan de Barahona (these two were from Jerez de la Frontera), and Pedro de Valencia (Montano's disciple).[15] Mostly these were learned clerics or wealthy gentlemen who avidly collected medals, coins and inscriptions with the prime objective of throwing light on questions of local history.[16] But already among these men we may discern an aesthetic appreciation of their antiquities. In his will of 1596 the Sevillian painter Pedro de Villegas bequeathed to his close friend Montano his library, his numismatic collection, various bronze figures and 'other antiquities', which must have included the 'three large figures in marble and two heads and a child in marble' which in an earlier will he had intended to leave to the Cathedral 'so that artists and teachers might benefit from them', in other words, that the sculptures might be used as models.[17]

The most important collection of antique statuary in late-sixteenth-century Seville was the one formed by Don Per Afán de Ribera, 1st Duke of Alcalá. It was displayed in his palace, the Casa de Pilatos [figs 2.4, 2.5 & 2.6], and the painter Francisco Pacheco had frequent access to it as, presumably, did Velázquez himself.[18] The collection was formed while Alcalá was Viceroy of Naples (1558–71) and its nucleus was the collection which had previously belonged to the Neapolitan antiquarian Adrián Spadafora. To this were added acquisitions made in other parts of Italy through a network of agents.[19] Alcalá sent an Italian architect, Benvenuto Tortello, from Naples to Seville, to oversee the installation of the collection and Tortello added to the old *mudéjar* palace series of *loggie* with niches and tondi in the Roman style.[20] The collection eventually passed to Alcalá's nephew and heir, Don Fernando Enríquez Afán de Ribera, 3rd Duke of Alcalá, a friend and patron

fig 2.2
Francisco Pacheco
Doctor Benito Ariás Montano
(Lázaro Galdiano Museum, Madrid)

fig 2.3
Francisco Pacheco
Prebendary Pablo de Céspedes
(Lázaro Galdiano Museum, Madrid)

fig 2.4
Casa de Pilatos, Seville

fig 2.5 The Bust of Trajan, Casa de Pilatos, Seville

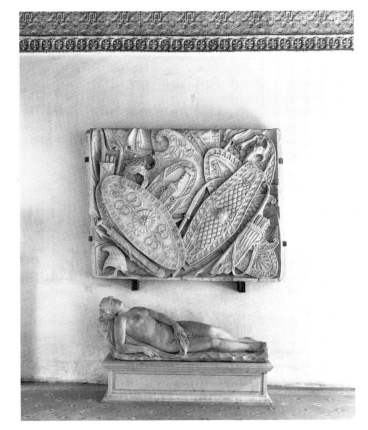

fig 2.6 Casa de Pilatos, Seville

of Pacheco and also of Velázquez,[21] who enriched it with new pieces acquired in Italy or obtained from Spanish sites. There was no comparable collection in the city, nor indeed in the whole of Spain, and those who visited it never failed to express their admiration.[22]

The example offered in Seville by the Duke of Alcalá[23] inspired the formation of other collections. Caro lists some of them and highlights those of the Duke of Medina Sidonia, the Conde de Castellar, the Licenciado (a title signifying a holder of a university degree) Sancho Hurtado de la Puente, and his own, which was divided between his houses in Seville and Utrera.[24] It is possible that some of these collections were accessible to young artists so that they could practise drawing from sculpture, as Pacheco recommended.[25] It seems practically certain that the Alcalá collection was available, at least to Pacheco and his closest disciples. The matter is of interest since it is connected with the problematic question of whether or not there were 'academies' in Golden Age Seville.[26]

One looks in vain for academies which follow the Italian model, with a constitution, ceremonies and regular sessions, but there were informal meetings of learned men, artists (Pacheco, Céspedes [fig 2.3], Jáuregui) and illustrious nobles united by their common interest in antiquity, poetry and matters of iconography.[27] The inventory of the *camarín grande* (great hall) in the Casa de Pilatos, whose ceiling was decorated with Pacheco's *Apotheosis of Hercules*, seems to have functioned as an artist's studio since it contained unpainted canvases, an easel of inlaid wood, as well as numerous bronzes both ancient and modern which could have served as models.[28] Some sources state expressly that the 3rd Duke of Alcalá was an amateur painter,[29] although if the *camarín* was his studio then he had little chance to use it since between his appointment as Viceroy of Catalonia and his death in Ger-

many in 1637 he was only in Seville for six years. It is possible, however, that Pacheco, who seems to have acted as Alcalá's artistic adviser (and who, on at least one occasion, restored a work in his collection), used it himself,[30] although from 1628 at least, the Flemish painter Jakob van der Gracht, who is referred to in documents as Jacobo Grachet, lived and worked in the palace.[31]

Unfortunately, the Duke of Alcalá's collection of classical sculpture is today largely dispersed and parts of it are inaccessible.[32] If it were ever possible to bring it together it would be of great interest to examine its relationship with Sevillian painting and sculpture of the first quarter of the seventeenth century. We would then have a clearer understanding of the basis of this supposedly local variety of classicism.

Seville then, at the beginning of the seventeenth century, was the city of the picaresque novel and of poor government, but it was also the home of a cultivated élite with a passionate interest in antiquity which debated the most abstruse iconographical and literary questions and whose members formed rich collections of archaeological material. Seville also attained greater heights than perhaps any other city in Spain in the field of scientific inquiry, largely on account of the work undertaken by the House of Trade, the institution which had responsibility for all affairs concerning the Indies, including geographical, astronomical and navigational questions.[33]

This seems also to have been ignored by art historians, despite the fact that inventories of artists' libraries list a significant number of scientific texts. Velázquez owned an exceptional number,[34] and Pablo de Céspedes,[35] too, had several, as presumably other artists.[36] Of even greater significance is the fact that there were close links between artists and men of science, and here too Pacheco is a key figure.

In the preceding generation the proportion of scientific pub-

25

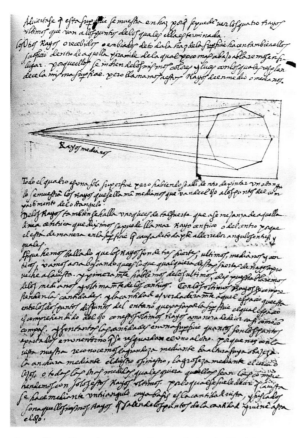

fig 2.7 Page from the manuscript translation by Rodrigo Zamorano of Leon Battista Alberti's *Della Pittura* (Biblioteca Capitular y Colombina, Seville)

fig 2.8 Illustration in Benito Daza y Valdés's *Arte y uso de los antojos,* published in Seville, 1613

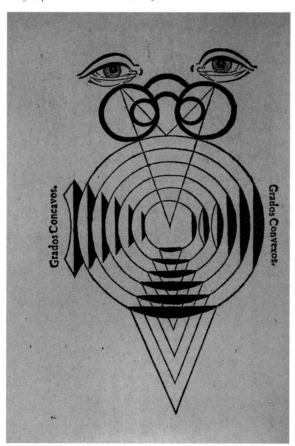

lications relative to all books printed in Seville was double the average for the rest of Europe,[37] and the city's learned men were in contact with their European colleagues through the great thinker and scripture scholar, Benito Ariás Montano.[38] Their science was essentially experimental in contrast to the antiquated teaching methods of the university. There were naturalists, like Simón de Tovar, who cultivated and studied the plants which arrived from the Indies; physicians, like Bartolomé Hidalgo de Agüero who in his role as surgeon in the Hospital del Cardenal experimented with new therapeutic methods; metallurgists, like the goldsmith Juan de Arfe, author of the first monograph on the laws of precious metals, as well as astronomers and navigators, like Pedro de Medina, whose works were translated into almost every European language.[39]

It comes as something of a surprise to realise how intense the interest of the men of science of around 1600 was in matters intimately connected with artistic theory, specifically in optics and perspective, in other words, with the laws that govern the processes of vision and representation. The study of the science of perspective becomes so popular that a personification of Perspective appears as an allegorical figure together with Mathematics and Astronomy in the festivities held in 1617 by the Colegio Mayor de Santa María de Jesus in honour of the Immaculate Conception.[40]

The majority of the treatises on perspective written in this period are known only from references since they remained unpublished and are now lost. Pacheco mentions that he owned one by Andrés García de Céspedes, a cosmographer to the House of Trade.[41] Benito Daza mentions a perspective treatise by another cosmographer, Antonio Moreno Vilches, 'which will soon be published'.[42] Moreno Vilches was also a good friend of Pacheco.[43] The most interesting case is that of yet another cosmographer, Rodrigo Zamorano (died 1620), who was known not only for his books on navigation but also for his translation of Euclid's *Geometry* (Seville, 1576) dedicated to Canon Luciano de Negrón, a good friend of Canon Francisco Pacheco, whom the painter Pacheco describes as an 'astronomer, mathematician and philosopher'.[44] Zamorano's broad interest in artistic theory is revealed by a collection of his papers recently discovered in the Biblioteca Capitular y Colombina of Seville Cathedral.[45] These include an incomplete translation of the first book of Alberti's *Della Pittura* [fig 2.7], which is devoted to geometry and perspective, as well as an incomplete translation of Carlo Tetti's *Discorso delle Fortificazioni.* One of these papers reveals that Zamorano was the translator of the 1582 Toledo edition of Alberti's *De Re Aedificatoria*, which has the name of the Madrid architect, Francisco Lozano, on the title page. Zamorano complains that the translation lacked 'refinement because it had been taken from me while still in draft form'.

Along with the remarkable interest in perspective in Seville at the end of the sixteenth and the beginning of the seventeenth centuries, there is a parallel development in the study of optics, although we are less well informed about this. Licenciado Benito Daza y Valdés's *Arte y uso de los antojos* (The Art and Use of Telescopes), an absolutely pioneering work in its field, was published in 1613 [fig 2.8].[46] Spyglasses and telescopes (or *visorios*, as Daza calls them) are known to have been in use in Barcelona from at least 1593,[47] but Daza's book reveals the existence in Seville of a veritable industry dedicated to their manufacture, producing examples giving eighty times magnification. Daza, an Inquisition notary, was familiar with Galileo's works[48] and he describes experiments with spherical mirrors and *camera obscura*. He also established a system of measuring diopters which he terms *grados*.

The third book of Daza's treatise contains a series of dialogues between the *Maestro* (presumably himself) and a group of friends. The dialogue form is a convention of classical literature, but certain features of Daza's dialogues suggest that they are rooted in real experiences: for example, the group's ascent of the Giralda, the Cathedral tower, to test the range of a *visorio* (viewfinder), and the specific references to the topography of the city, suggest that these dialogues on questions relating to optics reflect gatherings which actually took place.

At practically the same time as the publication of Daza's treatise, the Sevillian writer Rodrigo Fernández de Ribera composed an amusing satire entitled *Los anteojos de mejor vista* (Spyglasses for Better Vision).[49] The author tells the story of a magic spyglass which enables the wearer to see the true nature of people beneath their outer appearance. Certain details suggest that the authors knew each other: the owner of the spyglass is called *Maestro*, as in Daza's work, and he is an extravagant Licenciado who climbs up tall buildings to observe the city. The link between the two men is once again the painter Francisco Pacheco. Fernández de Ribera was a friend of Pacheco and dedicated to him his satire *Epithalamium on the marriage of an old widow, with a dowry of one hundred escudos, to a drunken soldier from Flanders, bald from birth* (Seville, 1625). Pacheco's friendship with Daza is attested to in the laudatory sonnet on the *Arte y uso de los antojos*, which for some reason was not included in the published edition of the treatise.[50]

It is tempting to think of the early patrons of Velázquez, and of other 'modern' painters, as belonging to this cultivated élite interested in science and antiquity of which we get a glimpse from the pages of Pacheco, from Caro's correspondence and the dialogues of Daza. There can be little doubt that *bodegón* paintings, at that time a radical novelty, must have been attractive to these men on account of their objective, scientific representation of reality, and also because of the illustrious classical precedents offered by painters like Piraeicus and Dionysius the Anthropographer, both cited by Pacheco. What little is known about the Sevillian collectors who owned paintings by Velázquez would seem to confirm this. All three were persons 'of quality': the Duke of Alcalá had two *bodegones* (one of which is perhaps identifiable with the *Two Young Men at a Table*, cat 24); Canon Don Juan de Fonseca y Figueroa, later a court chamberlain (*Sumiller de Cortina*), was the owner of *The Waterseller of Seville* [cat 31];[51] and the Caballero Veinticuatro, Don Luis de Medina y Orozco, owned three unspecified *bodegones*.[52]

If this hypothesis is correct and Velázquez's early patrons did in fact come from this small circle of connoisseurs with modern taste, this would help explain why his name is almost never listed in the contracts which are preserved in the Archivo de Protocolos in Seville. Unlike the great altarpieces or cycles of religious paintings commissioned by monasteries and convents, Velázquez's pictures would have been sold directly to his clients, perhaps in his studio and without any recourse to a public notary. These exceptional circumstances could not have continued for very long. Velázquez's move to the Court coincided with the beginning of Seville's decline, a decline which was not only economic. The small group of humanists and intellectuals gradually began to disperse, largely on account of the attraction of the Court in Madrid. The most melancholic testimony of this decline is to be found in a letter from Rodrigo Caro to the scholar Don Juan Francisco Andrés y Ustarroz dated 23 May 1644: 'Your Lordship should pity us who live in this last age of Bética (Andalusia), for having been mother through all the ages to so many illustrious intellects, she now finds herself so prostrated that I cannot say if in this great city, beacon of the old and new worlds, there may be found even three people who devote themselves to these studies, and if there is such a one, he does it either out of vain ostentatiousness and without public benefit, or he does it in ignorance of the true principles of surveying the glorious dust of Antiquity...'.[53]

fig 3.1 Francisco de Zurbarán *The Apotheosis of St Thomas Aquinas* (Museo de Bellas Artes, Seville)

Ronald Cueto

The Great Babylon of Spain and the Devout:
Politics, Religion and Piety in the Seville of Velázquez

The late twentieth-century admirer of Diego Velázquez may be Catholic or Orthodox, Protestant or agnostic, Muslim or Buddhist. This essay is intended to describe the spiritual as opposed to the economic or social forces in the society that produced Velázquez. The deceptively simple assertion that he is the product of the Counter-Reformation invites further exploration and elaboration.

* * *

On the afternoon of Friday 1 March 1624, Velázquez's young master, Philip IV, King of Spain, and his younger brother, Don Carlos, made their royal entry to the sound of trumpets into Seville, 'the Great Babylon of Spain'.[1] The royal carriage was accompanied by four great noblemen on horseback – the Duke of Infantado, the Count of Olivares, the Admiral of Castile and the Count of Carpio. As one American scholar has observed, 'public ceremonies were a means for the Habsburgs to demonstrate their political authority'.[2]

The courtiers in the mule-drawn coaches who attracted attention and were named by an eyewitness were all clerics. In one coach there was the Confessor Royal 'with three people'; in another the Nuncio; in another the Patriarch of the Indies in solitary splendour; and in yet another Cardinal Zapata, the administrator of the primatial see of Toledo.[3] Clearly, it was deemed right and proper at that time that the institutional Church should have a high profile in that worldwide Habsburg monarchy whose sovereign bore the proud title of Catholic Majesty.

A few years later, on Thursday 1 December 1628, that same Patriarch of the Indies, Don Diego de Guzmán [fig 3.2], by that time Archbishop of Seville, left his see to accompany the new Holy Roman Empress, the Infanta María, to Vienna. The whole city turned out to witness his departure. The prelate's splendid litter was surrounded by twelve lackeys in white hats. His many servants were mounted on mules bedecked in velvet trappings bearing his coat of arms with silver adornments. One mule bore panniers containing silver pitchers.[4] It was a sight not to be missed by contemporaries and was a pertinent illustration of the power enjoyed by the Church in general and the hierarchy in particular. A Spanish scholar has recently stressed the sheer expense involved in this kind of display which presupposed a strong financial infrastructure.[5] Archiepiscopal Seville was well endowed with its twenty-four parishes, its plutocratic Cathedral Chapter of more than fifty canons and over a hundred assistant clergy, as well as countless privately endowed chaplains. Furthermore, as another leading authority has explained: 'Contrary to those of the nobility, the clergy's economic interests did not suffer from the effects of devaluation, because their main source of income (tithes) consisted of wheat and other crops, whose value carried on increasing.'[6]

Archiepiscopal rents of 80,000 ducats at the beginning of the sixteenth century had increased in value to 130,000 ducats in Velázquez's lifetime, making Seville one of the richest sees in Catholic Christendom, even though a long way behind the rich-

est, Toledo, which had annual rents of around 250,000 ducats. Seville was the largest Iberian city in the Monarchy, with an estimated population of 135,000, just slightly greater than Lisbon's 130,100. Yet neither could compare with the Monarchy's biggest city, Naples, with 275,000 inhabitants.[7] But there is more than economics, finance or demography to be taken into account when exploring the complex religiosity of Velázquez's Seville which seems so strange to us today. Display was only one of many factors – social, devotional, spiritual, and so on – in the political makeup of the Hispanic world during this period: the young Philip IV [fig 3.3] was the head of a dynastic confederation known, tellingly enough, as the Catholic Monarchy.

During their Sevillian sojourn of almost a fortnight in March 1624, the King and the Infante stayed in the monastery of San Jerónimo de Buenavista as guests of the Hieronymites, whose liturgical needs were greatly to influence the development of Spanish ecclesiastical architecture throughout the period.[8] This was, possibly, the religious order most favoured by the Spanish Habsburgs, with lavish houses such as the Escorial and Guadalupe decorated on a scale unthinkable today. Equally challenging to the modern mind is the sheer amount of time taken up by visits to religious foundations during the royal brothers' stay. After greeting the Cathedral Chapter and the Inquisition on Saturday, and hearing Mass in the cathedral on Sunday, the royal party called during the following days on the Carthusians of Santa María de las Cuevas, the Franciscans of San Francisco, the Dominicans of San Pablo, the Mercedarians of Nuestra Señora de la Merced, the Jesuits of the House of the Professed and of San Hermenegildo, and then the Hieronymites of San Isidoro del Campo [fig 3.4].

This programme had significant inclusions as well as notable exclusions. There is some difference of opinion, however, as to the exact number of religious houses in early seventeenth-century Seville. According to the most reliable authority, in 1617, 'in the year of Murillo's birth, there were thirty-three monasteries and twenty-seven convents; another ten institutions (nine for men and one for women) were founded before 1649. From then on, foundations were virtually suspended'.[9]

The number of orders – eight in total – visited by His Catholic Majesty in Seville in 1624 was clearly both selective and select. Many feathers must have been ruffled at a time when the religious orders were deeply divided. The orders favoured by the visitors were preponderantly monastic or mendicant, with the only clerks regular, that is the only recently founded order, being the Jesuits. However, all had communities running into three figures. None of the new discalced orders receives a mention. Neither is there any reference to orders such as the Trinitarians or Augustinians, orders favoured by the Crown during the reign of the late Philip III.[10]

It would seem that the orders committed to learning and scholarship were singled out for marks of royal favour. Dominicans invariably filled the Royal Confessional, the King's second name was Dominic, and the new Chief Minister (*valido*), Don Gaspar de Guzmán, although he had Jesuit confessors, was in fact a relation of St Dominic himself. The King's late mother, Queen Margarita, like all the Styrian Habsburgs, had greatly esteemed the Society of Jesus, as her magnificent Jesuit foundation, the Clerecía in Salamanca, confirms. Aside from these family considerations, the Dominicans with their renowned College of Santo Tomás, the Franciscans with their equally famous College of San Buenaventura and the Jesuits with their highly prized College of San Hermenegildo were all obvious candidates for royal support. Less evident were the claims of the Mercedarians, an order founded to ransom Christians from the Muslim infidel. However, their Seville house was their finest in Spain.[11] Furthermore, it was precisely at this time that this order's commitment to scholarship was being emphasised. Indeed, it was Velázquez's exceptional fellow painter, Francisco de Zurbarán, who was soon to be commissioned in Seville to exalt not only Mercedarian men of letters as models for the order's own would-be scholars, but likewise St Thomas Aquinas for the Dominicans [fig 3.1], St Bonaventure for the Franciscans and St Alfonso Rodríguez for the Jesuits.[12] The most obvious implication to be drawn from these royal visits concerns the importance of Seville and its clergy to the continuing policy of the defence of Catholicism and the evangelisation of Andalusia, particularly of the remnants of the former non-Christian ethnic minorities, as well as in the Indies, both Occidental and Oriental. In Seville the Crown had sound historical reasons for its concern with the purity of the faith.

*   *   *

In Velázquez's youth in Seville, indeed right up to the expulsion of the Moriscos in 1609, the supply of well-educated and vigilant priests was a major preoccupation of the authorities, both civil and ecclesiastical. Thus it was that Archbishop Don Fernando Niño de Guevara, in the constitutions approved by the synod in the cathedral of Seville in 1604, reminded his clergy of their obligation to instruct Morisco children between the ages of five and eight in sound Catholic doctrine.[13] For this same reason a most anxious cleric was less than happy with the performance of Niño de Guevara's successor, the aged Don Pedro Vaca

de Castro [fig 3.5], who was to rule the archdiocese from 1610 till his death in 1623 at the age of ninety-nine. According to this critic, Don Pedro, a principal promoter of Our Lady's own purity, had been appointing priests who did not bother about the healing of souls, and were unlettered and without a firm grasp of doctrine.[14] Undoubtedly the task was perceived as enormous. On Saturday 22 February 1625, the new Archbishop, Don Luis Fernández de Córdova, stayed in his cathedral till 4 o'clock in the afternoon ordaining more than 500 ordinands.[15] Only one year later, his successor, Don Diego de Guzmán, was again in the cathedral till 4 o'clock in the afternoon ordaining candidates for the priesthood.[16]

In this very special post-Tridentine world the clergy in general, and the regulars in particular, were seen in Catholic Christendom as the very sinews and tendons of the body politic.[17] For this same reason, so many altarpieces of the period have religious figures as literal and symbolic pillars supporting the entire spiritual structure of Catholicism.[18] In the then current Counter-Reformation view, the orders, the Inquisition and preachers were seen as physicians and surgeons with responsibility for the health of all the faithful.[19] It was not merely a question of what is now called social welfare, with the orders and confraternities committed to poor relief, hospital work and other charities. *Salus*, or health, by definition involved not only physical well-being but also spiritual salvation. It is in this context that the Habsburgs, with their three recurrent themes of 'military prowess, pious devotion to the Faith and dynastic greatness', were seen as an irreplaceable bulwark and essential defence of Catholic Christendom.[20]

For a dynasty provided with an impeccable pedigree by its scholars, piety was an important part of its policy. At the beginning of the 1640s, in spite of all the evidence to the contrary, an influential Dominican had not the slightest doubt that the invincible and glorious House of Habsburg owed the greater part of its prosperity to its piety, and that 'God has made its arms formidable as a prize for its piety', which is unsurprising since His Catholic Majesty claimed to be the direct successor of the Kings of Israel of the House of Judah.[21] From the fifteenth century on-

fig 3.2 Sevillian School, seventeeth-century
Don Diego de Guzmán
(Archbishop's Palace, Seville)

fig 3.3 Velázquez *Philip IV*
(Prado, Madrid)

fig 3.4 The High Altar in the Monastery of
San Isidoro del Campo, Seville

wards the Habsburgs – through painting, engraving, sculpture, architecture, literature, numismatics and preaching – had succeeded in projecting themselves as having a very special relationship with the Court of Heaven. As has been observed: 'The Habsburgs were masters at using ephemeral art to convey their perceptions of the world and their ideals'.[22] In this Habsburg ideology the doctrinal decrees promulgated at the Council of Trent became central. Everything challenged by the Protestants – good works, intercession of the Virgin and saints, relics, the Papacy, the religious orders, the Mass and the seven sacraments and so on – was defended. All were seen to be interconnected. Thus the defence of relics, for example, was seen to be linked with the defence of the apostolic succession.[23] Above all, the defence of the Blessed Sacrament was regarded as crucial. According to the dynasty's apologists, the first Habsburg Holy Roman Emperor, Rudolph I, owed his election to his devotion to this Catholic sacrament *par excellence.* It was therefore quite natural that the feast of Corpus Christi should have been given particular prominence in all Habsburg lands and cities, including Seville. As a distinguished historian of Seville points out, not even the famous processions organised by the city's confraternities (and now so inextricably associated with Holy Week in Seville) could compete at that time with the magnificence with which the feast of the Body of Christ was celebrated.[24]

For some critics, the whole corpus of southern Counter-Reformation religiosity is flawed by certain overtones still regarded as excessively crude. However, much less obvious, but no less real, is that same corpus's strong doctrinal backbone. Even the most unpalatable cases have to be placed in context. For example, in Velázquez's Seville a condemned infidel, if willing to be baptised, would have been dressed in fine clothing and given noble godparents. Yet as soon as his christening was completed, the poor wretch was whisked off for immediate execution.[25] Clearly, Velázquez's fellow Sevillians were preoccupied by the real possibility of the new convert falling from his recently acquired state of grace, and ending up in hell rather than heaven, just as Shakespeare's Hamlet is distressed by the real possibility of his odious stepfather entering into a state of grace, and so ending up in heaven instead of hell. Likewise, those self-same Sevillians were obsessed with purity of blood (*limpieza de sangre*) as proof of orthodox Catholicism through genealogical demonstration of the absence of Jewish or Moorish forebears.

Even terms such as *religiosity, devotion* or *spirituality* can turn out to be very elusive. An appreciation of present-day Catholicism, Spanish or otherwise, does not really help. For one Spanish specialist the main characteristics of Sevillian spirituality during this period are devotion to the Immaculate Conception, to the Blessed Sacrament, to Sevillian saints and to penitential practices.[26] However, as Jonathan Brown has justifiably observed: 'It is a truism to say that seventeenth-century Spanish painting is predominantly religious in content. But this simple truth veils a complicated reality, because the Spanish Catholic Church was not a monolithic institution'.[27]

Litigation was the order of the day in most Iberian Cathedral Chapters, and Seville was no exception. The University College of Santa María de Jesús and the Dominican College of Santo Tomás were constantly opposing each other in the law-courts. The orders were divided amongst themselves, and it was not just over the now notorious disputes over the Immaculate Conception of the Virgin. The Dominicans were at loggerheads with the

Franciscans over the relative claims of Thomas Aquinas as opposed to Duns Scotus. The Dominicans and the Jesuits divided permanently on the *de auxiliis* controversy, that is, on the very nature of the operation of grace within the soul. The Carmelites resolutely stood out against all the other orders on the question of antiquity, a serious matter in a society that invested so much in prestige and in lineage. The Mercedarians could never agree with the Trinitarians on questions of privilege relating to monopolistic rights to collect alms. Furthermore, the orders were deeply divided within themselves. Again it was not just a question of the calced against the discalced, there were also deep divisions on the deployment of resources, on the filling of offices and the formulation of policy. Moreover, the regulars were not always on good terms with the seculars. During Velázquez's youth in Seville there was a time when Archbishop Vaca de Castro forbade the Austin friars to preach in his archdiocese.[28] It was in the midst of this sort of minefield that painters had to execute their commissions.

A typical example of this complexity is provided by the English Jesuits who had a college in Seville. It was dedicated fittingly enough to St Gregory the Great. Its enormous main altarpiece, now in Ushaw College, Durham [cat 4] celebrates the fact that it was Pope Gregory who first sent missionaries to England.[29] These Jesuits, like their brethren at the Court of Philip III, were a constant reminder to the faithful of the sufferings of their co-religionists in the British Isles. During the same period Francisco Pacheco, Velázquez's father-in-law, was commissioned to celebrate the sanctity of English Kings and Queens in at least two series of royal portraits now to be found in Oscott Semi-

fig 3.5 Sevillian School, seventeeth-century
Don Pedro Vaca de Castro (Archbishop's Palace, Seville)

nary, Birmingham and the English College in Valladolid [cat 6].[30] The Jesuits of Seville provide ample proof of the enduring attraction of martyrdom throughout this period. They participated enthusiastically in the promotion of the thriving cult of St Hermenegild, whose devotees had transformed his place of martyrdom into a lavishly adorned temple in 1616.[31] It was a Jesuit author of a slightly later date who pointed out that the altarpiece of their college church dedicated to this popular Sevillian saint, as well as its most precious relics, were all to the greater glory of this King and martyr who had given his life in defence of the Catholic faith against the heretic.[32] Likewise, the martyrdom of the Catholic Monarchy's Franciscan and Jesuit missionaries in Japan in 1594 had been celebrated throughout the length and the breadth of the land. Seville itself had been visited by a Japanese embassy on its way to Rome.[33]

In general, the very Catholicness of Velázquez's religious painting is immediately perceptible, as are its orthodoxy and pedagogical purpose. For one Jesuit, Martín de Roa, there was no doubt that 'painting with its colours and visible features can greatly teach the understanding with its immediacy; and the sight of it can engrave things more deeply on the soul with its liveliness.' Equally, he noted with regard to sculpture that many of the Church Fathers called images the books of the ignorant.[34] So, as in preaching, it was not just a question of doctrine but also the cultivation of an inner response, of an inner spirituality.[35] For the believer it was, and still is, not so much a matter of seeing or hearing as heeding.

With particular reference to Velázquez, it is Enriqueta Harris who, with her customary lucidity, has analysed the master's exiguous Sevillian production of religious subjects.[36] Naturally enough, the young painter's *Virgin of the Immaculate Conception* [cat 33] takes pride of place from an iconographical point of view. Contemporary Sevillian writers were convinced that their city was the most Marian of Catholic Christendom.[37] The Dean and Chapter reminded Pope Paul V in 1616 that Seville had a special obligation to the Virgin, for it was through her intercession that the holy King Ferdinand III had recaptured the city from the Moors.[38] Thus arose the paradox that Andalusia, 'the land of Mary Most Blessed' in Spanish, with its main city of Seville dubbed 'the Great Babylon of Spain' because of its worldliness, was passionately committed to this doctrine. This was in spite of the opposition of the Catholic Monarchy's most influential academic order, the Dominicans, who had no less than six friaries in the city at this time. Yet the sons of St Dominic were devoutly Marian in all but the doctrine of the Immaculate Conception. After all, the ever popular Rosary was held to be a devotion that had been given to their founder by the Virgin herself. However that may be, the scandalous debate was re-kindled in Seville in 1613 when a Dominican quoted, 'Quam pulchri sunt gressus tui in calceamentis Filia Principis': 'How beautiful are your feet in your sandals, O prince's daughter', from the *Song of Songs* (VII,2). He was preaching on the feast of the Nativity of Our Lady. He applied the text to the Virgin and argued that this demonstrated her subjection to Original Sin, because her footwear was made from dead animal skin.[39] And *scandalous* is not too strong a word, for throughout Velázquez's youth the faithful of Seville, with the aged Archbishop Vaca de Castro in the forefront, were utterly convinced of the Virgin's care for Spain and all things Spanish.

They firmly believed that she had appeared in person to St James in Saragossa to encourage him in his Spanish apostolate. The Monarchy itself was full of Marian shrines which confirmed in manners marvellous and miraculous her constant solicitude. Ironically it was a Dominican writing in 1604 who maintained that Our Lady had shown herself to be committed to Spain and had given ample proof of the fact.[40] Indeed, certain devotees could actually quantify this Marian concern. It would be claimed that, from the beginning of Christianity up to 1492, of the 150 major victories engineered by the Virgin, no less than eighty had been granted to the Catholic arms of Spain, and only seventy to all the other Christian powers.[41]

For the people of Seville during this period the Immaculate Conception was much more than a question of fashion. It had become an issue of dogma, that is, for them it was self-evidently true that Mary Most Pure had been conceived without the stain of Original Sin. But the polemics did not stop there. Velázquez's *Immaculate Conception* [cat 33], with all its apocalyptical symbolism, was meant to be hung in a house of the Carmelite Order alongside his *St John the Evangelist* [cat 34] with the Virgin appearing in a cloud, an image with far-reaching Carmelite implications.[42] It is this order that was perceived as the prophetic order *par excellence* of the Catholic Church, for they claimed to have been founded by the Old Testament prophet, Elijah. Just as the immensely popular Carmelite reformer, St Teresa of Avila, was convinced that her beloved sons were destined to play a leading role in the imminent ending of the world,[43] so were many Spanish theologians certain that the Old Testament predicted the special part to be played by Spain in hastening the fulfilment of that tremendous event.

It was not just a case of holy missionaries like the valiant Poor Clare, Mother Jerónima de la Fuente [cats 42 and 43], setting out at the age of sixty-six to found a potent spiritual centre in far-off Manila. She in turn, like her brethren in the New World, thought that she was engaged in the advancing of the completion of the fullness of time, when all nations and peoples will have heard the good news of the Lord. For scholars of the calibre of the humanist Benito Ariás Montano or the Jesuit Juan de Mariana, but above all the Augustinian poet and scripture scholar, Luis de León, there was a clear prophecy in the Bible of Spain's apocalyptic, imperial mission. Hence for León, the Old Testament made it clear that Spaniards 'will occupy by force of arms and preaching of the Gospel, the cities of the New World'.[44]

This type of what now appears to be arcane erudition was not foreign to Velázquez's Seville, where learned academies flourished. At the same time there existed secret societies such as the Congregation of the Pomegranate. A future sitter of Velázquez's, the highly respected sculptor Juan Martínez Montañés, was a member. Their leader was thought to have the spirit of Jesus Christ, and all the members were apparently destined to fight against the Antichrist at the end of time. In this kind of context *The Adoration of the Magi* [cat 36], portraying the manifestation of the Infant Saviour to the world at large, is but the start of the missionary process that is destined to reach fulfilment, when the prophecies of the Apocalypse come to pass.[45] All this would be equally consonant with the Jesuit provenance of the picture, for the Society of Jesus is the first specifically missionary order of the Catholic Church.[46] By the same token martyrdom was seen to be an integral part of the same eschatological process. Martyrdom whether in Jacobean England or Shogunate Japan, whether Franciscan or Jesuit, was therefore of immediate and passionate concern to all believers, for it was also an unequivocal sign of the one true Church.

The other two overtly religious themes painted by Velázquez

in Seville are both ostensibly kitchen scenes [cats 21 and 22], and so deal with food and the serving of food. Associations of St Teresa of Avila finding the Master amongst the pots and the pans may be hard to resist for some.[47] However, in the kitchen at Bethany it is the servant who catches the eye, and the teaching of the Council of Trent may be seen to be confirmed. The knowing and the loving of the Lord in this world are primary duties of the Catholic Christian. The same applies to the serving of the Lord, if the believer is to *gozar*, that is, to be happy with Him forever in the next. The Tridentine Fathers had been quite specific in St James's assertion – so damning to the Protestant case – 'that by works a man is justified, and not by faith only'.[48] Equally clearly, Christ dining at Emmaus has quite specific eucharistic connotations. It brings to the Catholic faithful's mind Our Lord's own celebration of Mass. It was in Emmaus that the risen Christ gave Himself in the form of bread and wine to His disciples, who recognised Him in the breaking of bread. Just as there is the portrayal of food for physical sustenance, so there is the reminder of another food in the form of the Body of Christ for the soul, *pabulum vitae*, or food of life, in every sense.

The second theme, the discussion between Martha and Mary, between the pragmatist and the mystic, was topical not only in Seville, but throughout the whole Catholic Monarchy. At the beginning of the modern period there had taken place a quickening of the mystical pulse, particularly, but not solely, amongst women. An Italian humanist at the Court of Ferdinand and Isabel had written of *beatas* or lay holy women 'pullulating'.[49] A contemporary of Velázquez was of the opinion that their numbers were so copious 'that no pen could count them, because as they are spread throughout the world and are not enclosed or in convents and do not need dowries, ... they thus exceed all other orders put together ...'[50] In Seville the Inquisition had eventually been forced to take action. As early as the 1570s the phenomenon of *Alumbradismo* or pseudo-mysticism was, according to some, taking on epidemic proportions.

In seventeenth-century Seville some thought that relics provided the best cure for this type of contagion, and that Protestants could provide nothing as efficacious.[51] For the Inquisition, heresy and depravity went together; for this reason its edicts were against *la herética pravedad*, that is, heretical depravity. Dread was the order of the day, for the most feared result of depravity was venereal disease. The number of whores plying their trade in the the red-light district of El Compás in Velázquez's Seville meant that syphilis was perceived as a major problem.[52] Calls for a reformation of manners abounded.[53] At the same time in such a situation of stress and tension, it was only to be expected that there should have been massive popular recourse to the very remedies defended by the Council of Trent, as a counter to Protestant criticisms, with the defence of the Blessed Virgin's own exemplary purity and the effectiveness of her intercession to the fore. Precisely because these evils were perceived in personal terms, rather than in what are now called social terms, individual sanctity was a top priority. It is difficult now to appreciate not only the extent of the popular appeal of the sanctity, but also the very exuberance of its many manifestations in Seville. For instance, during Velázquez's youth the whole city seems to have been aware of the twenty-three hour long Masses of a dancing Portuguese priest, who was to die of shame because he did not go to meet his Maker when he predicted he would. This would-be mystic was but one of many acclaimed as saints by the populace of Seville.[54] But, of course, this was a problem throughout the whole

of Catholic Christendom during this period. In the words of a French scholar: 'the cult of saints remains the liveliest, the most authentic and the most spontaneous cultural creation of popular religiosity'.[55] This in turn helps to explain why Pope Urban VIII through his decree of 30 October 1625 should have tightened up canonisation procedures.

For the Holy Office of the Inquisition it was all a question of correct diagnosis and appropriate clinical treatment. This was not limited to amputation and cauterisation of the infected body politic. A healthy diet had to be assured. Hence the importance of the fish and eggs – with their obvious Easter symbolism – so lovingly painted in Velázquez's Bethany kitchen scene [cat 21]. Healthy and appetising food – hence the garlic and capsicum – was synonymous with sound doctrine, as the Council of Trent reminded the faithful: 'all who in any manner have charge of parochial and other churches to which is attached the *cura animarum*, shall ... feed the people committed to them ..., in order that they may escape eternal punishment and obtain the glory of heaven'. The same point is made in the Tridentine Catechism: 'But, as the preaching of the divine word ought never to be intermitted in the church, so at this time with much greater piety and industry it ought to be practised, that with sound and uncorrupt doctrine, as with the food of life, the faithful should be nourished and confirmed.'[56] Food had been provided by Our Lord to His disciples sacramentally at Emmaus and to Martha and Mary verbally at Bethany. The Fathers of the Church had assembled at Trent in order that 'the darkness of heresy, which for so many years has covered the earth, being dispelled, the light of Catholic truth may, with the aid of Jesus Christ, who is the true light, shine forth in splendour and purity'.[57] Clearly, in Velázquez's world purity of faith firmly based on sound doctrine was crucial.

The early Sevillian paintings of Velázquez are deceptively simple, which, paradoxically, underlines the fact that they are a product of a complex world now lost and remote, even to Spanish Catholics. It was a world which sought in religion the protection and reassurance that the civil authorities could not provide. Hence the importance of processions, rogations, conjurations, confraternities, penance, shrines, relics, the intercession of saints, guardian angels, the Rosary, the scapular of Our Lady of Mount Carmel, and deep devotion to the Blessed Sacrament of the Altar. In the words of Jean Dulumeau, Baroque insurance policies may have been different to ours, but they were still insurance policies.[58] Nonetheless, post-Tridentine religion was not solely concerned with insurance. As well as the spiritual and theological concerns here touched upon, there was also the important consideration of civic pride and social prestige, still on display to this very day in Seville's spectacular Holy Week processions. Particularly notable was the public rejoicing throughout the Catholic Monarchy in 1622 on the canonisation of four Spanish saints: Isidore, Teresa, Ignatius and Francis Xavier. A special account of the celebrations at Court was published in Seville.[59] Later the news of papal authorisation of the investigation of the sanctity of Ferdinand III, the liberator of Seville from the Muslim yoke, was celebrated publicly, as had been papal approval of the offices of several local Sevillian saints.[60] Seville, like Lisbon, Madrid, Brussels, Besançon, Milan, Naples, Palermo, Cagliari and Barcelona, formed part of the global Catholic Monarchy. Thus it was that 'the Great Babylon of Spain' figured in the Europe of the devout, a Europe in which devotions and devout practices 'left their mark on the evolution of lived religion'.[61]

VELÁZQUEZ IN SEVILLE · II

VELÁZQUEZ

fig 4.1 Pedro de Campaña *Mariscal Altarpiece* 1555–6 (The Cathedral, Seville) detail showing the portraits of Diego Caballero's wife, sister-in-law and daughters

Juan Miguel Serrera

Velázquez and Sevillian Painting of his Time

FRANCISCO Pacheco states that painters are born. Thus it was with Velázquez, although his father probably apprenticed him in the profession without fully recognising his natural ability. However, though it is true that painters are born, they only become great masters as the result of living and working in a specific environment. This has always been so and particularly with Velázquez, whose career would have been very different had he not been fortunate enough to live in Golden Age Seville.[1] The same may be said of the other great masters of Sevillian painting such as Zurbarán and Murillo and also of the prominent figures in other fields, especially sculpture and literature. In this context a recent observation about Cervantes is particularly apt: 'Seville herself was the great teacher'.[2]

To what extent and in what way, then, did Seville influence the origin and development of Velázquez's painting in his early years? Velázquez lived and worked in the city which was known as the 'Port and Gate of the Indies' and this explains the richness and complexity of his sources of inspiration. Following the discovery of the New World and, above all, during the period of colonisation, Seville became one of the most important centres for the production and distribution of works of art. With the new demand came picture merchants who would place large orders for series of paintings with workshops specialised in satisfying this market. To meet the requirements of such commissions (in which the number of works and speed of execution were important factors) painters set up commercial partnerships usually made up of two or three artists who would share equally the costs and profits.

The importance of artistic commerce with the Americas brought a large number of foreign artists to Seville, particularly from the Netherlands and Italy, as well as thousands of paintings and prints, mostly Netherlandish and Italian, which were destined for export. These artists and works of art played an important role in determining the distinctive development of the Sevillian school of painting. Indeed, the 'Sevillian' character of painting in the city in the sixteenth century and the first third of the seventeenth is due to this combination of influences, a combination which was paralleled in this period in Spanish Naples.[3]

Both these influences can be discerned in Velázquez's Sevillian works, but it is the Netherlandish which is predominant and this also applies to the majority of Sevillian painters. This predominance was due not only to the presence in Seville, of Netherlandish paintings and painters, but also to the combined impact on local painting of the style and forms employed by the many glass-makers, sculptors, embroiderers, tapestry workers, ceramicists and printers from the Netherlands who had settled in

fig 4.2 Francisco Pacheco *St Agnes* 1608 (Prado, Madrid)

Seville in the sixteenth century. It is thus more appropriate to speak of the general influence of Netherlandish art on Sevillian painting rather than simply that of Netherlandish painting.

This Netherlandish predominance is not fully accounted for by the fact that there were more works and artists from the Netherlands than from Italy in Seville. There was also a large and wealthy Flemish colony in the city whose artistic preferences, especially with regard to painting, coincided with those of Sevillians. In religious painting, for example, there was a great affinity between Sevillian and Netherlandish artistic modes of expression, which in both instances combined mannerist tendencies with a certain Gothic flavour.

The majority of Pacheco's paintings partake of this character, including the works he executed during the period when the young Velázquez was in his workshop, from 17 September 1611 until at least 14 March 1617, the date of his guild examination as a painter. During these years Pacheco not only taught him all that related to his craft but also, that the works of artists of earlier generations could serve as models for his own. Velázquez would thus have looked beyond such works by Pacheco as the *Christ Carrying the Cross* of 1589 and the *Virgin of Bethlehem*, signed and dated 1590, to the originals upon which they are based: the former repeats the composition of a mural painted in 1561–2 by Luis de Vargas on the exterior of Seville Cathedral and the latter is a copy of an original by Marcel Coffermans still in the former Jesuit church of the Compañia in the city. Pacheco's figures of the Virgin and St John painted in about 1600 as the background to a sculpture of *Christ on the Cross* are closely modelled on figures in the central panel of the large triptych by Frans Francken I which was then in the Hospital de las Bubas in Seville and is now in the Museo de Bellas Artes, a work which later on Pacheco unabashedly copied in his *Crucifixion* of 1638.

Velázquez would have known the altarpiece which Pacheco executed in 1602 for Capitán García de Barrionuevo, still in the church of Santiago, Seville, and his familiarity with sixteenth-century Sevillian painting would have enabled him to recognise that the panel showing *The Virgin and Child with St Anne* is an adaptation of the central panel of the *Holy Kin* by the North Netherlandish painter Hernando de Esturmio (Ferdinand Sturm, active in Seville from 1537 until his death in 1556) painted in 1549 for the parish church of Santa María de la O in Pacheco's home town of Sanlúcar de Barrameda. Velázquez would also have noted that Pacheco's paintings of *St Catherine* and *St Agnes*, now in the Museo del Prado (the latter signed and dated 1608) [fig 4.2], are modelled on Esturmio's half-length saints in the predella of his altarpiece of the *Evangelists* in Seville Cathedral.[4] Some of Pacheco's compositions are derived from those of Pedro de Campaña (the Netherlandish painter Peter Kempeneer, who was in Seville from 1537 to 1562, when he returned to Brussels), for example his *Fathers of the Church* from the altarpiece of the convent of San Clemente dated 1613.[5] Velázquez might have been surprised to realise that the *Evangelists* in this altarpiece are directly based on those painted in 1601–2 by Alonso Vázquez (documented in Seville from 1588 to 1603, when he departed for Mexico) in the predella of the main altarpiece of the Hospital de la Sangre in Seville.[6] Pacheco and Vázquez had worked together on the commission to produce canvases to decorate the large cloister of the Convento de la Merced in Seville between 1600 and 1603.

All Sevillian painters raided the compositions of earlier masters for their own works, and to some extent so did Velázquez, although in his case one cannot speak of copies but rather of creative adaptations. Before analysing Velázquez's debt to the Sevillian painting of his time, however, one should consider whether he simply adopted his master's procedures and thoughts on painting and made them his own or whether he sought to test their validity.

The preoccupations of the painters of Seville tended to be of a practical and pragmatic nature. The disputes of 1480 and 1599 which mark the history of the guild of Sevillian painters were concerned with curbing the activities of unlicensed practitioners and halting the fall in prices and the growth of picture shops. At no point was the question of the status of painting as a liberal art, or other matters of this kind, ever raised. Pacheco was the only Sevillian painter to deal with these subjects, but Velázquez must have been aware that what his master practised often contradicted his theoretical writings. Velázquez could, however, turn to the lettered men of Seville to whom his master introduced him in order to have some light shed on such questions. We know that members of the Sevillian literary world were present at his wedding and Baltasar de Cepeda's poetic account of the festivities held in Pacheco's patio to mark the occasion makes reference to competitions of wit and ingenuity.[7]

The writers Mal Lara and Fernando de Herrera, who are frequently cited in Pacheco's *Arte de la pintura*, could have provided him with some valuable material for reflection. In writings like Mal Lara's prologue to his *Filosofía vulgar* of 1568 and Herrera's *Anotaciones a Garcilaso* of 1580, the authors express their grave concern at the backwardness of Sevillian letters which they wanted to raise to the level of its rivals. Towards the end of his prologue Mal Lara appeals for the adoption of certain foreign customs:

Although not employed in Spain, it is the praiseworthy custom in other nations that writers receive assistance from learned men; they read their works in special academies established for this very purpose where all express their views and make pertinent observations and the author can thereby benefit without having to give these men credit for their kindnesses. The books are then completed and published in amended form to the applause of the learned men of the time. We, on the other hand, continue giving free rein to envy and pride which keeps some men busy with praising their own works and others with disparaging those of their fellows.[8]

Statements such as these would have encouraged Velázquez to draw freely on all kinds of works as occasion required, in addition to those of his master. He made use of prints which were widely exploited as sources by Sevillian artists of the Golden Age, especially by Pacheco. The list of Pacheco's possessions made at the time of his marriage in 1593 includes books of prints by Dürer and Lucas van Leyden. These had previously belonged to Vasco Pereira, a Portuguese painter who settled in Seville in 1561 and whose posthumous inventory of 1609 lists a total of 2,407 prints.[9]

The use of prints accounts for Velázquez basing the composition of his *Adoration of the Magi* of 1619 [cat 36], on the painting of the same subject by Alejo Fernández, a painter of German origin who settled in Seville from 1508 until his death in 1545, made for the crossbeam above the high altar of Seville Cathedral, 1509–12 [fig 4.3].[10] In adapting this composition he must also have realised that it was based in its turn on a print by Schongauer. Later on in Madrid he did not hesitate to make use of a print by Dürer as the model for his *St Anthony Abbot and St Paul the Hermit* (Museo del Prado). It is interesting that this work shares the same composition as the panel painting of the same subject by Pedro de Campaña which was also based on the Dürer.

fig 4.3 Alejo Fernández *The Adoration of the Magi* (The Cathedral, Seville)

figs 4.4 and 4.5 Pedro de Campaña *Mariscal Altarpiece* 1555–6 (The Cathedral, Seville) and detail showing *St Ildefonso Receiving the Chasuble from the Virgin*

This is not purely coincidental since Campaña, who wins high praise from Pacheco, was one of the artists whom Velázquez studied most closely, as is apparent from the many points of comparison between works by the two painters.

One of the works Velázquez paid close attention to was the *Mariscal Altarpiece* painted by Campaña in 1555–6 for a chapel in Seville Cathedral [fig 4.4], especially the scene of *St Ildefonso Receiving the Chasuble from the Virgin* [fig 4.5] and the portraits in the predella. There are interesting similarities between the former and Velázquez's treatment of the same subject [cat 39], particularly in the blaze of glory, in the figure of the saint and above all in the types of the angels. The angels who accompany the Virgin in Velázquez's picture have always engendered curiosity and they have been thought of as saints or even young Andalusian girls. Their peculiar character has been explained in terms of their dependence on the androgynous angels of El Greco, who has also been seen as the source of the whole composition. However, it is quite clear that the starting point for these figures is the winged and female angels which appear in all Campaña's Sevillian works.

Indeed, such was the impact of Campaña's angels on Sevillian painters that even Pacheco, who declared that angels should be painted beardless but male and not 'with the forms and faces of women' (*con figuras y rostros de mujeres*), or with their heads adorned with curls and plaits, imitated them when he painted his large canvas of *Christ Served by the Angels in the Desert* in 1616 (Musée Goya, Castres).

Campaña's portraits of members of the family of Mariscal Diego Caballero in the predella are of great interest [fig 4.6]. The female portraits are painted in the purest Netherlandish manner. Not only do they constitute the formal starting point for Velázquez's portraits of *Mother Jerónima de la Fuente* [cats 42 and 43] they lie at the basis of his uncompromising realism in capturing his sitters. In fact Jerónima de la Fuente's disquieting presence, both spiritual and physical, closely recalls the portraits of Diego Caballero's wife, sister-in-law and daughters [fig 4.1]. Campaña painted them without making any concessions to idealisation or flattery in a conscious effort to represent natural appearances as realistically as possible. Indeed, Campaña can be

credited with painting the cruellest and most merciless portraits of children in the whole of Sevillian painting.

Velázquez, however, also studied portraits by other Netherlandish painters, and in particular those actually executed in the Netherlands. In the church of San Vicente, the parish in which Pacheco lived during the period of Velázquez's apprenticeship, there is a triptych by Jan van Hemessen painted in Antwerp in about 1530.[11] On the interior of one of the wings there are portraits of various members of the Alfaro family, in whose chapel the painting was recorded as early as 1540 [fig 4.7]. The portraits of Hemessen and Campaña helped form the taste among Sevillians for a certain kind of portraiture, and painters between about 1570 and 1630, including Velázquez, conformed to this taste.[12] It has been claimed that Velázquez's early portraits represent a logical progression from the portraits by Pacheco now in the Museo de Bellas Artes of Seville. However, these are usually dated about 1630, when Velázquez was already in Madrid, and more relevant to Velázquez's portraits are earlier ones by Pacheco, in particular that of Capitán García Barrionuevo in the altarpiece commissioned in 1602, and that of Don Miguel Jerónimo and his son, signed and dated 1612.

Pacheco's portraits rely in their turn on those painted at the end of the sixteenth century by artists like Villegas Marmolejo and Alonso Vázquez. The same is true of the portraits by Juan de Uceda, the other painter who, together with Pacheco, examined Velázquez on 14 March 1617. Uceda's portrait of Don Bernardino de Escalante, administrator of the Hospital de San Hermenegildo in Seville, in the large altarpiece of the *Death of San Hermenegildo* illustrates this dependency [fig 4.8]. This painting was commissioned by Don Bernardino and begun by Alonso Vázquez in 1603. Following Vázquez's departure for Mexico in 1604, it was completed by Juan de Uceda. As the work of two artists of different generations and training, the altarpiece combines the late mannerist style, still dominant in Seville at the end of the sixteenth century, of the one, with the nascent naturalism of the other. The two tendencies may be discerned in the portraits in the lower right-hand corner. In the foreground is Cardinal Cervantes, who had died a century earlier, painted by Vázquez [fig

fig 4.6 Pedro de Campaña *Mariscal Altarpiece* 1555–6 (The Cathedral, Seville) detail showing male portraits of the Caballero family

fig 4.7 Jan van Hemessen *Members of the Alfaro Family* c.1530 (Church of San Vicente, Seville) photographed during restoration

fig 4.8 (left) Alonso Vázquez and Juan de Uceda *Death of San Hermenegildo* (Museo de Bellas Artes, Seville)

fig 4.9 (above) Alonso Vázquez *Cardinal Cervantes* (left) Juan de Uceda *Don Bernardino de Escalante* (right) detail from the *Death of San Hermenegildo* (Museo de Bellas Artes, Seville)

fig 4.10 Alonso Vázquez, ceiling detail, 1601 (The House of the Poet Arguijo, Seville)

fig 4.11 (above) Pacheco *The Fall of Icarus* 1604 (Casa de Pilatos, Seville)

fig 4.12 (left) The Gallery of the Archbishop's Palace, Seville

40

4.9]; behind him is the portrait of Don Bernardino de Escalante, executed by Uceda [fig 4.9], whose career runs from 1593 until his death in 1631. Of the two it is obviously the latter that constitutes the clearest precedent for Velázquez's portrait of *Cristóbal Suárez de Ribera* [cat 41] of 1620.

But what of Velázquez and Italian painting? Was there none to be seen in Seville and did he have to wait till he reached the court to discover it? Although Seville did not have the Royal collections, for a painter like Velázquez the Italian paintings which could be seen in the city certainly provided visual nourishment and served to kindle his interest in seeing the great collections of Madrid and in visiting Italy.

One of the first painters to employ the Italian style was the Sevillian Luis de Vargas who returned from his second trip to Italy in 1550 and whose art is filled with references to Perino del Vaga, Francesco Salviati and, above all, Vasari. Towards the end of the century three Italian painters on their way to the New World, Bitti, Medoro and Pérez de Alesio, the last named of whom had executed one of the frescoes in the Sistine Chapel, passed through Seville reinforcing the Italian 'presence' in the city. It was not only painters, however, who made of Seville a 'New Rome'; the patrons of art, both ecclesiastical and secular, played an important role and it is significant that in 1584 a large number of the canons of Seville Cathedral had been in Rome.[13]

A sign of the increasing adoption of Italian forms is apparent in the gradual supplanting in the palaces of Seville of the traditional gilded wooden *mudéjar* ceiling with Italianate painted ceilings with elaborate iconographic programmes of mythological or religious subject matter. Ceilings of this type survive in the house of the poet Arguijo, dated 1601 and executed, probably, by Alonso Vázquez [fig 4.10]; in the Casa de Pilatos, painted in 1604 by Pacheco [fig 4.11]; and in the hall and gallery in the Archbishop's Palace, executed by anonymous artists apparently also in 1604 [fig 4.12].[14]

The young Velázquez, who avidly studied all the paintings of Seville, would have been afforded access to these places by his master. On entering the great hall of the house of Arguijo he would have imagined himself transported to Mount Olympus. The gods painted by Vázquez must have appeared awesome to him, especially when he compared them with the unconvincing figures which Pacheco had painted on the ceilings of the Casa de Pilatos. Velázquez must have studied each figure carefully, probably paying particular attention to the Mars, which is based on Goltzius's engraving of *Publius Horatius,* and which is reminiscent of Velázquez's own *Mars* (Museo del Prado) painted many years later in Madrid. Pacheco's Mars in the scene of the *Apotheosis of Hercules* in the Casa de Pilatos is also a distant relation of Velázquez's *Mars.*

Velázquez seems, in fact, to have all but ignored Pacheco's ceiling paintings. He was much more interested in those in the Archbishop's Palace which, though not of great quality, supplied him with several ideas for his own works. In 1604 Cardinal Niño de Guevara held a diocesan synod and decided to mark its achievements in establishing the norms for the good government of the diocese by commissioning decorations for the great hall, which at that time was accessible to the people of Seville. The ceiling appears to be the work of two Sevillian painters, and the scenes in it are based on a variety of northern prints. The iconographic programme celebrates the triumph of the Catholic Church, with which the Sevillian prelates identified themselves, and is spread across seventy paintings of figurative and emblematic subjects. It is the latter which attracted Velázquez's attention and through the inscriptions attached to them he learnt that a simple dove, a nest of swallows, or a raven perched on a rock, could have further meaning. Perhaps Pacheco accompanied him on his first visit to the palace and explained to him the symbolic content of the scenes, but Velázquez would probably not have required much guidance, since from the time he entered Pacheco's workshop he would have become familiar with exercises in wit and ingenuity, common amongst the Sevillians of his day. Cardinal Niño de Guevara so delighted in them that the prebendary Porras de la Cámara dedicated to him an anthology of the witty aphorisms of Padre Farfán.

The iconographic programme of the ceiling canvases in the so-called Galería de Paso (known as the Connecting Gallery or the Prelate's Gallery) in the Archbishop's Palace is rooted in the same culture which gave rise to these exercises in ingenuity. There are twenty-seven paintings in all: five large pictures, flanked by eight smaller ones and framed by fourteen long rectangular panels. The programme has a moralising character and relates to the function of the room, which serves to connect the two lateral wings of the palace. It combines serial representations

fig 4.13 Unknown artist, *Kitchen Scene c.*1604
(The Prelate's Gallery, Archbishop's Palace, Seville)

fig 4.14 Unknown artist, *Apples c.*1604
(The Prelate's Gallery, Archbishop's Palace, Seville)

of the elements, the seasons and the activities of man, and alludes to life as a passage or transit. The large central scene shows the god Vertumnus disguised as a woman. According to classical mythology, he ordered and governed the seasons, and personifications of these complete the painting. The other four large canvases represent the elements: Earth is represented by a kitchen [fig 4.13], Air by huntsmen, Water by fishermen, and Fire by a forge. Four of the eight medium-size paintings which are arranged around the Vertumnus show scenes from the story of Noah and the Ark, and four allude to the seasons through the activities represented. The rest of the programme is composed of still-life paintings of fruit illusionistically set in the long rectangular panels positioned adjacent to the pictures of the seasons with which the fruits are associated [fig 4.14].

The paintings are of mediocre quality. Those of the seasons are copies after Leandro Bassano, and those of Noah are after his father, Jacopo. They, like the large canvases, were probably brought from Italy. The panels with fruit may have been painted in Seville. The young Velázquez was hardly concerned with questions of provenance, authorship or even quality, however, and he was probably anyway familiar with works by the Bassano family since Pacheco owned a 'Nativity', listed among the possessions which Pacheco brought to his marriage in 1593, and a 'Nativity' and 'Annunciation' are listed in 1609 in Vasco Pereira's estate. What may have interested him about the ceiling was the complex web of symbolic meanings. This could provide the background against which one attempts to gain further understanding of some of Velázquez's Sevillian works, especially the

bodegones, which could be laden with symbolism, both religious and secular.

Another relevant source may have been the series of prints of the Months which Antonio Tempesta dedicated to Cardinal Pietro Aldobrandini in 1599, in which *January* and the *Sign of Aquarius* are represented by large kitchen scenes. Velázquez could have known these, since a set of 'Months by Tempesta' is recorded in the inventory of Vasco Pereira. It may be also that the kitchen scene in the Archbishop's Palace of the allegory of Earth underlies Velázquez's *bodegones* both in subject and meaning. This painting reflects the style of the Cremonese artist Vincenzo Campi, and contains elements common to the paintings and prints of the Netherlandish painter Pieter Aertsen and his followers, which Velázquez also knew.

This combination of Netherlandish and Italian influences characterises the style of most of the Sevillian painters of Velázquez's youth. Juan de Roelas [cat 4], who was in Seville from 1603 to 1616, is an exception, as his manner is wholly Italian. The colour and light in his pictures are so reminiscent of Venetian painting that it is almost certain that he made a trip to Italy. The Jesuits favoured the new style propagated by Roelas and in 1604 commissioned the Italian Girolamo Lucente da Correggio, who was then resident in Seville, to paint the great high altarpiece of their Casa Profesa. They specified, however, that if his first canvas failed to please, as indeed occurred, they reserved the right to give the commission to another painter, and they duly turned to Mohedano whose effort was also unsuccessful. In comparison with Roelas, their style must have seemed dis-

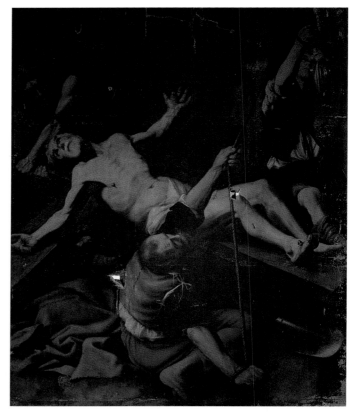

fig 4.16 After Caravaggio *Crucifixion of St Peter* (Church of San Alberto, Seville)

fig 4.15 Juan de Roelas *The Vision of St Bernard* (Archbishop's Palace, Seville)

appointingly old-fashioned and so eventually Roelas himself undertook the commission. Between 1604 and 1606 he executed some of the most impressive canvases painted in Seville in the first thirty years of the century [fig 4.15]. The impact of these works was extraordinary, and from the time of their completion the Casa Profesa became a sort of Escorial for Sevillian, Portuguese and Mexican painters. Velázquez, too, must have observed the power of Roelas's works which broke so forcefully with the Sevillian tradition, but he may not have been willing to adopt a manner which was so forthright and immediate and, as such, diametrically opposed to that of his own master. What he did absorb, however, was Roelas's incipient naturalism, his effort to promote the language of truth to the humble and everyday, an aspect of painting that was fiercely criticised by Pacheco.

In one of the chapters of his *Arte de la pintura*, Pacheco did, however, include a section in which he praises the naturalism of Velázquez, Ribera and Caravaggio, a copy of whose *Crucifixion of St Peter* he cites, although without saying where or when he saw it. It could be the derivation which is today in the former Convent of San Alberto in Seville, and which in 1894 was attributed to Ribera [fig 4.16]. This is a free variant of indifferent qual-

ity and, despite being based on a famous work, it qualifies for the category of paintings known in seventeenth-century Seville as *pinturas comunes* or *ordinarias*. The same can be said of a copy after Caravaggio's *Taking of Christ* now in the Museum of the Cathedral of Sucre, Bolivia, which was probably sent there in the seventeenth century from Seville.[15]

If the *Crucifixion of St Peter* now in Seville is the one that Pacheco knew, then Velázquez may have seen it. However, its low quality would have prevented Velázquez from learning much about the Italian master, despite claims to the contrary. What it would almost certainly have done is encouraged him to see original works by Caravaggio and increased his desire to go to Madrid to study there and in the Escorial. When he settled in Madrid he did not forget what he had learned from his Sevillian masters. His Crucifixions recall those of his master; his *Christ Contemplated by the Christian Soul* (National Gallery, London) is modelled on Roelas's versions of the subject, and when he painted the portrait of *Juan Martínez Montañés* (Museo del Prado) he evidently recalled Francisco Varela's portrait of the sculptor of 1616 [figs 4.17 and 4.18]. But Velázquez in Madrid is a separate subject, another story.

fig 4.18 Francisco Varela *Juan Martínez Montañés* 1616 (Ayuntamiento, Seville)

fig 4.17 Velázquez *Juan Martínez Montañés* c.1635 (Prado, Madrid)

fig 5.1 Francisco Pacheco *The Virgin of the Immaculate Conception with Miguel Cid* c.1616
(The Cathedral, Seville)

Enriqueta Harris

Velázquez, Sevillian Painter of Sacred Subjects

IN DISCUSSING what he calls 'the ingenious invention of portraits from the life', Francisco Pacheco, Velázquez's teacher and father-in-law, takes pride in having trained his pupil in the true imitation of nature. This, he says, cannot be achieved without drawing. Velázquez, he recalls, used to bribe a young country lad who served him as model 'to adopt various attitudes and poses' and different expressions and 'thereby gained assurance in his portraits'. None of these drawings have survived, but Velázquez's youthful paintings in Seville, both sacred and secular, are evidence of his studies from the life of familiar models. By the same means, Pacheco might have added, he gave verisimilitude to his religious subjects. But, strangely, Pacheco makes no mention in his treatise *Arte de la pintura* of any such subjects painted by his pupil in Seville or, for that matter, after he moved to Madrid. He claims to have recognised his pupil's natural genius already when he was nineteen years old, when he gave him his daughter in marriage in 1618. By the time he was writing (the *Arte* was finished by 1638 and published posthumously in 1649), his pride in the achievement of his by then famous pupil was centred on his success at court, as portrait painter to Philip IV. He was writing, he says, not only in praise of his pupil but also out of gratitude and deference to the king who so greatly honoured him.[1]

Velázquez's career at court and his prowess as portrait painter also dominate the first full biography of him published in 1724 by Antonio Palomino, the 'Spanish Vasari'.[2] Palomino gives full praise to the few religious subjects painted for the king but makes no mention of any from the artist's youth in Seville. True, the latter do not appear to have been very numerous, judging from the few that are extant. Together with his early genre paintings, they were mostly lost sight of until the late eighteenth and early nineteenth century, when they began to be rediscovered, and they have been appreciated particularly by British collectors. Portraits from Velázquez's youth in Seville are even rarer than his sacred subjects. These youthful works, the subject of this paper, are few but varied in character and certainly testify to the great natural genius that Pacheco was quick to recognise in his pupil. They all date from after he left Pacheco's studio in 1617 until his move to the court in 1623, at the age of twenty-four. If their sequence is not altogether clear (only four are dated), that they were all painted during these six years is undisputed and so too is their authorship.

It has been said that what was matter for theological debate elsewhere was a subject for popular discussion in Spain.[3] Pacheco's studio was a meeting place for theologians, poets and artists. A poem celebrating the wedding of his daughter to Velázquez describes a discussion of the Eucharist and other such subjects as well as details of the wedding feast.[4] Pacheco, of course, must have been fully aware of Velázquez's exercises in religious paintings. Like every Sevillian painter, Velázquez won his licence (1617) as 'Master painter of religious images [the polychrome wood sculptures that were a feature of local churches]

and in oils'.[5] Pacheco, one of his examiners as well as his teacher, is known to have coloured some of these images made by the chief sculptor of Seville, Juan Martínez Montañés. It gave them life – as he put it.[6] Pacheco must also have known and approved Velázquez's religious paintings since he had been appointed by the Inquisition in 1618 'censor and inspector of all sacred subjects'. As an artist, Pacheco was known chiefly as a religious painter and, as a theoretician, he devoted a large portion of his treatise to the orthodox treatment of the Christian mysteries. His own practical concern for portraiture was manifested in his projected *Libro de descripción de verdaderos retratos de ilustres y memorables varones*. For this he made a collection of more than 150 drawings to be accompanied by biographies and verse eulogies, taking as models the most authentic likenesses or descriptions available.[7]

Pacheco apart, it was inevitable that the young Velázquez should have devoted himself to sacred subjects. Seville in his time was a major centre of religion and religious art and still a city of great wealth as chief port of trade with the New World. It was a point of departure for missionaries and a centre for the export of quantities of works of art. An engraving of 1617 records the centre of the city with the skyline filled with numerous church spires and the river busy with shipping [cat 2]. The foreign artist's tribute is expressed in the inscription with a version of the popular saying: *Quien no ha visto Sevilla no ha visto maravilla*.

Seville today is still remarkable for the number of its churches and religious houses and holy images, many of them of seventeenth-century origin, for the daily scenes of popular piety and for the splendour of the displays of public devotion, especially during Holy Week. In Velázquez's time, in the words of a contemporary, 'the services for Holy Week were so sumptuous that they leave Rome, summit of the world and heart of the church, far behind'.[8] It must, however, have been then as it is today a scene of great contrasts between splendour and solemnity, between the images of the Virgin – the *mater dolorosa* – adorned with rich silks and laces and precious jewels and the scenes from Christ's Passion, tragic and dramatic.

In addition to the regular religious feasts, Velázquez in his youth would have witnessed the celebrations for the beatification of St Teresa in 1614 and for her canonisation in 1622 together with that of two Spanish Jesuits, St Ignatius and St Francis Xavier, and St Isidore, patron of Madrid. But the event of the greatest importance for every citizen of Seville, a city long devoted to the Virgin Mary, was the so-called Marian War: the dispute over the doctrine of the Immaculate Conception of the Virgin, which began there in 1613 with an attack by a Dominican preacher, and ended four years later. Nowhere in Christendom was the mystery more zealously defended or the papal decree of 1617 more enthusiastically received, though it went no further than to forbid public denial. This was celebrated with festivities that lasted many days. Typical of royal and religious celebrations, they included a mixture of the secular and the sacred: fireworks, pageants, jousting, church services and religious processions.[9]

The large canvas now in Valladolid records the elaborate ceremonial in honour of the mystery in 1615 [fig 5.2]. Painted by the Sevillian artist Juan de Roelas (a contemporary of Pacheco) to present to King Philip III, it shows, in the upper part, around the figure of the Virgin, a theological compendium of all the sayings of preachers and writers and the prophetic words of Church Fathers that could be interpreted as support for the notion of her Immaculate Conception. Below, are the processions to the Cathedral in which all the clergy, nobility and populace, including the artist, took part. Among the crowds on the left are children holding banners with the couplets composed by the ballad writer Miguel Cid and set to music by Bernardo de Toro, one of the promoters of the dogma, to provide the battle cry of the Marian party, sung by children as they paraded the streets: *Todo el mundo en general / A voces, Reina escogida / Diga que sois Concebida / Sin pecado original.*[10]

Though it was by no means a new devotion and it was not until 1854 that the Immaculate Conception of the Virgin was defined as an article of faith and declared dogma, this was an appropriate moment to establish an orthodox image of the Virgin. Both Pacheco and Velázquez played an important part in establishing this image in Seville, where it survived with variations for many generations.[11] Not long after Roelas produced his complex record of the city's celebrations, Pacheco made the first of many paintings illustrating the rules for the orthodox treatment of the Immaculate Conception of the Virgin as set down in his treatise. In the version in Seville Cathedral, he includes, in the attitude of donor, the portrait of Miguel Cid holding a paper bearing the words of his popular refrain [fig 5.1].[12] Pacheco prided himself on working from life, as he had taught his pupil to do. But beside his still and mannered figure, Velázquez's one and only painting of the subject [cat 33] presents the Virgin as a more lifelike and three-dimensional figure that seems to owe more to the naturalistic polychrome wood sculptures of Juan Martínez Montañés [cat 32] than to Pacheco.[13] In fact, Pacheco's

rules for the representation of the subject come closer to his pupil's painting than to his own. According to Pacheco, the image of the Virgin, derived from the mysterious woman seen by St John the Evangelist, should represent her as a beautiful young girl of twelve or thirteen, with flowing golden hair, serious eyes and perfect nose and mouth, surrounded by the sun, standing on the moon and crowned by twelve stars. Neither artist has followed the rule that she should be wearing a blue cloak over a white robe, as she appeared to the Portuguese nun Beatriz de Silva. For representing the moon, Pacheco adds, he has followed the learned opinion of his friend Luis del Alcázar, Jesuit author of a Latin treatise on the Apocalypse, published in Antwerp in 1614. The crescent moon points downwards so that the woman stands on a convex surface and is lit by the moon receiving light from the sun. The landscape below contains traditional symbols from the litany of the Virgin: garden, fountain, temple, city, hills, the dawn – the *atributos de tierra* mentioned but not listed by Pacheco.[14]

Velázquez, in representing this image of the Virgin as companion to the figure of *St John the Evangelist* [cat 34] appears to be exceptional, and there is no doubt that they were intended as pendants. The canvases, close in style and nearly identical in size, were most probably painted for the place where they were first recorded some time before 1800: the chapter-house of the monastery of Shod Carmelites in Seville, an Order committed to the defence of the dogma of the Immaculate Conception. Here St John, on the island of Patmos, is seated with pen poised to describe his vision, which appears above represented on a small scale. Velázquez has disregarded Pacheco's advice that the Saint at this time was an old man and has portrayed him as a handsome youth who bears some resemblance to the sitter of one of his early portraits, which is possibly a self-portrait.[15] Luis del Alcázar, author of the treatise consulted by Pacheco, was one of the illustrious sons of Seville represented in his portrait gallery and uncle of the brothers who looked after Velázquez on his ar-

fig 5.2 Juan de Roelas *Ceremony in Honour of the Immaculate Conception of the Virgin* 1616 (Museo Nacional de Escultura, Valladolid)

fig 5.3 Illustration by Juan de Jáuregui of *The Vision of St John the Evangelist* for Luis de Alcázar's treatise on the Apocalypse published in Antwerp 1614

fig 5.4 Illustration by Antón Pizarro of *The Virgin Bestowing the Chasuble on St Ildefonso* in Salazar de Mendoza, *El Glorioso Doctor San Ildefonso,* published in Toledo 1618

rival at court. While the young painter may not have studied the text of this theological treatise, he based the vision of St John on the full-page illustration in Luis del Alcázar's work [fig 5.3].[16] Seen together, Velázquez's paintings testify to the origin of the mystery of the Immaculate Conception of the Virgin and of her devotional image. Unlike the woman in the vision of St John, Velázquez's Virgin is portrayed as a real person like the Saint but on a smaller scale, to indicate perhaps her mystical meaning.

At the height of the controversy over the doctrine of the Immaculate Conception of the Virgin, there was a revival of Spain's devotion to St Ildefonso, the seventh-century Archbishop of Toledo. Two important treatises were published, one in Madrid in 1616, the other in Toledo two years later, by El Greco's patron Pedro Salazar de Mendoza.[17] St Ildefonso's tract on the perpetual virginity of Mary, a defence against attacks by infidels and heretics (first printed in 1556) was now interpreted as an early vindication of her Immaculate Conception. The scene of her miraculous appearance in Toledo Cathedral to reward the Saint by investing him with a chasuble won increased favour as a subject for art not only in Toledo and not least in Seville.[18] Here, Archbishop Pedro de Castro, formerly of Granada, was honoured for his championship of the Virgin Mary and her Immaculate Conception as 'a second St Ildefonso'.[19]

Velázquez's painting of *St Ildefonso Receiving the Chasuble from the Virgin* [cat 39], much damaged and restored, owes little to any pictorial tradition (the subject is not mentioned by Pacheco). The illustration in Salazar de Mendoza's work faithfully represents his account of the miracle: the appearance of the Virgin in the Cathedral, seated on the episcopal throne, and in the company of female saints, to present a chasuble to St Ildefonso, who kneels before her with hands clasped [fig 5.4]. This is more or less how the subject is most often treated, though the saints are sometimes replaced or joined by angels. Velázquez, however, has treated it differently. The Virgin appears among clouds, an imprecise figure among a group of women, holy no doubt but not identified as saints. In contrast, attention is focused on St Ildefonso, who is represented as a realistic portrait-like figure dressed as a cleric, as if intended to be recognised, kneeling in an indeterminate place. His rapt expression suggests that his is a vision as Salazar de Mendoza describes it, *en cuerpo y en alma* (in body and in soul). The chasuble, at least in the present condition of the painting, is not the rich vestment seen in most versions of the subject.

The Adoration of the Magi [cat 36], probably painted a year or two before the St Ildefonso, is one of the few dated canvases and one of the few traditional religious subjects that Velázquez painted in Seville. The date, 1619, is on the stone on which the Virgin's feet are resting. Velázquez has followed once again Pacheco's rules for the orthodox treatment of the subject.[20] The scene takes place at the mouth of a cave. The presence of Joseph, though not mentioned in the Gospel, is sanctioned by tradition. The Virgin *muy alegre y hermosa* (here she is beautiful but hardly lively) holds the Infant Christ in her arms. Contrary to usual practice, Pacheco argues for the Child being in swaddling clothes, on the authority of St Bernard and an obscure passage in the spiritual writings of Luis de Granada, one of the illustrious members of his portrait gallery. Velázquez's scene is distinguished by the sobriety of the costumes of the Magi – not *de gala* as Pacheco had it – and the lack of rich crowns and splendid gifts. Like St Ildefonso, all the protagonists appear to be portraits, based probably on the artist's early life studies of regular models. The same model for the Virgin had served earlier for *The Immaculate*

Conception [cat 33]. The boy attendant in the background on the left is present in some of the *bodegones*: in the picaresque kitchen scene: *An Old Woman Cooking Eggs* [cat 16], dated a year earlier, and together with the Magus in front of him in *The Waterseller* [cat 31]. Their lifelike appearance and apparent ages invite the suggestion that we have here a group of the artist's own family: Pacheco as the older Magus, Velázquez himself as the younger one, the Virgin the likeness of the wife he married in the previous year and the Child – a little older than usual in this scene – the daughter born in May 1619. But there is no evidence to support such an ingenious notion.

Apart from one portrait, the only paintings from Velázquez's Seville days that Pacheco mentions are the *bodegones* and, like the drawings, he praises them as preparation for the portraits. Taking up the challenge of a rival at court, who dismissed such subjects as unworthy of esteem, he declared: 'Of course they are except when they are painted as my son-in-law paints them ... then they deserve the highest esteem. From these beginnings and in his portraits he hit upon the true imitation of nature.'[21] In the same chapter, Pacheco recalls Pliny's story of the painter Piraeicus, who won fame with humble subjects of shops, food and the like. Palomino, who knew Velázquez's *Waterseller* and some of his other *bodegones*, goes further and cites – without acknowledgement – a similar story in Baltasar Gracián's *El Heroe*. Believing it to refer to Velázquez, he tells of the artist who took to painting rustic subjects with bravado. Asked why he did not paint more serious subjects with delicacy and beauty (like Titian), he replied that he preferred to be first in that kind of coarseness than second in delicacy.[22] Though Velázquez was not the hero of this topos, he may well have known Pliny's version as he owned Italian and Latin editions of his *Natural History*.[23]

Velázquez's *bodegones*, admired by both Pacheco and Palomino, must have enjoyed great popularity, judging from the number of copies, variants and some parodies known today. But neither writer offers any interpretation, literary, allegorical, reli-

fig 5.5 Francisco Pacheco *St Sebastian in Bed Attended by St Irene* 1616 (formerly in Alcalá de Guadaira, Hospital of St Sebastian, destroyed 1936)

gious or erotic, as some modern critics have done. Pacheco, in fact, gives a straightforward description of a *bodegón* which he himself painted in emulation of his pupil. 'When I was in Madrid, in 1625', he writes, ' I ventured ... to please a friend by painting a small canvas with two figures from the life, with flowers, fruits and other trifles ...' But he makes no mention of the moralising *bodegones* or *bodegones a lo divino* as they have come to be called, of which only two examples are known. These present a very different kind of religious imagery from those discussed previously.

What is remarkable about the *Kitchen Scene with Christ in the House of Martha and Mary*, is the mastery of technique by a nineteen-year-old artist (there are traces of the date 1618) in the portrayal of the two women and of the still life on the table in what at first sight appears to be an everyday domestic scene [cat 21]. Nearly as remarkable is the amount of ink spilt in modern times in attempts to read meaning into the painting as a whole and into every detail – the eggs, the fish, the mortar and pestle – attempts too many and too diverse to mention here.[24] Not that the meaning is crystal clear. What is clear is that the scene in the foreground belongs to the artist's world, with women dressed in contemporary costume, the young woman even wearing an earring, the old woman a bracelet, while the scene in the background, on a much smaller scale, is a biblical one illustrating the visit of Christ to the house of Martha and Mary. According to the Gospel of *St Luke* (X, 39–42):

Mary sat at Jesus's feet and heard his word. But Martha was cumbered about much serving, and came to him, and said, Lord, dost thou not care that my sister hath left me to serve alone? ... And Jesus answered and said unto her, Martha, Martha, thou art careful and troubled about many things: but one thing is needful: and Mary hath chosen that good part, which shall not be taken away from her.

In the scene in the background, Mary is seated at Christ's feet while the woman standing behind her is usually taken to be Martha (crucial to the scene) with a gesture interpreted as one of remonstration, rather than an attendant like the old woman in the foreground. Here, her gesture and the expression on the face of the young woman beside her as she pauses in her work, as if they were addressing the spectator, relate them to the biblical scene behind. One of the questions that has been much discussed is whether the biblical scene is a picture on the wall, a mirror, or a view into the next room seen through an opening in the wall. It is tempting to imagine that it is a mirror and that the young woman is looking at the scene that takes place behind us, as the poet Ruth Fainlight eloquently surmised:

> *You stare out of the picture, not at me.*
> *Your sad, resentful gaze is fixed on what*
> *Is only seen reflected in the mirror*
> *On the wall behind your shoulder ...*
> *That old servant by your side is whispering*
> *Admonitions and consolation – her*
> *Country wisdom ...*[25]

The sides of the opening in the wall, however, make it clear that it is this and not a mirror, so the scene is not visible to the young woman, though her awareness of it would explain her expression and the attitude of her companion.

The double scene with a view through a window or in the background was a commonplace in the sixteenth century and later. Pacheco, two years before Velázquez painted this *bodegón*, had painted for a hospital outside Seville a canvas, *St Sebastian in Bed Attended by St Irene*, with the martyrdom of the Saint on a small scale, seen through a window [fig 5.5].[26] Still closer as the probable source for Velázquez's composition are the sixteenth-century kitchen and market scenes with biblical subjects represented on a small scale in the background, associated in particular with the Netherlandish artists Pieter Aertsen [cats 17–20] and Joachim Beuckelaer. Velázquez, who could have known these in later engravings if not in the original, has transformed the Netherlandish formula into something modern, local and personal. His composition is much simpler, and while the attitudes, gestures and facial expressions suggest that they are addressing the spectator, at the same time they relate them directly if not obviously to the Gospel story. We are reminded of how Velázquez as a boy used to get his models to adopt various poses and expressions. The young cook's expression, as she pauses in her work, is no doubt intended to identify her as a modern reference to Martha, troubled about many things, while the old woman, as the poet suggests, is whispering consolation and admonitions perhaps – as has also been suggested – as St Teresa offered consolation to her nuns with the words: 'The Lord walks even among the kitchen pots, helping you in matters spiritual and material.'[27] The model for the old woman is the same as for the cook in the *An Old Woman Cooking Eggs*; the pestle and mortar and the green glazed earthenware jug also appear in her kitchen [cat 16]. The garlic, pimento, fish and eggs, the basic ingredients of a Spanish meal, is presumably a reference to a meal of abstinence.

The *Kitchen Maid with the Supper at Emmaus*, similar in size and format to the *Martha and Mary*, is the only other *bodegón* with a religious meaning [cat 22]. The scene in the background representing the supper at Emmaus was only uncovered in 1933, and it is unmistakably viewed through a hatch. The young woman seated at the table, usually described as a mulatto kitchen maid, has an expression which is not easy to read. She has been seen as rapt in thought, alternatively in a trance-like state suggesting awareness of the miracle enacted behind her, the moment of the disciples' recognition of Christ as He took bread and blessed it: 'And their eyes were opened and they knew Him and He vanished from their sight' (*Luke* XXIV, 32). The *Supper at Emmaus* has also been related to the message of St Teresa: 'The Lord walks even among the kitchen pots.'[28] The jug on the table and the basket on the wall are, like details of the other *bodegón* with *Martha and Mary*, also to be seen in *An Old Woman Cooking Eggs* [cat 16] but this young woman, like the modern Martha, appears in no other known painting by Velázquez. Rosemarie Mulcahy has brought to notice the suggestion of the Prior of the Escorial (1575) that *Christ in the House of Martha and Mary* and the *Supper at Emmaus*, together with *Abraham Receiving the Three Angels* were the subjects most suitable to hang in the monastery's reception room, all themes of charity, of hospitality to the stranger.[29] Velázquez's paintings of the first two subjects would also appear to be suitable to hang in the refectory of a nunnery, possibly above a hatch, but they have no early history to indicate their original location.

It may appear strange that I have chosen to include in this selection of sacred subjects painted by Velázquez in Seville the portrait of a Franciscan nun, the venerable *Mother Jerónima de la Fuente* [cat 42]. In fact the nun was on her way to becoming a saint when Velázquez painted her portrait in Seville, though she has still not been canonised. Like many other holy persons in seventeenth-century Spain, she was a subject of veneration in her lifetime, but claims to her sanctity failed to win approval from Rome. Velázquez's portrait is his first known attempt at a full-length portrait and Mother Jerónima is the first of his sitters to be identified. It was no doubt with pride that he signed his painting, as he rarely did, and dated it 1620. The nun is in the traditional pose of a saint or holy person, similar to that of Father Simón, a priest in Valencia who was venerated locally but failed to reach sainthood [fig 5.6]. (He appears in the painting by Francisco Ribalta in the National Gallery, London, dated 1612.)[30] Velázquez's portrait was rediscovered only in 1927 when it was lent by the sitter's convent in Toledo to an exhibition of Franciscan art held in Madrid. When it was acquired soon afterwards by the Prado Museum, the inscription on the banderole, now hardly visible, was removed on the grounds that it was alien to the artist – as it must have seemed at that time – and was therefore considered a later addition.[31] But it survives in a replica of the portrait that also came from the convent in Toledo, and is now in a private collection [cat 43]. This inscription and another across the top of the canvas (from *Psalms* and *Lamentations*) affirm the religious character of the portrait. The inscription across the lower part of the canvas – certainly a later addition – reads: 'This is the true portrait of Mother Jerónima de la Fuente, a nun of the Convent of San Juan de los Reyes in Toledo, who set out in April 1620 at the age of 66 with two nuns and a novice to found and become the first Abbess of the Convent of St Clare of the Immaculate Conception in Manila.' One of several biographies, published in Madrid in 1717, tells how she was chosen as a model of religious fervour and for her fame of sanctity to go to Manila, and how on her way to embark she stayed for three weeks in Seville, in the Franciscan Convent of Santa Clara. It was there that Velázquez must have painted her portrait, which was sent back to Toledo, where replicas were made. After her death in Manila in 1630, it is recorded that

crowds came to see and pay homage to her corpse and the Governor of the Islands sent an artist to paint her. To help him, she closed her mouth and opened her eyes, though they remained half closed as if out of humility. This was one of the many miracles listed in the cause for her beatification promoted in 1734. The apostolic process has never been completed, yet Mother Jerónima has won a place in more than one dictionary of saints, where her acts of penitence and humility, her gift of prophecy and her performance of miracles are recorded. Among her writings she left a mystical work dedicated to the Immaculate Conception of the Virgin.[32]

Velázquez's portrait of this remarkable woman, with book in one hand and brandishing a crucifix in the other, gives a vivid impression of the appearance of the missionary, with martyrdom in mind, that she must have presented when she set out to join the forces of the Jesuits and Franciscans in the Philippines. Illustrating, as it does, the narrow line between the sacred and the profane, it foreshadows the young artist's future brilliant career as a portrait painter. As chief artist in Seville, it is likely that Pacheco played a part in Velázquez being given permission to paint this important sitter. His own talents for portraiture were limited. For his version of a true likeness, he was satisfied, in his book of drawings, with a portrait to copy or a description of the sitter. Thus, his posthumous portrait of Luis de Granada, for example, based probably on a painting or an engraving, gives the impression of a literal rather than a living likeness [fig 5.7].[33] Pacheco may well have realised that Velázquez by 1620 had fulfilled his promise and, thanks to his early studies from the life, he had gained what Pacheco called 'assurance in his portraits'. 'A master is more to be honoured than a father-in-law – he claimed – 'and I consider it no disgrace for the pupil to surpass the master', citing with less modesty the examples of Leonardo and Raphael, Giorgione and Titian.

This essay is reprinted from Symbol and Image in the Iberian Arts *(Trinity & All Saints, Leeds, 1994) with kind permission of the editor, Margaret A. Rees*

fig 5.6 Michel Lasne, after Francisco Ribalta
Father Simón

fig 5.7 Francisco Pacheco *Fray Luis de Granada*
(Museo Lázaro Galdiano, Madrid)

fig 6.1 Velázquez, detail from *An Old Woman Cookings Eggs* 1618 (National Gallery of Scotland, Edinburgh)

David Davies

VELÁZQUEZ'S BODEGONES

HE [VELÁZQUEZ] *took to painting with most extraordinary originality and remarkable talent animals, birds, fish-stalls and bodegones with perfect imitation of nature, with beautiful landscapes and figures; different foods and drinks; fruits, and poor and humble furnishings, with such mastery of draughtsmanship and colouring that they appeared real.*   Antonio Palomino, 1724[1]

Although this range of genre subjects is not evident in the extant work of Velázquez, it is testimony to the keen interest in such subjects that was shared by Velázquez and his patrons and collectors. His extant genre paintings are referred to as *bodegones* and are composed of figures in humble settings, domestic utensils and food and drink.

According to a contemporary dictionary compiled by Sebastián de Cobarruvias (1611), *bodegón* was the name given to the cellar or lower entrance area of a *bodega* (wine-vault) where those who did not have anyone to cook a meal for them were provided with food and drink.[2] Cobarruvias also noted the opinions that *bodegón* was derived from 'budello', Italian for tripe sold in similar circumstances, or the Hebrew word for 'to eat' since the *bodegón* was the place where one was given food.[3] What is implied in Cobarruvias's definition is clearly stated in the *Diccionario de Autoridades* (1726). The people provided with food and drink in the *bodegón* were the poor and the common.[4] In taverns, wine was sold and depending on the region, simple food was sometimes available. Etymologically, *taberna* was associated with stalls where vendors sold wine, in particular, and some comestibles.[5]

These verbal definitions reflect and evoke scenes of poor or humble people preparing, serving, eating and drinking or selling simple food and drink in lowly and, by inference, dimly-lit settings. There is no reference to the world of dandies, riff-raff, confidence tricksters, pimps and prostitutes. At worst, Cobarruvias characterises the owners of *bodegones* as fat and greasy, and drunks in taverns as proverbially sad or happy, singing or weeping, and all tipsy and befuddled.[6] Nor is there any reference to an excessive quantity of food, since this would be totally inappropriate in these settings. Consequently, these verbal references are at odds with Netherlandish and Lombard paintings of kitchen scenes or market stalls in which there is often a glut of food and drink. Likewise, they do not conjure up the world of Caravaggio's wistful, hedonistic youths or knowing fortune-tellers. Nevertheless, some of the earliest recorded references to paintings of *bodegones* in Spain reveal that they were associated with these foreign traditions, which is understandable since the Netherlands and the Duchy of Milan were dominions of the Spanish Habsburgs. Two Flemish *bodegones* were presented by Philip II to the Hieronymite monastery of El Escorial in 1593.[7] The painter royal of Philip II, Pantoja de la Cruz, completed three *bodegones de Italia* in 1592 for Agustín Álvarez de Toledo, a member of the Council of the Indies.[8] At court, these styles became increasingly popular.[9] Listed in the 1600 inventory of the collection of Juan de Borja, Count of Ficallo and son of San Francisco de Borja [see cat 9], were four *bodegones*, one of which was described as 'another canvas of a kitchen scene from Flanders' (*otro lienza de la cocina de flandes*).[10] Courtly taste for these paintings of daily life is best exemplified in the 1623 inventory of the newly rebuilt Pardo Palace. Seven *bodegones* were recorded, six of which were of Flemish origin. The scenes depicted were of stall-holders selling fish, fruit and vegetables, cheeses and eggs.[11]

Pacheco himself only gives a sketchy characterisation of a *bodegón*. It includes various scenes of figures eating and drinking.[12] Figures may also be shown with various still-life objects, as can be inferred from his description of a *bodegón,* now lost, that he painted in Madrid for his friend, Francisco de Rioja: 'a small canvas with two figures from the life and flowers, fruits and other trifles'.[13]

Velázquez's *bodegones* are a different kettle of fish! They are firmly rooted in the verbal tradition and what it describes – scenes of humble people in humble settings. Velázquez never loses sight of this basic meaning and always interprets it with compassion. Thus, although he is aware of the Netherlandish and, probably, Lombard styles of painting, his images are never derivative because his eye is constantly focused on what he sees around him. That is why looking at a chipped, glazed, earthenware jug in one of his *bodegones* is an exciting and novel experience.

Yet underlying his visual perception is a profounder truth. The world that Velázquez and his Christian contemporaries looked at was perceived as created by God and controlled by Divine Providence.[14] Thus, at the very beginning of his address to the reader of his *Tesoro de la Lengua*, Cobarruvias affirms that God created Adam and Eve and that the language in which they communicated was neither acquired nor invented by them but instilled in them by God.[15] This sentiment is clearly and emphatically spelt out in the prologue and the first and final chapters of Pacheco's *Arte de la pintura*.[16] Indeed, it is a leitmotiv. Since God created the natural world in his divine wisdom, it is the function of the Christian artist to learn to know God through the imitation of nature. For that reason, Pacheco stresses the importance of drawing, that is, the recording of nature. Yet he does not perceive painting as a literal copying of nature. Instead, the painter has to transcend nature in order to communicate his perception of it. For Pacheco, this is not copying but imitating nature. It involves not merely manual skill but especially the intellectual capacity to discern what is appropriate to the painter's vision (of nature). Therefore, painting is not a mechanical but a liberal art. It is an intellectual exercise whereby the painter can imitate nature and God himself, as far as that is possible. This belief in a theocentric world was taken for granted, especially among learned Spaniards, and to ignore its fundamental importance is to fail to appreciate fully the context and, therefore, the meaning of genre images such as Velázquez's *bodegones*.

In order to analyse that context and assess what was traditional and what was novel in Velázquez's response, some brief mention of the history of genre painting may prove helpful. Genre imagery was integral to Medieval and Renaissance series of 'Labours of the Months', 'Seasons' and 'Liberal and Mechanical Arts'. All were imbued with the Christian ethic that man must perform good works to merit grace for his salvation. In the case of the 'Labours' and 'Seasons' [see fig 6.9], these 'good works' took the form of tending God's creations. 'In those days no incongruity was felt in placing these pictures of daily life side by side with scenes from the legends of the saints. The dignity and sanctity of labour were expressed in this way.'[17] Perhaps this response to God and His creation also explains the seemingly incongruous display of religious and genre paintings together on the walls of various rooms in many sixteenth- and seventeenth-century Spanish collections.

The sixteenth and seventeenth centuries witnessed significant changes in the representation of genre subjects. They are treated as independent compositions, not parts of a series; their content is often overtly didactic, especially moral; and they are peopled with peasant types whose behaviour is usually far from exemplary. Whereas such types were accepted for what they were in the 'Seasons' or 'Labours of the Months', because they dutifully engaged in manual labour or innocently enjoyed the pleasures of God's creation, they came to be increasingly perceived and represented as sinful and foolish, and were ridiculed.

The emergence of independent genre painting or sculpture (for example, Giambologna) was probably inspired or encouraged by the desire of educated Renaissance patrons and collectors to possess re-creations of works of art described in ancient and famous literary sources, such as Pliny the Elder's *Natural History*. This practice is termed 'ekphrasis'.[18] This was part of a wider interest in the rediscovery of classical antiquity, in particular the Renaissance achievement of liberating classical forms from their medieval and often moralised trappings, and restoring them to their classical content. In the context of genre painting, Pliny's well-known description of 'a minor style of painting' is relevant:

Among these was Piraeicus, to be ranked below few painters in skill; it is possible that he won distinction by his choice of subjects, inasmuch as although adopting a humble line he attained in that field the height of glory. He painted barbers' shops and cobblers' stalls, asses, viands and the like, and consequently received a Greek name meaning 'painter of sordid subjects'; in these however he gives exquisite pleasure, and indeed they fetched bigger prices than the largest works of many masters ... [19]

It is noteworthy that Pliny makes no reference to any of these subjects having a moral meaning. Yet it does not follow that they had none.

In Northern Renaissance art, however, the moralising legacy of the medieval world was earnestly preserved and overtly displayed. A striking example is Hieronymous Bosch's *Table of Seven Deadly Sins* in which 'Gluttony' is epitomised by fat and vulgar peasants [fig 6.2]. Similarly, in 'Peasant Brueghel's' art, the blind who lead the blind are crude and menacing paupers.[20] They are the 'sturdy beggars' of contemporary society, whom Brueghel has chosen to represent the blind ignorance of those who lack faith. This moralising sentiment underlies both Brueghel's *Peasant Wedding* and *Peasant Dance* [fig 6.3].[21] Thus both Bosch and Brueghel vividly use negative examples to awaken man's consciousness, to expose ignorance and superstition, and to exhort virtue. Such food for thought was not for peasants. The moral meaning and the novel imagery was for the consumption of the educated and the sophisticated.[22] As such, they are pictorial counterparts to the 'Adages' and 'Apophthegms' of Erasmus, the celebrated Christian reformer and humanist. Here were pithy sayings on plebeian subjects addressed to a literate and learned audience.

A similar moralising sentiment, but expressed in a different pictorial idiom to that of Bosch and Brueghel, can be discerned in the work of two other sixteenth-century Netherlandish artists, Pieter Aertsen [fig 6.4], and his nephew Joachim Beuckelaer. It is characteristic of their religious imagery that the Biblical episodes are visible in small scale in the background, and the foreground usually filled with a profusion of still life, mainly food, and humble figures, one of whom normally looks at or addresses the beholder (for example in their respective versions of *Christ in the House of Martha and Mary* in the Rijksmuseum, Amsterdam and Boymans-Van Beuningen Museum, Rotterdam). This visual inversion of the traditional religious image serves to compel the beholder to meditate on the continuing relevance of Christ to the modern, that is, sixteenth-century world. To a twentieth-century viewer the message could be ambiguous. Does the excessive quantity of food symbolise the beneficence of God or man's sinful indulgence in material pleasures? Since Christ upholds the poor in spirit (*Matthew* V, 3), the moral would seem to be that Christ is only present to those who renounce these earthly vanities.[23] Even where the subject is not explicitly religious, the

fig 6.2 (left) Hieronymous Bosch *Table of Seven Deadly Sins* (Prado, Madrid)

fig 6.3 (above) Peter Brueghel the Elder *Peasant Dance* (Kunsthistorisches Museum, Vienna)

frequent inclusion of excessive quantities of food and vulgar peasant types, some of whom make obviously lewd gestures, suggests a moral intention (for example Aertsen's *Market Scene,* Kunsthistorisches Museum, Vienna, and *Pancakes,* Boymans-Van Beuningen Museum, Rotterdam; and Beuckelaer's *Country Market,* Capodimonte Museum, Naples). As in the images of Bosch and Brueghel and the sayings of Erasmus, humour is often used by Aertsen and Beuckelaer to mock the folly of these peasant types. Rarely are they treated as individuals or with compassion.

Unlike the terse, vivid and distinctively individual styles of Bosch and Brueghel, the blander imagery of Aertsen and Beuckelaer was more easily disseminated. Its influence on sixteenth-century Lombard painters such as Vincenzo Campi has long been recognised.[24] For example, in his *Christ in the House of Martha and Mary* the scriptural episode is relegated to the background while the foreground is filled with a variety of poultry, fish, fruit and vegetables [fig 6.5]. Similarly Campi has adopted a horizontal format, not for narrative purposes, since the religious scene is in the rear and reduced in scale, but for the display of food. The different shapes and textures attest to the skill of the artist and appeal to the senses of the beholder, especially sight, touch and taste. These sensations are heightened by the viewpoint whereby the spectator has the illusion that he is close to this spread of plenty. It is a feast for the eyes. The kitchen maid, too, who is young and buxom, is ripe for the picking! Similarly in the *Kitchen Scene* (Museo Provincial de Bellas Artes, Málaga) a grinning, lecherous peasant fondles the maid as she penetrates a plucked chicken with a skewer, as does her counterpart in Beuckelaer's *Christ in the House of Martha and Mary.* Yet such overt display was surely a vanity. As the author of *Ecclesiastes* reminded his readers:

I ... planted vineyards. I made gardens, and orchards ... I got me manservants and maidservants ... and herds of oxen, and great flocks of sheep ... I heaped together for myself silver and gold ... And whatsoever my eyes desired, I refused them not ... (*Ecclesiastes* II, 4–10)

Yet they were worth nothing.

Vanity of vanities, says the Preacher, Vanity of vanities! All is vanity. (*Ecclesiastes* I, 2).

Instead, he upheld what was to be the ethos of the 'Seasons' and 'Labours of the Months':

Is it not better to eat and drink, and to shew his soul good things of his labours? And this is from the hand of God.' (*Ecclesiastes* II, 24)

Sensual appetites had to be curbed if man was to receive spiritual nourishment.[25] Viewed in the contemporary context of Catholic reform and renewal, it is probable that these paintings by Aertsen, Beuckelaer and Campi were also meant to be read on a moral level. Such moralising was intended for an educated, well-off and, probably, male audience. In reality no peasant would have been presented with such a profusion of food. This was a time when pauperism was rapidly increasing to an awesome degree throughout Europe, and the situation was exacerbated and clearly evident from the influx of the rural poor into the towns to seek employment and sustenance.[26] Probably because of their evil condition, paupers were identified in much pictorial imagery of the period with sensual instincts and appetites.

Yet this pictorial perception was soon to be challenged and changed dramatically by a later Lombard painter, Caravaggio. In his *Supper at Emmaus* the two disciples appear stocky and strong, rough and robust, and are shabbily dressed [fig 6.6]. One has a weather-beaten face and powerful hands, the other has big shoulders and a thick neck. These are poor men who work with their hands. In addition, one wears a jerkin with a hole at the elbow. In the same realistic vein, one of the wickers of the plaited basket is broken, and a rotten apple is among the fruit. Such are the players and props in Caravaggio's religious dramas. Obviously, they do not conform to the classical ideal which, although based on nature, is selected and perfected to create a harmonious and graceful whole, that is more perfect than anything found in nature. Traditionally in the wings, these lowly types are brought to the front of the stage where, under a bright spot-light, they act their parts with forceful rhetoric. As always with Caravaggio, only those players are chosen who have a powerful physical presence. They are bony and burly rather than tall and thin or short and fat. They are as carefully selected as any classical figure, but with different intent.

Pointedly and compassionately, Caravaggio identifies the two disciples with the poor. Hierarchical status is of no consequence. The sentiment echoes that of the celebrated Franciscan spiritual exercises, the *Meditations on the Life of Christ,* attributed to a follower of St Bonaventura:

fig 6.4 (above) Pieter Aertsen *Christ in the House of Martha and Mary* (Boymans-Van Beuningen Museum, Rotterdam)

fig 6.5 (right) Vincenzo Campi *Christ in the House of Martha and Mary* (Galleria Estense, Modena)

fig 6.6 Caravaggio *Supper at Emmaus* (National Gallery, London)

But also attend to the humility of the Lord in another thing, that He did not disdain these disciples of lower degree. For these were not of the apostles ... yet He joined them familiarly, walking and talking with them. Not thus do great men do; for they do not wish to converse and walk with anyone except important men of great wealth.[27]

The implications of Caravaggio's dramatic presentation of the disciples as poor men in modern dress are profound. The 'poor in spirit' (*Matthew* V, 3) are rewarded with Christ's presence. Therefore they, too, are deserving of sympathy and charity. Consequently, the moral message is not addressed to the poor – the avant-garde style, the novelty of representing Christ and his disciples as unidealised, and the price of such a large canvas would have precluded this. Instead, it must have been intended for sophisticated patrons who had the intellectual capacity and moral inclination to appreciate and reflect on its significance. Whatever the precise relationship of Caravaggio with individual clerics, it is clear that his interpretation of this and other religious subjects should be seen in the context of the distress of the poor in Rome and the response of zealous Catholic reformers to provide physical and, especially, spiritual nourishment. Caravaggio's paintings mark a watershed in the pictorial representation of the poor. Directly or indirectly they would seem to have been of signal importance for the young Velázquez.

Although it is the religious rather than the genre imagery of Caravaggio that seems to have influenced Velázquez's *bodegones*, it is noteworthy that the Aragonese painter Jusepe Martínez, who

visited Rome and Naples 1620–5, characterised a painting of the Supper at Emmaus in terms of a *bodegón*:

Christ our Lord of eighteen years, looking more like the figure of a youth in a bodegón *than Christ, and the disciples Luke and Cleophas treated with such little decency that it can even be said that they look like two vagabonds.*[28]

The artist is not named, but the characterisation suggests that it was painted in the style of Caravaggio.

Yet there is no documentary evidence that Velázquez had seen in Seville any paintings by Caravaggio or copies after them or by his followers.[29] However, such paintings are recorded elsewhere in Spain during this period. According to Bellori, Caravaggio's *Crucifixion of St Andrew* was acquired by the Count of Benavente, Viceroy of Naples, and taken by him to Spain. He left Naples on 11 July 1610, and installed the painting in his palace in Valladolid.[30] Bellori also records that the Count of Villamediana owned two paintings by Caravaggio, a *David* and a *Youth with an Orange Blossom in his Hand*, and that these too were sent to Spain. It is likely that they belonged to the second Count of Villamediana, Juan de Tarsis y Peralta, and that they were brought to Spain in 1617. He had been living in Naples 1611–17, and was assassinated in Madrid in 1622.[31] A copy after Caravaggio's *Crucifixion of St Peter* [fig 6.7] exists in the Colegio del Patriarca, Valencia, which was founded by San Juan de Ribera (d. 1611). Whether acquired by the latter or after his death, it is likely that it was in the Colegio at some time during the first two decades of the seventeenth century since Ribalta's copy (Principe

Pio Collection, Mombello) would seem to have been made after this version.[32] The popularity of Caravaggio's image is attested to by the fact that Pacheco refers to other copies, presumably in Seville, when he lauds the practice of working from the life: 'That is what Michelangelo Caravaggio did with such success, as one can see in the *Crucifixion of St Peter* (although copies)'.[33] Perhaps one of these copies was the painting which Ponz later recorded (1777) in the church of San Felipe Neri in Seville.[34] However, Pacheco does not reveal whether these copies were in Seville when Velázquez was there.

A tantalising piece of evidence reveals that Caravaggio presented a gift of paintings to the prior of the hospital in Rome where he was nursed. Were they subsequently sent to Seville or Sicily? Both places are variously cited in two manuscript copies of Mancini's *Considerazioni sulla pittura* (1617–21).[35]

Paintings by Italian artists who worked in the style of Caravaggio are also said to have been sent to Spain, though not specifically Seville, during this period. Giulio Mancini cites the work of Gramatica and Cavarozzi. In fact, the latter accompanied Crescenzi, an architect and a painter of still life, to the court in Madrid in 1617.[36] Moreover, three canvases by Saraceni were sent to Toledo (1613–14) to be installed in the chapel of the Virgin del Sagrario in the Cathedral.[37]

Paintings by the Spanish emigré Ribera were sent from Italy to Spain, but whether any were sent during the period of Velázquez's activity in Seville is not known. According to Mancini, Ribera painted in Rome for a Spaniard (not named) a series of the *Senses* [see cat 11 and fig 6.8]: *Cinque mezze figure per i cinque sensi, molto belle*.[38] This series was painted before Ribera's move to Naples in 1616 but whether it was sent to Spain is not known. Another early work, *St Peter and St Paul c*.1616 [cf. cat 12], was later recorded in the royal monastery of El Escorial in 1657.[39] It seems unlikely that the paintings by Ribera which were brought from Naples to Osuna by Pedro Téllez Girón, Duke of Osuna and Viceroy of Naples (1616–20) were accessible to Velázquez before his departure to Madrid.[40] Nevertheless, on stylistic evidence it would appear that the early work of Ribera may well have been the conduit for the Caravaggesque style that must have fired the imagination of the young Velázquez.[41]

During this period, some native Spanish artists did respond to the style of Caravaggio. Probably in Valencia, Ribalta made a reduced version of the copy of Caravaggio's *Crucifixion of St Peter*

in the Colegio del Patriarca.[42] In Toledo, Maino's altarpiece in San Pedro Mártir 1612–13, clearly reveals his debt to this tradition.[43]

Literary evidence supports the view that the art of Caravaggio was well known in Spain during the second and third decades of the seventeenth century. In 1615 in Madrid, C. Suárez de Figueroa's *Plaza Universal de todas ciencias y artes* was published in which 'Micael Angelo Caravachio' was included among 'modernos insignes en pintura'.[44] Pacheco was well aware of its contents.[45] In the following decade, Juan de Butrón's *Discursos apologéticos ...* (Madrid, 1626) contains a reference to 'Michael Angelo Carabaghio' as being one of those illustrious painters whose work was esteemed in Italy and Spain.[46] Caravaggio was also lauded by Pacheco in his *Arte de la pintura*, which was published posthumously in 1649. Although the text was completed in 1638,[47] it is too late in date to confirm that Velázquez was familiar with the style of Caravaggio. Nevertheless, it is surely significant that when Pacheco extols Caravaggio as an artist working from life, citing the example of the *Crucifixion of St Peter*, he also mentions Ribera and Velázquez: 'That is what Jusepe de Ribera does, for of all the great paintings belonging to the Duque de Alcalá his figures and heads look alive and the rest painted, even beside Guido Bolognese [Reni]. And in the case of my son-in-law [Velázquez] who follows this course one can also see how he differs from all the rest because he always works from the life'.[48] Pacheco acknowledges the novelty of Velázquez's style and relates it to the Caravaggesque tradition. And he is fully aware of a basic element of that style – foreshortening, the dramatic projection of three-dimensional forms:

The most important of the three parts into which we divide colouring is ... relief ... sometimes you might find a good painting lacking beauty and delicacy. If it possesses, however, force and plastic power and seems round like a solid object and lifelike and deceives the eye as if it were coming out of the picture frame, in this case the lack of the other two requirements is forgiven. These other two are not as important as the first one. Many spirited painters, such as Bassano, Michelangelo Caravaggio and our Spaniard, Jusepe de Ribera, did without beauty and delicacy but not without relief ...[49]

The connection between the style of Caravaggio and that of Velázquez is further supported by Antonio Palomino (1724), who had been trained by Juan de Alfaro, an intimate friend of Velázquez in his later years:

fig 6.7 After Caravaggio *Crucifixion of St Peter* (Colegio del Patriarca, Valencia)

fig 6.8 Jusepe de Ribera *The Sense of Taste*, c.1615 (Wadsworth Atheneum, Hartford, Connecticut)

fig 6.9 Pieter Coecke van Aelst *Autumn* from the series *The Triumph of the Seasons*, 1537

Velázquez rivalled Caravaggio in the boldness of his painting ... He admired Caravaggio for his extraordinary and subtle talent ... He was called a second Caravaggio because he imitated nature so successfully and with such great propriety, keeping it before his eyes in all things and at all times.[50]

In addition to these pictorial and literary references, there were important political, religious and economic connections between Seville and the cities in which Caravaggio worked, thereby facilitating the dissemination of his novel style. The Spanish Habsburgs ruled the Duchy of Milan, the Kingdom of Naples and Sicily. They also contributed largely to the defence of Malta. The archbishop of Seville was second in the ecclesiastical hierarchy to the archbishop of Toledo, the primate of the Catholic Monarchy. Thus the archbishop and his clerics were undoubtedly thoroughly conversant with Milanese, Roman and Neapolitan ecclesiastical affairs. Cardinal Niño de Guevara, whose portrait had been stunningly painted by El Greco, and who was responsible for the remarkable decoration of the Prelate's Gallery in the Archbishop's Palace in Seville, had spent part of his life in Rome. Dynastic connections may also have been of crucial importance. The 3rd Duke of Alcalá, Fernando Enríquez de Ribera (1583–1637) was related to San Juan de Ribera, son of the 1st Duke of Alcalá. He was Patriarchal Archbishop of Valencia, patron of Ribalta and, possibly, responsible for the acquisition of the copy of Caravaggio's *Crucifixion of St Peter* in the Colegio del Patriarca. There is also a link with the Duchess of Osuna, Doña Catalina Enríquez de Ribera, whose husband had acquired paintings by Ribera when Viceroy in Naples.

It is also relevant to note the Genoese connection. Some of Caravaggio's patrons were related to families from Genoa – the Marchese Vincenzo Giustiniani, Prince Marcantonio Doria, and Ottavio Costa. The latter probably commissioned a *Conversion of the Magdalen* (possibly the version in the Detroit Institute of Arts), a copy of which is exhibited [cat 10]. It may also be significant that in Rome Costa was a banking partner to a Spaniard, Juan Enríquez de Herrera, to whom he had left, in a provisional will, a painting probably by Caravaggio.[51] Whether Enríquez de Herrera had connections with Spain or Seville is apparently not known, but there were important Genoese bankers in Seville owing to the lucrative trade with the Indies. In fact, the Genoese community in Seville was the largest foreign one there; one of its quarters was known as the 'Barrio de Génova' and a street famed for its printing houses was named 'Calle de Génova'.[52]

These particular connections may have had no bearing on Velázquez's early development. Nevertheless, that he was exposed to the Caravaggesque style seems obvious. Nor is it surprising. Caravaggio's influence was not only widespread but also embraced by many young artists in France, Holland, the Spanish Netherlands, Rome, and the Spanish Duchy of Milan and Kingdom of Naples. It was a European phenomenon, albeit short-lived. It was as if a rock had been hurled into a stagnant pond. In these circumstances it would have been remarkable if this young, imaginative, independent-minded and highly intelligent Sevillian painter was either disinterested in, or unaware of, Caravaggio's achievement, especially since he had completed his training only seven years after the death of Caravaggio and approximately seventeen years after the *Supper at Emmaus* was painted [fig 6.6]. The contrary begs disbelief.

If it is accepted that Caravaggio had provided a new and striking manner of depicting reality, the question remains – what genre imagery was already availabe to Velázquez in Seville? In the city itself there were two major schemes of decoration in which genre elements were incorporated and with which Velázquez would have been familiar. In the Casa de Pilatos, a long room on the first floor was decorated with the *Triumph of the Seasons*, painted by Diego Rodríguez in 1539 and based on engravings by Pieter Coecke van Aelst of 1537 [fig 6.9]. The fusion of classical personifications and rural genre, all in a Christian ethical context, epitomises some of the basic ideals of Sevillian culture. These same ideas imbue the decorative scheme on the ceiling of the Connecting Gallery in the Archbishop's Palace [see also J. M. Serrera's essay pp.37–43].[53] The decoration was probably commissioned by Cardinal Niño de Guevara, Archbishop of Seville (1601–9) and patron of art and architecture. Since the gallery was lauded by Luis de Góngora [see cat 47] in a sonnet dated 1607, it is likely that the scheme dates from the early years of Niño de Guevara's tenure as archbishop.[54]

The figurative compositions represent scenes from the story of Noah, the Four Elements (Earth, Air, Fire and Water) and the Four Seasons. That of Earth is a kitchen scene [see fig 4.13] in which a cook or maid holds a plucked chicken in one hand and a skewer in the other and is surrounded by a profusion of food. In a far room, one maid serves a man at table, another seems to be washing kitchen utensils. In the borders are pictures of fruits and birds, framed within cartouches and separated by grotesques. The treatment of the fruit and birds evokes the story of Zeuxis's illusionistic painting of a *Child carrying Grapes*, as recorded by Pliny the Elder.[55] The scheme of decoration, as has been convincingly and perceptively pointed out, is in praise of God's creation.[56] God restores the elemental forces of nature and the cyclical seasons (*Genesis* VIII, 22) and gives Noah power over the 'beasts of the earth and upon all the fowls of the air' and delivers to him 'all the fishes of the sea'. (*Genesis* IX, 2). And God tells Noah 'Behold I will establish my covenant with you, and with your seed after you' (*Genesis* IX, 9). Undoubtedly this is the reason why the kitchen scene – a *bodegón* – is included and presented in modern dress. Whereas the action of the kitchen maid would appear to be lewd in the pictorial imagery of Aertsen and Campi, it is presumably innocent in this ecclesiastical context. Similarly, the profusion of food is unlikely to be considered a vanity but a manifestation of the natural world that was created by a beneficent God for mankind.[57]

Pictorially, this *bodegón* clearly reflects the images of Aertsen and Campi. Set in such an auspicious setting, it may well have inspired painters in Seville to follow this tradition. Certainly the young Velázquez would refer to such compositions, especially via Matham's engravings, when he painted his *Kitchen Scene with Christ in the House of Martha and Mary* [cat 21]. Yet the copious detail, uniform finish, feeble modelling and bland expression of this kitchen scene in the Archbishop's Palace and in others by Aertsen and Campi clearly failed to impress the young Velázquez. Instead, he observed forms separately and intensely, emphatically modelled their every plane, accentuated their physical presence through foreshortening and strong contrasts of light and shade, stripped away incidental detail, focused the light only on what was essential, boldly designed the composition and endowed his characters with a profound sense of human dignity. He must have been aware of the ripples on the pond.

An Old Woman Cooking Eggs [cat 16] clearly exemplifies the manner that Velázquez himself evolved. Serious in expression, dignified in countenance, and soberly dressed with only a small necklace for adornment, an old woman is depicted cooking two eggs in a glazed earthenware dish, chipped at the rim [cat 16, and fig 6.1]. With bony fingers she holds deftly in one hand a smooth wooden spoon and in the other a gleaming white egg. Lips slightly parted and with a tooth just visible, she pauses, as if about to speak, and gazes intently and expectantly at the young boy. Simply, but respectably dressed, he clasps a glass flask in one hand and in the other holds a melon, tied with string that is frayed at the ends. As he is about to pour the contents of the flask into the dish he, too, pauses, but to turn his head away in intro-spection.

Stage directions are kept to a minimum. There is no narra-tive, no dialogue and action is suspended. Yet it is riveting. The uncanny intensity with which Velázquez records, uncompromis-ingly, these humdrum characters and objects is astonishing. Each is observed separately and studiously modelled in line and tone rather than colour. Their three-dimensional form is accentuated by their being seen against a dark background so that they stand out. Weight is also conveyed. The modelling of the hands of the boy and old woman indicate that the melon and flask are much heavier than the egg and spoon. The crumpled grey cloth and basket hang differently from the heavier oil lamps. There is, too, a gamut of textures. The sallow complexion of the old woman contrasts with the smooth, fresh complexion of the boy. The sheen on the mortar contrasts with the parts of the jugs where the potter's finger-marks are clearly visible. The shiny, thin skin of the onion is different from the matt uneven surface of the melon.

The representation of these characters and objects is realistic – it is both convincing and uncompromising. The melon is dis-coloured – like the rotten apple in Caravaggio's basket of fruit – the earthenware is variously chipped, the old woman's hands are darkened and reddened through toil in the kitchen. Yet this is not trompe l'œil painting. Each object is scrupulously based on nature and, accordingly, has its identity but it is subordinated to a larger, unified and more complex vision, one which reflects the artist's perception of nature. Velázquez's imitation of nature in-volves the selection, arrangement, colouring and lighting of forms to create a unified pictorial composition. His vantage point is in line with the face of the old woman, the dominant charac-ter. From here he scrutinises all the forms separately and relates them through their rounded shapes. Thus as one normally reads a picture from left to right, so he creates rhythmic patterns by repeating these shapes. The treatment of the still life on the table exemplifies this technique. The circular shape of the white dish is repeated in the rim of the mortar and grooves and glazed edges of the two jugs. The round cast shadows on the table sustain the rhythm.

The treatment of light is also calculated. The direction is uni-form but the reflection is selective. Only those forms relevant to the artist's conception reflect strong light. Extraneous details are submerged in deep shadow. Moreover, in spite of its intensity, it does not illumine the background, for example, so that it is un-naturally dark and devoid of texture. Where it does fall its re-flections are sharply delineated and contrast markedly with the shadows. Furthermore, there is little evidence of reflected light from the surrounding atmosphere. Consequently, forms are mainly seen in silhouette rather than in space. This is not atmos-pheric light. The radiance of dust that pervades the airy space of Las Meninas has yet to be realised.

Colours, too, are carefully chosen. Earth colours are used to convey earthy settings. Sombre browns, yellows, oranges, greys, blacks and dull whites predominate. Limes, lemons, apples, au-

bergines, fresh red peppers and water-melons are nowhere present in this humble kitchen. Colours are also carefully bal-anced: orange melon and yolks of egg; yellow brass pan and mortar; white dish with dark knife and white glazed jug with dark markings.

Space is no less calculated, though not according to a scien-tific system of perspective. Forms are observed separately and recorded empirically, which explains why the still-life elements appear to be on different levels. Space is enclosed and shallow. It is terminated immediately behind the figures by the dark back-ground and confined on all sides by the frame that abuts on to the basket, table, boy and white glazed jug. The deep recession in the engravings of Matham after Aertsen, for instance, is ab-sent. Instead, Velázquez focuses greater attention on the fore-ground. The viewpoint is closer and the figures are brought nearer to the picture plane, though the dramatic foreshortening of Caravaggio is not apparent here.

Viewed closely, fully modelled, strongly lit and dramatically set off against the dark background, the realism of each figure and object is heightened. Since each is observed and recorded with intense concentration, each has a separate identity and in-trinsic value. Yet it is not only this aspect that relates the style of Velázquez to the Caravaggesque tradition. Velázquez also ex-plores the psychological relationship between the figures in his compositions, a signal characteristic of Caravaggio's paintings and clearly evident in Christ in the House of Martha and Mary [cat 21]. In response to the direct, open gaze of the old woman in An Old Woman Cooking Eggs, the boy looks aside, lost in thought. His shadowy eyes tempt the beholder to read into his thoughts: 'Heard melodies are sweet, but those unheard are sweeter' (Keats).

By means of this enigmatic expression, Velázquez subtly evokes, as did Leonardo in the Mona Lisa, the workings of the mind. The passage of time is suspended, as it would be in The Waterseller [cat 31], the Surrender of Breda and Las Meninas, while the beholder ponders on the musings of the boy. Nuances of thought, not rhetorical flourishes, are the concern of this sophis-ticated young painter. As he evokes the psychological relation-ship between the two figures so he endows them with thought and elevates them from genre types to individuals. Their intrin-sic worth as human beings – God's creations – is acknowledged. On that principle it follows that there is no reason to idealise or satirise them. They can be depicted objectively. Therein lies the young artist's compassion, a quality that will be reflected in his portrayal of dwarfs and buffoons at the court of Philip IV.

He continues to explore these ideas and refines his style in order to articulate them more concisely. Within a few years he has made astonishing strides in terms of design, space, model-ling, light and colour, as well as psychological awareness. A comparison of An Old Woman Cooking Eggs with The Waterseller is instructive [figs 6.10–15]. The characters are similar – young boy and old woman/man – and their positions are the same – the young boy is on the left and seen in a three-quarter view, the old woman/man is on the right and in profile. The direction of light and range of colours are basically the same. But what a difference!

In The Waterseller, the format is vertical, thereby elevating the old man; the figures are brought closely together, to intensify the intimacy of their relationship, and overlapped to convey spatial recession as opposed to the emphasis on the surface plane in An Old Woman Cooking Eggs. The forms are more three-dimensional because they are foreshortened and more accurately observed in light. More planes are observed and the reflections of light at the edges of each form more sensitively rendered. Indeed there is a far greater range of tone. The faces of the young boy and waterseller are no longer seen as brightly lit and in silhouette. Transitions from light to dark are less abrupt. Light flows over the form. The head of the waterseller is more three-dimensional than that of the old woman. Similarly the water-jug is rounder and more solid than any of the still-life objects in *An Old Woman Cooking Eggs*. The sense of texture, too, is enhanced. The surface of the water jug, indented slightly before it had been fired, is dry and dusty, in contrast to the moist glistening surface of the other jug and, especially, the glass held by the waterseller. Although the colours are similarly balanced – the dark clothes of the boy on the left and the brown garments of the old woman and man on the right – the orange egg yolks and melon have been eliminated to suggest greater chromatic unity. This formal harmony enhances the quiet stillness of the figures. With solemn dignity the waterseller ceremoniously offers the elegant glass of clear water that is respectfully received by the young boy. How different is this old man from the crude and cursing waterseller in the *View of the Alameda* [cat 3] or those others who share the company of pimps and prostitutes in picaresque literature. This waterseller is imbued with sobriety and sensitivity. Velázquez accepts him for what he is and rejects the traditional type-casting of those engaged in menial tasks. Thereby the mundanity of the subject is transcended and the spectator is made aware of the dignity of man – man created in the image of God.

In this approach to the figures, Velázquez has effected a subtle play between the psychological and the physical or sensual. As a consequence, both are heightened and their existence made real. By this means a mundane subject of an old woman cooking two eggs is transcended and the contemporary beholder is made aware of the variety and complexity of the human condition and, fundamentally, the profundity of God's creation. For Velázquez, painting is clearly a Liberal Art. It is the intellect that guides the hand that holds the brushes.

Clearly, Velázquez's painting is based on the imitation of nature. Yet, as demonstrated, it is not a literal interpretation. His selection and adaptation of nature conforms to established conventions of picture making. Not the idealised images of the classical tradition, but the intense and uncompromising realism of the Caravaggesque idiom seems to have captured his imagination. As Pacheco recounted, 'Velázquez hit upon the true imitation of nature, thereby stimulating the spirits of many artists with his powerful example'.[58]

Scenes are set in kitchens or taverns rather than refectories or banqueting rooms. Nor are there scenes of any other forms of daily life in Seville and the cast of characters is limited. The action in Velázquez's *bodegones* always revolves around food and drink. Yet, in spite of the spare settings and simple repasts, all the participants are healthy and well nourished. They are not starving, like beggars. Nor are they dirty or shabbily dressed or crippled, as were many of the destitute. Nevertheless, the conventional perception of Velázquez's 'poor' was later repeated by Antonio Palomino who in describing *The Waterseller*, perceived the old man as 'very badly dressed in a shabby coat, torn so as to show his chest and stomach with its scabs and thick hard callouses'.[59] Nor are his characters (for example the boy) fancifully or theatrically dressed with plumed hat, as so often in the genre images of Caravaggio and the Caravaggisti.

Similarly, their frugal meals were typical of those eaten by the poor labourers. A near contemporary record of the eating habits of the poor is provided by Henry Piers, an Anglo-Irishman, when he lodged the night of 4 November 1598 at a farmhouse outside Seville (*of one of the Ritche merchants of Civill*). The meal he described was the staple diet of the ploughman, that is *gazpacho*:

I did obserue the allowance of meate gyven vnto his plowmen, which was only bread oyle and garlicke, and there Drincke water, they Did Cooke there meate in this sorte followinge, first they boyled som water then they brake there breade into small peeces, and putt it into great boules and scalld it, there breade beinge soaken they Caste oute the Remainder of the water and sprinckled oyle vpon it minglinge the same, with good stoore of garlicke, and eate the same, with spownes, there wadges as they told me was 1 x d str. a day...[60]

Thus the excessive quantities and varieties of food that encumber the tables in the foregrounds of paintings by Aertsen and Beuckelaer are nowhere evident. Even the meal in Caravaggio's *Supper at Emmaus* [fig 6.6] is a feast in comparison.

In sum, these stylistic and thematic elements in Velázquez's *bodegones* constitute their realism and clarify their relationship to the tradition of genre painting. However, in order to assess their meaning for a seventeenth-century Sevillian audience, it is necessary to examine their contemporary context. Firstly, to whom were they addressed? Certain evidence may allow conclusions to be drawn. Obviously, they were not painted for the peasant types represented in the paintings. The subject-matter was too novel, the style too avant-garde and, judging by Velázquez's own valuation of *The Waterseller* (400 reales), the price prohibitive.

As in the case of Caravaggio, the earliest known patrons of Velázquez were wealthy and sophisticated. Velázquez either presented or sold *The Waterseller* to Don Juan Fonseca y Figueroa, chaplain to Philip IV. It was after Fonseca's death in January 1627 that Velázquez made a valuation of the paintings in his collection and appraised *The Waterseller* highest of all.[61]

Two other *bodegones* by Velázquez are recorded in the collection of Don Fernando Enríquez de Ribera, the 3rd Duke of Alcalá. In the inventory of his possessions in the Casa de Pilatos, his Sevillian residence, there are listed: 'A small canvas of a kitchen where a woman is crushing some cloves of garlic' and 'A canvas of two men, in half-length, with a small glass vase'.[62]

In the Casa de Pilatos there were also mural paintings of illustrious Romans, such as Cicero, Croesus, Titus Livius, Cornelius Nepos and Curtius, executed by Andrés Martín, Alonso Hernández Jurado and Diego Rodríguez (1538–9), and of the *Triumphs of the Seasons* by Rodríguez (1539). These had been commissioned by Fadrique Enríquez de Ribera, Marqués de Tarifa. His successor, Per Afán de Ribera, was also given the title of Duke of Alcalá and amassed a celebrated collection of classical sculptures. The interest in the classical tradition was sustained by the 3rd Duke of Alcalá, who commissioned Pacheco to decorate a ceiling with mythological subjects, notably the *Apotheosis of Hercules* (1603).[63] The fact that he was only twenty years old when he gave this commission is not surprising. In the *Anales* of Diego Ortiz de Zúñiga, he is described as having acquired a 'perfect knowledge of Latin...' as being 'well-versed in everything appropriate to Princes, [and] classical antiquity, religious and secular history and, not least, in the liberal arts.'[64] It was in the Casa de Pilatos that the Duke convened literary gatherings – *tertulia* – to

figs 6.10–6.15 (opposite) Velázquez, details from *An Old Woman Cooking Eggs* (left column) and *The Waterseller* (right column)

fig 6.16 Velázquez, detail from *An Old Woman Cooking Eggs*

which were invited writers, such as Rodrigo Caro, Juan de Arguijo and Cristóbal de Mesa, and painters, notably Francisco Pacheco. Pacheco, too, lauded Alcalá's artistic bent: '... our Duke of Alcalá, viceroy of Naples, [is one] who has joined to the exercise of letters and arms that of painting as a thing worthy of such a great prince',[65] while Mesa hailed him as the *Nuevo Mecenas* (new Maecenas) who had made Seville a *Nueva Atenas* (new Athens).[66]

Why then did paintings of 'peasants' appeal to princes? Their lineage, wealth and education would have distanced them, as well as the young Velázquez, who claimed he was of noble descent, from those on the fringes of society.[67] The question of status applies not only to the social position of the patron but also to the artistic merit of the subject-matter. Genre, like landscape, was generally deemed to be much inferior to religious history and portrait painting.

In his *Discursos apologéticos, en que se defiende la igenuidad del arte de la pintura*, Madrid, 1626, Juan de Butrón writes:

The only Painters worthy of the name are those who imitate human nature, painting the parts and the perfections of man, bringing life to a canvas or a board: not those who, having become Landscapists through an inability to reach the heights of Art, stoop to copying fields and meadows.[68]

It is against this critical background that Pacheco obviously felt compelled to defend the *bodegón*:

Well, then, are bodegones *not worthy of esteem? Of course they are, when they are painted as my son-in-law paints them, rising in this field so as to yield to no one; then they are deserving of the highest esteem.*

From these beginnings and in his portraits, of which we shall speak later, he hit upon the true imitation of nature, thereby stimulating the spirits of many artists with his powerful example. Thus, I myself ventured on one occasion, when I was in Madrid in the year 1625, to please a friend by painting him a small canvas with two figures from the life and flowers, fruits and other trifles, which belongs today to my learned friend Francisco de Rioja. And I was so successful that compared with this other works by my hand look painted.[69]

In Pacheco's opinion, the *bodegón* is a worthy subject for a painting if it is skilfully painted. Were Velázquez's *bodegones* admired solely for this reason? Pacheco adds that they were intended to give pleasure. There is no hint that they were to be viewed otherwise.

Yet 'pleasure' does not preclude other levels of meaning. El Greco's genre image of a *Boy Lighting a Candle* [fig 6.17] undoubtedly not only delighted the eye of the learned and sophisticated patron, Cardinal Alessandro Farnese, but also appealed to his intellect, since it was a modern re-creation of a picture painted in antiquity by Antiphilus and described by Pliny the Elder.[70] It may also have had a moral meaning, that is a warning not to play with fire and inflame sexual passions.[71] Although there is no documentary evidence to confirm this moral interpretation, it is surely significant that two owners were distinguished ecclesiastics at the forefront of the reform of the Catholic Church – Cardinal Farnese and San Juan de Ribera, Archbishop and Patriarch of Valencia,[72] and, another, D. Juan de Borja, Conde de Mayalde y Ficallo, was the son of San Francisco de Borja.[73] Two expanded versions of the subject, which included a monkey and a man[74] were almost certainly intended to be moralistic,[75] and were recorded in the inventories of the possessions of San Juan de Ribera (1611) and García de Loaisa Girón (1599), Archbishop of Toledo.[76] If El Greco's paintings had not been skilfully painted and did not please the eye they would never have been commissioned or collected by these learned individuals. Yet they were obviously appreciated on other levels.

Similarly in literature, common sayings, such as proverbs, were entertaining but they were also food for thought. Thus, in the prologue to Alonso de Barras's *Proverbios Morales*, (Madrid, 1598) which was dedicated to García de Loaisa, the reader is told that proverbs are a delight to read, music to the ear, encapsulate the truth and mirror life in an instructive manner. These lines were written by the Sevillian, Mateo Alemán, the author of *Guzmán de Alfarache*, a celebrated picaresque novel with moralising intent.[77]

Pacheco also mentions that Francisco de Rioja, the friend who owned Pacheco's only known *bodegón*, was learned. Rioja, interestingly, had been a witness at the wedding of Velázquez and Pacheco's daughter Joana de Miranda.[78] Rioja was a priest and was consulted on religious matters by Pacheco when the latter wrote his *Arte de la pintura.*[79]

It is surely meaningful that the collectors mentioned in connection with the *bodegones*, as well as El Greco's genre images, were erudite, had a profound knowledge of the classical tradition and were involved with the Church. In this context, Velázquez's own upbringing and education would appear pertinent. According to Palomino:

His parents brought him up, without fuss or grandeur, on the milk of the fear of God. He applied himself to the study of the humanities, surpassing many of his contemporaries in his knowledge of languages and philosophy ... he displayed ability, quickness and aptitude in every subject ...[80]

Undoubtedly, these men admired the skill with which these images were painted and found them pleasing to the eye, otherwise they would not have acquired them. Very likely, they also found them a relief from the rigorous didacticism of much religious art. Yet it does not follow that they viewed them merely as skilful and decorative. If they were appreciated only on that literal and trivial level, scenes of dimly-lit kitchens and taverns with peasant types in drab clothes would seem incongruous in palatial settings with Flemish tapestries, gilded and painted tooled leather hangings, *bargueños* [see cat 49] and other items of fine furniture. It is highly unlikely that they were perceived in this way. The crucial factor is that these men gathered together, whether in the *cigarrales* (country retreats) and academies of Toledo or the *quintas de recreo* (rural retreats) and the Casa de Pilatos in Seville – probably as a relief from the serious matters of Church and State – to discuss and reflect on the Liberal, not the Mechanical Arts, to commune with nature, and to seek a 'sweet tranquility' that enables one 'to live within oneself'. Such was the ideal expressed by Juan Antonio de Vera in his *Embaxador* (1620).[81] Thereby these men recognised the immanence of God and sought to attain knowledge of Him. In this context, painting was allied with poetry, music, grammar, rhetoric, dialectic, mathematics, medicine and philosophy. It was an intellectual exercise that appealed initially to the senses but ultimately to the mind. Thus it enabled the painter and patron alike to gain a deeper understanding of God's creation. These ideas are clearly and emphatically spelt out in the prologue, and first and final chapters of Pacheco's *Arte de la pintura*.

In the highly sophisticated and profoundly Catholic context of these Sevillian literati it is evident that the art of painting was not deemed a craft and that art for art's sake was not a viable concept.

What, then, was the intellectual appeal of Velázquez's *bodegones*?

Reference has been made to the serious interest of the Duke of Alcalá and others of his circle in the classical tradition. It is conceivable, therefore, that the *bodegones* were seen as re-creations not necessarily of specific paintings described in antiquity but of similar types of paintings. Recapturing the spirit of antique art may well have been perceived as more inventive. The *Natural History* of Pliny the Elder would have been an obvious source of inspiration. Velázquez himself possessed three copies of Pliny's *Natural History*, two in Italian translation and one in Latin.[82] Although the date of their acquisition is not known, since they are recorded in the inventory of his possessions after his death, it is likely that he was aware of Pliny's book owing to his education and association with Pacheco and his circle.

It is conceivable, therefore, that Velázquez's *bodegones* were painted in response to the general classical tradition fostered by the Duke of Alcalá, Pacheco and their learned friends. However, none of these *bodegones* appear to be derived specifically from paintings described in antiquity. Yet the modern genre of the *bodegón,* similar to subjects described by Pliny, would undoubtedly have reminded erudite viewers of classical precedents.

In this connection, it may be significant that Velázquez, like El Greco and others who engaged in 'ekphrastic' exercises, studiously avoided painting his *bodegones* in a style *all' antica*. Instead, he endeavoured to create them in a contemporary idiom, thereby stressing their relevance to the seventeenth-century Sevillian spectator. What relevance might this have had? Is it feasible that Velázquez was also alluding to some proverb or pithy saying?

In the tavern scenes, the peasant types may have served as a warning: 'Shun evil company; which brings mischief' (*Huye del malo, que trae daño*); or as edification: 'Very poor but very merry' (*Pobrete pero alegrete*); or, with reference to the loaf of bread, as seeking sympathy; 'To the hungry man no bread is bad' (*A la hambre no hay pan malo*).[83] Any one of these different proverbs could have been applicable. Yet it does not follow that any was intended. The possibility of alternate meanings of genre subjects would seem to preclude the tavern scenes from being illustrations of proverbs. It is conceivable that some punning reference was made to other items, such as the silver-gilt salt cellar or dish of mussels, but none has been convincingly identified. Whether puns or proverbs were intended, it is likely that they were adornments of the subject, rather than the subject itself.

Did the *bodegones* have a moral significance? Were they part of that moralising tradition, as exemplified in the works of Bosch and Brueghel, in which peasants were castigated and displayed as examples of imprudent and intemperate behaviour? Do the peasant-types in Velázquez's *bodegones* manifest sins of foolishness, gluttony and lust? The strolling players in *The Musical Trio* [cat 25] may well be raucous, and the drinkers in the other tavern scenes [cats 26, 28–30] look rowdy and slightly tipsy. Yet their obvious pleasure seems innocent rather than sinful. The tables are not piled high with food and drink as in many moralising Netherlandish paintings, nor are the characters gluttonous, aggressive or deceitful. Pick-pockets, pimps and prostitutes are nowhere to be seen. They are plying their trades on the other side of the river, in the underworld of Triana. In the *bodegones* no devilish mischief is afoot. Indeed, who could be more upstanding than the waterseller? If in other scenarios, designed by other artists, as in the view of the Alameda [cat 3], the waterseller appears coarse and behaves crudely, in Velázquez's painting he has the aura of a man of dignity. It would seem most unlikely that Velázquez's *bodegones* were intended as images of immoral behaviour.

Is it valid to associate the *bodegón* with the vogue for low-life characters in contemporary fiction, notably the picaresque novel? The *pícaro* was a young delinquent who lived by his wits on the fringes of society. The escapades of these artful dodgers are notorious but, at times, amusing, which is part of their attraction. On the literary scene they are, like the characters in the *bodegones*, a breath of fresh air.[84]

In *Lazarillo de Tormes* (1554) the *pícaro* recounts, in autobiographical form, and in down-to-earth language, his devilish tricks. On one occasion he deceives his blind master into jumping across a gutter headlong into a stone pillar:

'Hey, jump all you can' ... *the poor blind man charged like a goat and with all his might came on, taking a step back before he ran, for to make a bigger jump, and struck the post with his head, which sounded as loud as if he had struck it with a big gourd, and fell straight down backwards half dead and with his head split open.*[85]

To the reader, this shocking scene is almost comic, and sympathy for the blind man is qualified by his evil nature.

Another celebrated picaresque novel was *Guzmán de Alfarache* (2 vols, 1599–1604) written by Mateo Alemán, the son of a *converso* prison doctor of Seville.[86] In one episode an old woman cooks eggs for the young *pícaro* but, unlike the eggs in Velázquez's painting, these are addled! This scene of the devious *pícaro* and the wicked old woman seems a far cry from the pregnant calm and quiet dignity of the characters in Velázquez's rendition. Although the irresponsibility of the *pícaro* and the comic episodes must have had some appeal, the intention of the author, which was reiterated in Alonso de Barros's eulogy, was to condemn immoral behaviour. The reader was dissuaded from aping these parasitic rogues, and urged to assume responsibility for his or her actions, and save himself or herself by repentance. 'Though the book does not deal explicitly with the larger social problems of Alemán's own time – the stagnation of the economy, the decay of agriculture and depopulation of the countryside, etc – the picture that Alemán gives us is the product of his own observation of a declining society diagnosed in the only terms familiar to him, those of Christian theology.'[87] In the context of seventeenth-century, low-life imagery in Europe, it would seem noteworthy that *Guzmán de Alfarache* was translated into French, German, Italian, Dutch, Latin and English.

Yet there is no direct evidence that any specific episode in *Guzmán de Alfarache* or in any other picaresque novel furnished the subject of a *bodegón* by Velázquez. As a painter he would have responded more to pictorial conventions than to literary ones. Nevertheless, there are distinctive elements common to both. The characters are young and lowly – though they do not appear to be low-life in the *bodegones*. They have a mind of their own, they hold the centre of the stage and they exude vitality. The idiom, like the characters, is down-to-earth, terse and vigorous. The novels and, presumably, the paintings, are addressed not to the *pícaro* or the humble but the educated, the literate, those who could appreciate the essential meaning of the subject. *Guzmán de Alfarache* was dedicated to Francisco de Rojas, Marqués de Poza and President of the Council of Finance. It is also conceivable that literary-minded patrons and other collectors would have been more appreciative of Velázquez's *bodegones* because they were reminded of picaresque fiction.

What is relevant to an understanding of Velázquez's

bodegones is that there is an observable change in attitude towards paupers in both secular and religious literature of the period. As already noted, *Guzmán de Alfarache* signifies that man has the free will to contribute towards his salvation. Eventually Guzmán undergoes a moral and spiritual conversion. Divine Providence is at hand for the repentant sinner, no matter how destitute.[88] The virtue of assuming responsibility, in accord with one's station, whether it be king or peasant, is upheld in Calderón's religious drama, *El Gran Teatro del Mundo* (performed in 1649). When one of the players protests that he is given the part of the peasant, the producer points out that what matters is how well he plays the part. 'Judged subjectively, therefore – from the standpoint of the men performing the tasks – one perfectly performed task represents the same moral perfection ... as another perfectly performed task, however wide apart they might be in their hierarchical grading.'[89] In literature, as Paula Jojima reveals in her forthcoming doctoral thesis, there is a perceptive change in attitude towards the poor in Spain during the course of the sixteenth and seventeenth centuries. The same is discernible in art, both in Spain and the rest of Europe. One can trace the change from the gluttonous peasants in Bosch's *Seven Deadly Sins*, to Brueghel's foolish peasants and on to the arresting images of Caravaggio, in which the poor are now shown with dignity and compassion. Poverty is no longer sinful. Likewise in the *bodegones* of Velázquez there is a profound sympathy for 'the poor in spirit'. As in the paintings of Caravaggio, their feelings, their psychological awareness, are recognised.[90] The movement reaches its climax in the art of Murillo, in which urchins are represented not as ugly or dirty or foul-mouthed but as angelic. Certainly they do not reflect the appall-ing misery of the life of the destitute on the streets of Seville. Perhaps these idealised images of children were intended to assuage the minds of those who wished to distance themselves from the deprived, or, more likely in that Sevillian context, elicit sympathy for orphans and other poverty-stricken children. In contrast to the street-wise delinquents in picaresque fiction, Murillo's are innocent. They may be impoverished but they smile benignly [fig 6.18]. Maybe they reminded the viewer of the first words of Christ's Sermon on the Mount:

Blessed are the poor in spirit: for theirs is the kingdom of heaven. (*Matthew* V, 3)

These changes in the pictorial representation of the poor complement changes in subject-matter. Peasants are increasingly seen in scenes of virtue than vice. In religious images, especially, the Virgin and Saints are frequently shown as exemplars of good works, such as succouring the poor.

These changes that have been detected in art and literature are also manifest in the attitudes of contemporary social, political and religious reformers. In the sixteenth century, civic and ecclesiastical institutions already faced the problem of an increasing number of the poor, their ranks swollen with old and maimed soldiers. The problem was exacerbated by the movement of the rural poor to urban centres in search of employment and, or, sustenance. The increase in the number of beggars was a European phenomenon and a major evil. It was addressed by Thomas More in his *Utopia* (1516) and Luis Vives in a pamphlet entitled *De subventione pauperum* (1526). In the view of the latter, able-bodied beggars should be compelled to work, idlers and fakers should be expelled from towns. The attitudes of beggars and civic

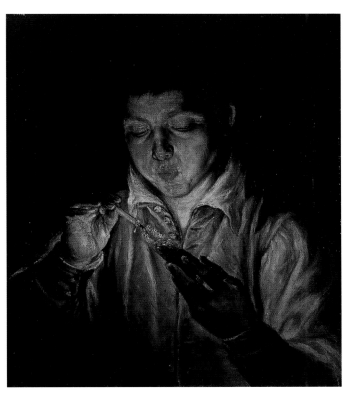

fig 6.17 (above) El Greco *Boy Lighting a Candle* (Museo di Capodimonte, Naples)

fig 6.18 (right) Bartolomé Murillo *A Peasant Boy Leaning on a Sill* (National Gallery, London)

authorities alike are encapsulated in Erasmus's colloquy *Beggar Talk* (1524):

Irides: *I wouldn't trade this 'misery' even for king's wealth ...*
This freedom, than which nothing is sweeter, belongs to no king more than it does to us ... Whether there's war or peace, we're safe. We're not drafted for the army; we're not called to public office; we're not taxed when the public is plundered by levies. No one investigates our lives ... The common people have a superstitious dread of harming us, as though we were under God's protection.
Misop: *But meanwhile you live filthy in rags and huts.*
Irides: *What have these to do with true happiness? What you're talking about are external to man. To these rags we owe our happiness.*
Misop: *But I'm afraid you're going to lose a good deal of this happiness before long ... citizens are already muttering that beggars shouldn't be allowed to roam about at will, but that each city should support its own beggars and all the able-bodied ones forced to work.*
Irides: *Why are they planning this?*
Misop: *Because they find prodigious crimes committed under pretext of begging. In the second place, there's not a little danger from your order.*[91]

Freedom from responsibility was characteristic of the *pícaro*, too, and it was probably attractive to the reader, beset with responsibilities. This perception of the beggar or vagabond as care-free seems to inform much genre painting of the period. For example in Gerrit van Honthorst's painting, *The Merry Fiddler* 1623 (Rijksmuseum, Amsterdam), the character grins foolishly and raises his glass to the beholder. It is this same spirit – and gesture – that is shown by the boy in Velázquez's *Tavern Scene* [cat 26].[92]

In view of the increasing size of the beggar population in Europe, the problem of distinguishing between legitimate and counterfeit became ever more acute. In Thomas Harman's *A Caveat or Warening for Common Cursetors* (1573 ed.), a rogue is unmasked after disguising himself as a beggar and pretending to be ill in order to be given alms.[93] Guzmán de Alfarache indulged in the the same devious tricks. Fiction mirrored fact. In 1597 the Royal Council instructed the civic authorities in Seville to give licences to beg only to the deserving poor. In that same year, four thousand licences were prepared, clearly indicating the very large number of legitimate poor in Seville.[94] It also reflected the chronic unemployment of the unskilled, whose abject state was compounded by severe shortage of food and the plague of 1599–1601.[95] In this context, a familiar saying in Toledo at the end of the sixteenth century is apposite:

God preserve you from the plague that comes down from Castile,
And from the famine that comes up from Andalucia.[96]

In addition to the civic licensing scheme intended to help the deserving poor in Seville, there were others designed for their benefit. During the period 1595–8, Cristóbal Pérez de Herrera, who was also associated with Mateo Alemán, published in Madrid a programme of social reform to be implemented in all the major cities. It involved the provision of shelter for legitimate beggars, retired soldiers, women and orphans, and the reform of false beggars. Orphans were to be educated and learn a trade.[97] On a more directly political level, the Toledan jurist, Jerónimo de Ceballos,[98] argued that those inferior to the King, such as those who perfomed the poorest offices, were needed and should be treated equally. They, too, were members of the body politic, like the ecclesiastical and military arms, and enabled the King, the head of the body, to conserve his monarchy and majesty.[99] Like Vives, Ceballos uses the metaphor of the head and the

feet – one is dependent on the other – and cites its source St Paul's Epistle to the Corinthians (*I Corinthians*, XII). In this chapter, celebrated for its importance for Christian political theory, St Paul expounds the mystic body of Christ. He specially recommends care for:

those that seem to be the more feeble members of the body ... And such as we think to be the less honourable members of the body ...'
(I *Corinthians*, XII, 22–3).

It is in this same context that St Paul speaks of God's design (Divine Providence) to allocate to each member different roles or offices to fulfil:

But now God hath set the member every one of them in the body as it has pleased him ... And God indeed hath set some in the church: first apostles, secondly prophets, thirdly doctors; after that miracles; then the graces of healings, helps, governments, kinds of tongues, interpretations of speeches.
(I *Corinthians*, XII, 18, 28)

This belief is crucial to Ceballos's discourse and the 'Producer's' response to the actor given the part of the 'Peasant' in Calderón's *El Gran Teatro del Mundo*.

At a time of zealous religious reform, the response of the Catholic Church to the deteriorating state of the poor was to embrace them into the mystic body of Christ. Hospitals, orphanages and prisons were founded, in addition to the giving of alms. The concern for the proper administration of hospitals was addressed by the Council of Trent in its twenty-fifth session (December, 1563). In its *Decree Concerning Reform* (ch. VIII), the Council admonished 'all who hold ecclesiastical benefices ... to exercise with promptness and kindness the office of hospitality ... being mindful that those who love hospitality receive Christ in their guests.' The reference is undoubtedly to *Matthew* XXV, 35:

For I was hungry, and you gave me to eat: I was thirsty, and you gave me to drink; I was a stranger, and you took me in.

The theme of hospitality is intimately associated with Velázquez's religious *bodegones, Christ in the House of Martha and Mary,* and the *Kitchen Maid with the Supper at Emmaus* [cats 21 and 22].[100]

It is also characteristic of the new and reformed religious orders that they should have devoted so much energy to the increasing plight of the poor. Their efforts are epitomised in the Bull of Canonisation of St Ignatius Loyola (6 August 1623).[101] Pope Urban VIII drew attention to Loyola's commitment to the poor and needy:

Tirelessly he served the poor in the hospitals. He distributed alms which he himself had assiduously requested from pious persons ... Afterwards he began to visit and help prisoners, a task in which he zealously persevered.[102]

This manifestation of faith and good works was fundamental to man's justification, according to Catholic doctrine. It was also widely reflected in wills and endowments in which the deceased left money to charitable institutions for the poor.

These forms of charity reflect the magnitude of pauperism during this period, the marked deterioration of those in its clutches, and the determined response of institutions and individuals to contain, reduce and alleviate it. This evil was endemic in many European societies. It was not confined to Spain. It has also been noted that in both European art and literature, the poor (good and bad) play an increasing role. Foolish peasants, young delinquents and sham beggars abound.

It is likely that the cultural phenomenon of 'ekphrasis' released genre from the wings and backgrounds of earlier Renaissance painting to give it an independent identity with its own pictorial conventions. However, it could not have been responsible for the discernible change in the visual representation of the poor; the change from them being emblematic of sin and folly (Bosch) to that of virtue (Murillo), with the art of Caravaggio forming a crucial watershed. Since this change was social, rather than cultural (albeit with religious, economic and political associations) it follows that an examination of the social context is essential for a proper understanding of genre painting in general and Velázquez's *bodegones* in particular. Failure to do so is comparable to the study of religious art without reference to religion; the study of Velázquez's *Immaculate Conception* without regard to either the Counter-Reformation or more specifically the theological disputes concerning its veracity.

Velázquez was obviously aware of the social conditions of his time, but his response to them, borne of his own free will, was one of personal choice rather than predetermination, and the nature of his choice is clearly evident.

Velázquez's interpretation of the gospel stories of Christ in the House of Martha and Mary and the Supper at Emmaus, as well as his representation of the humble characters in these and other *bodegones*, patently reveal his and his patrons' sympathy for the poor. They are neither starving beggars nor delinquent *pícaros* – though the young boys may be reformed ones. Nevertheless, they are lowly and on the margins of society. They do menial work or have simple meals in mundane settings.

However, it would be historically inaccurate to regard Velázquez's representation of them as advocating the dissolution of the social order. As far as the evidence indicates, his patrons were not only sophisticated but also privileged. In that social context, social hierarchy was rigidly maintained. Thereby, according to their perception, the rich could help the poor – and patronise artists! The poor would have to remain poor, but in better circumstances. Politically and socially they were needed.

They supplied the new armies with infantrymen, tilled the land and served those at the upper end of the social scale. It was characteristic of this society that among the privileged those who wished to join the élite military orders had to provide evidence not only of nobility and legitimacy, but also purity of blood, a lack of engagement in commerce and of never having worked with their hands. Hierarchy was firmly entrenched.

Yet the players on Velázquez's stage are also invested with human dignity. They have feelings and face life calmly, as the old woman and waterseller, or with zest, like the musicians and drinkers. As in his later paintings of dwarfs, they are treated with respect not revulsion. In this theatre of a world that was imbued with classical learning and profoundly Catholic, Velázquez created scenes and characters, possibly in the guise of classical imagery, that reveal his compassionate perception of the human condition, one that must have been appreciated, perhaps inspired, by his patrons. They also reveal that he, like Caravaggio and Sánchez Cotán, imitated and transcended nature in order to express his perception of it more intensely. In that sense, his painting of the *bodegones* constitutes a Liberal Art.

In his perception, and in that of his Christian contemporaries, Catholic and Protestant alike, all the characters have been divinely created and directed by Divine Providence (*I Corinthians*, XII, 18). Like the 'Peasant' in Calderón's *El Gran Teatro del Mundo*, they are seen to fulfil the various roles allotted to them (*I Corinthians*, XII, 28). Therefore they are accepted for what they do and what they are. Since they are all members of the mystic body of Christ, they are treated with respect and compassion. Surely, that is the moral of the *bodegones*?

In Christian Europe, north and south, this belief was fundamental. Genre images, whether intended or read as moral exempla or merely decorative, would have been perceived, ideally, as part of a world picture that was of God's design.[103] With profound sensitivity and acuity, Velázquez understood the essence of this scriptural truth and with paint and brush made it real.

fig 6.19 Velázquez, detail from *An Old Woman Cooking Eggs*

fig 7.1 José Garcia Hidalgo *A Drawing Academy* 1693 (Biblioteca del Palacio Real, Madrid)

Peter Cherry

ARTISTIC TRAINING AND THE PAINTERS' GUILD IN SEVILLE

ON 17 SEPTEMBER 1611, Juan Rodríguez, father of a twelve-year-old boy called Diego Velázquez, signed a document committing his son to a five year apprenticeship with the city's leading painter, Francisco Pacheco.[1] The contract was utterly conventional in its terms; Velázquez was to live as a servant in Pacheco's house, to be fed and clothed and in return to be taught the art of painting, without anything hidden from him (*sin le encubrir dél cosa alguna*).[2] In March 1617 Velázquez passed his guild examination, on the strength of a practical demonstration and questions he answered before guild officials, Pacheco and Juan de Uceda, and the young artist embarked on a career as a qualified painter of imagery and in oil (*pintor de ymaginería y al ólio*), the conventional title of all figurative painters in Seville.[3]

Since 1599, Pacheco had enjoyed a high profile in the Seville painters' guild of St Luke and by 1617 when he examined his pupil he had risen to the top elected post of inspector (*alcalde veedor*), along with Uceda.[4] The guild was the official corporation regulating the profession of painting in Seville, with a set of statutes supported by law.[5] The guild inspectors (*veedores*), for example, were authorised to enter the houses and studios of their members and to inspect and confiscate works which contravened their ordinances.[6] The guild could also invigilate for breaches of decorum, as in the case of seven painters in Cádiz in 1667 who were denounced before the Vicar General of the archbishopric for hawking around the city streets paintings of Christ, the Virgin and of the Saints, and particularly one painter, Francisco Núñez, who employed his mulatto slave to peddle these images, shouting 'Who wants to buy painted pictures?'.[7] From 1618, Pacheco himself held the complementary role of censor of sacred images for the Tribunal of the Seville Inquisition.[8]

The guild oversaw the four main professions (*oficios*) of the painters detailed in the civic ordinances (*ordenanzas de Sevilla*) of 1527, which were republished in 1632.[9] Foremost among these were the painters of imagery (*imageneros*), followed by gilders (*doradores*), painters of grotesques (*obra del Romano*) and other decorative work in fresco and oil, and *sargueros* or painters of altarpiece curtains and decorative cloth hangings (*sargas*).[10] Strictly codified divisions between the professions prohibited, for instance, a gilder from painting any kind of image, which was considered the work of the 'more learned and ingenious and those who have studied more and worked in such art'.[11]

Sculptors (*escultores*), wood carvers (*entalladores*) and carpenters (*carpinteros*) were also prohibited from receiving any commission for a work of painting, a rule which was tested on two occasions in the early seventeenth century. In 1610, Miguel Güelles, inspector (*alcalde veedor*) of the painters' guild, headed a lawsuit against the wood carvers' move to accept commissions for works of painting and gilding, as well as carving, in clear contravention of the ordinances of both guilds.[12] Francisco Pacheco himself invoked the relevant ordinances in a document he published in 1622 in rebuttal of the sculptor Juan Martínez Montañés, who assumed the right to contract for the sculpture, painting and gilding of a large altarpiece for the Convent of Santa Clara, and which resulted in a legal confrontation with the painters' guild.[13] This quarrel was probably fuelled as much by the economic implications of Montañés's intention to keep three-quarters of the remuneration for the Santa Clara altarpiece, as by the traditional rivalry between the arts of painting and sculpture. The debate between the sister arts, known as the *paragone* in Italy, took on an ironic dimension in Seville, which was home to one of the greatest schools of painted wood sculpture. There existed a symbiotic relationship between them in the production of religious images; the sculptor carved the wooden images which were brought to life and perfected by the polychromy of a skilled painter, and the normal professional title of figurative painters in Seville was *pintores de imaginería*, painters of imagery.[14] Pacheco, himself convinced of the superiority of painting over sculpture, was also one of the most accomplished polychromers of Montañés's sculptures [cat 7].[15] The major altarpieces erected in Seville during Velázquez's youth were predominantly sculptural ensembles and most painters in Seville, Velázquez included, were qualified in this specialisation. In altarpiece contracts, for example, Alonso Cano, a sculptor-painter, normally avoided the inevitable conflict of interests by engaging another artist to polychrome his sculptures, although he probably painted his own smaller works for private clients.[16]

Guild membership reinforced a strong sense of corporate identity which was normal in the highly conformist society in which Velázquez grew up. Many large-scale commissions in Seville were necessarily collaborative ventures and artists were used to working in professional companies (*compañías*), and it was not unusual for these teams to be cemented by family ties.[17] Velázquez's marriage to his master's daughter afforded him the professional and social benefits of Pacheco's connections, and this pattern was repeated at court in Madrid when Velázquez's pupil, Juan Bautista Martínez del Mazo, married Velázquez's daughter, Francisca. Alonso Cano married in 1631 the daughter of Juan de Uceda, a prominent guild member and colleague of Pacheco.[18] In the case of the painter Pedro de Camprobín (1605–1674), born in Almagro (Ciudad Real) and apprenticed in Toledo to Luis Tristán from 1619 to 1624, his marriage in Seville to the daughter of a local painter Antonio de Arnos in 1628 was an important step in his assimilation into the artistic community.[19]

Membership of one of the many religious confraternities was another means by which artists were integrated into the normal social fabric of Seville.[20] A branch of the painters' guild was the Brotherhood of St Luke of which Miguel Güelles became *mayordomo* in 1622, and which was obliged by statute to celebrate the feast day of Corpus Christi in its chapel in the Hospital of San Martín.[21] After 1672, the brotherhood settled in a chapel in the parish church of San Andrés, which was decorated with paintings donated by each of its successive *mayordomos*, including one of the Virgin as protector of painters.[22]

In theory, the most powerful form of control exercised by the guild was the issuing of examination certificates (*carta de examen*) since the civic ordinances stipulated that only examined masters could practise in Seville.[23] In reality, however, this was not always the case and most painters earned a living from their art on completion of their apprenticeship, or even before.[24] Nor did the guild have a monopoly, since the custom existed of the municipality issuing special licences to painters in lieu of examination, a practice which the guild challenged in 1606.[25] Some artists may have used these licences as a means of circumventing strict guild regulations as, perhaps, did the sculptor Pedro Roldán in 1658.[26] Other painters claimed they were too poor to pay the examination fee of three *reales*, and the plea of poverty was less a ruse than a real predicament for a host of minor artists.[27] However, the large number of painters' examination certificates found in Andalusian notarial archives testify to the efficiency with which this guild regulation was enforced.[28]

In principle, the purpose of the examination was to ensure technical competence, and the ordinances of the Córdoban guild of painters (1493) laid great emphasis on correct technical procedures.[29] The civic ordinances of Seville outlined the areas in which candidates were to be examined, including the preparation of painting surfaces and carved wood, how to work colours and to give a good account of themselves in drawing, 'be ingenious and good draughtsmen'.[30] The candidate for examination as a figurative painter had to know how to draw a male nude, how to represent faces and hair well, drapery and its folds, and landscape, and all that was considered conducive to a 'perfectly made image', and to demonstrate this verbally as well as by a practical demonstration.[31] These requirements were similar to those stipulated in the ordinances of Córdoba and Zaragoza, with the exception of the clause concerning the male nude.[32] Of course, in the Sevillian context it is also to be understood that the painter should be a qualified and skilled painter of sculptural imagery.[33] Representing the human figure was one measure of artistic competence in the examination of Sevillian sculptors as well as painters.[34] This heads the list of attributes in Pacheco's definition of 'diligence' in painting in his *Arte de la pintura*; 'to know how to draw and paint a man of all ages, a woman, a horse, a lion, a building, a landscape, and to compose and adorn these things generally with good proportion, style and skill, which few know how to do'.[35] In the case of the Flemish painter Adrián Escarabán, examined in Seville in 1619, he was tested in his speciality of landscape painting.[36] Examination certificates were awarded on the candidate's passing the practical and oral components of the exam, and while there is no record of the types of questions asked, it is likely that they pertained to technical matters, rather than being of a purely theoretical nature.[37]

The municipal ordinances of Seville show that the guild of painters did not enjoy any favour over other guilds in the city. Given the lowly professional status accorded to painting in Spain, guild membership may have been inconsistent with the desire of some painters to be considered unique creative individuals who practised an art akin to that of the poet rather than a cobbler or tailor. Generally speaking, it was the academies which conferred special status on painters, rather than the guilds, but early attempts to establish academies of drawing in Spain had failed.[38] Many artists, however, were suited to wholehearted involvement in the guild by conviction, and perhaps also by conservative temperament and limited artistic gifts. Pacheco was one such artist, along with his colleague and collaborator Juan de Uceda (*c*.1570–1631), and Francisco Varela (*c*.1585–1645), who was guild exam-

iner of some thirty painters in the 1620s and 1630s.[39] Another was the painter Miguel Güelles, whose works are unknown today, and who was first elected *alcalde veedor* in 1610.[40] This made him a sought-after teacher, and he took on at least seventeen apprentices between 1618 and 1633, none of whom are known today.[41] It does not appear that Güelles won commissions for painting altarpieces (*retablos*), not even for polychromy, and he may typify the majority of artists in Seville who were dependent upon decorative painting and the production of series of devotional easel paintings for private clients at home and in the Spanish colonies.[42]

During Güelles's career, the Seville guild asserted its authority in artistic life in the city by strict implementation of the ordinance concerning examinations. Painters who had completed their apprenticeships some years earlier were therefore obliged to sit the guild examination. Alonso Cano, who left Pacheco's studio in 1621, was examined in 1626 and himself rose to prominence in the guild.[43] Angelino Medoro, who returned to Seville from South America aged sixty, had to sit the painters' exam in 1627, for which one of the officials was Cano.[44] The examination was entirely consistent with the practices of other guilds, in which artisans graduated to master of their chosen profession by means of a supervised practical examination; just as the examination of a cobbler or tailor involved his making and showing a range of shoes and clothes before an examining tribunal, so the painter produced examples of his own work. This may have seemed an insult to the genius of some artists with a keener pride than most in their artistic individuality and there were two significant dissenters, Francisco de Herrera and Francisco de Zurbarán.

Francisco de Herrera (*c*.1590–*c*.1656) had probably left his apprenticeship before 1610, when Velázquez may have been one of his first pupils, and received a number of important commissions during his early career.[45] Herrera, who was independently minded, proud and notoriously irascible, had to be forced by the guild to sit the compulsory painters' examination in 1619. In fact, he was examined twice and the evidence from his two *cartas de examen* allows us to piece together the turn of events. The documents state that Herrera ran a workshop and took apprentices (*tenía tienda pública de pintor y obrador y aprendices*) but that he did not want to take the guild exam (*y no se quería examinar*). The guild took out a lawsuit against him and on 13 July 1619 the criminal tribunal ordered him to sit the statutory examination, which he did on the same day before Francisco Pacheco, who certified his competence as a *pintor de ymaginera* 'in oil, fresco, tempera and illumination, and in all types of *historia* and filigree work (*filigranas*)'.[46] Clearly this expedient was considered improper procedure and one month later Herrera was arrested and forced to repeat the exam before the tribunal.[47]

The guild did not tolerate mavericks. Herrera sat his exam at 4.00pm in the house of the Mayor (*Alcalde*) of the town council of Seville, Don Juan Arias de la Rua. Before the assembled company he was ordered to paint an image of the Immaculate Conception (on a small prepared canvas), which was judged to be perfectly made.[48] Herrera fielded a number of unspecified questions pertaining to the art of painting and was found 'capable, able and competent' (*capaz, abil y suficiente*) and issued with his *carta de examen* to practise his art. A non-conformist by temperament, Herrera probably saw no need for this formality, but was coerced into obeyance of guild regulations by the full force of the law. The tribunal's choice of the Immaculate Conception as the subject of Herrera's examination was not accidental; this reflected the passionate commitment of Seville to this devotion. This image was a staple of all its painters, suggesting that it was chosen in this case to exact obeisance.[49]

The case of Francisco de Zurbarán demonstrates the zealous protectionism of the Seville guild. Zurbarán had been trained in Seville (1614–17) and worked in the provinces, living in Llerena (Extramadura). In 1629, Zurbarán was officially invited by the town council (*Cabildo*) to reside in Seville, and called a 'consummate artist' (*consumado artífice*) on the strength of his work for San Pablo el Real and the convent of Nuestra Señora de la Merced Calzada.[50] Nearly a year later, on 29 May 1630, Alonso Cano petitioned the municipality that Zurbarán be subject to the guild examination.[51] Zurbarán argued that he was exempt from this since he had been officially invited 'as a famous man and as befits the glory of this city and for the works of its temples' (*por onbre ynsigne y que conbenia al lustre desta ciudad y obras de los templos*) and that he was not to be confused with the 'ignorant men' (*onbres ynorantes*) required to sit an examination. Moreover, he claimed that other painters were jealous of his favoured position *vis-à-vis* the *Cabildo* and, shielding himself behind its authority, claimed he was an officially approved master and therefore beyond the jurisdiction of the guild.[52] It appears that in Seville employment by the *Cabildo* traditionally conferred status on painters, which weighed more heavily with Zurbarán than membership of the guild.[53] Zurbarán's assertion of independence from the august body of the guild sprang from professional pride, and the belief that he was the most famous and sought-after painter in the city. It is not clear what economic benefits might have derived from his desire to operate on his own. The outcome of the confrontation is unknown, but no *carta de examen* has been found for Zurbarán. If he did manage to flout the ordinances, this was undoubtedly facilitated by the painter's good connections with members of the *Cabildo* itself, who sided with him and for whose chamber he was commissioned to paint an *Immaculate Conception* in June 1630, perhaps in lieu of his exam. Zurbarán's name is conspicuous by its absence from Pacheco's *Arte de la pintura*.

Most apprentice painters in Seville were from the lower classes. Many were the sons of widows or poor orphans, and only a small number ever became future masters of any distinction. Although older apprentices may have shown artistic inclinations, most of the younger ones probably did not; painting, like any other trade, was regarded as a means of earning a living. It was normal for a master to have three or four apprentices living with him at any one time and older apprentices earned their keep by working as assistants in the productions of the studio. Apprenticeships taught the practical necessities to enable the apprentice to earn a living by painting at the end of his contract and were geared to the acquisition of technical knowledge and skills. Much teaching would have been by example, including skills such as the preparation of surfaces for painting, the application of pigments and the range of procedures associated with the polychromy of wood sculpture, as well as any tricks of the trade which the master was prohibited by contract from hiding from apprentices.[54] Gifted apprentices like Velázquez and Alonso Cano were exceptional. Most were content with acquiring a practical knowledge of painting, some formulas and recipes, and went out to join the ranks of the semi-anonymous painters in the city whose works are indistinguishable today. Francisco López Caro, apprenticed to Pacheco in 1608 and a friend and imitator of Velázquez, achieved a measure of distinction early in his career,

but died in poverty and obscurity.[55] And of Velázquez's own Sevillian apprentice, Diego Melgar, apprenticed in 1620, nothing is heard of again.[56]

It is difficult to reconstruct the exact means of artistic instruction in Sevillian workshops of the early seventeenth century, given the lack of written and graphic accounts, and we know next to nothing of the physical layout of studios there. However, the third book of Pacheco's *Arte de la pintura* deals with the practice of painting and is based on a lifetime of experience in the exercise of his profession and as a teacher, and some of the advice he committed to this treatise surely reflects that available to apprentices under his tutelage.

One of the principal means of instruction in the finer points of painting must have been through the graded discipline of drawing.[57] In Seville, as elsewhere, students learned the elementary principles of drawing by copying from the master's drawings and from prints.[58] Pacheco concurred with the Córdoban artist Pablo de Céspedes (c.1538–1608) in recommending that the beginner learn by drawing simple contours, and progress by degrees from drawing the parts of a face to eventually drawing the whole body, from parts to the whole, from comparatively easy to more difficult forms.[59] In this synthetic process, masters availed themselves of the prints of Italian primers, and Jusepe Ribera's etchings of eyes, ears, noses and mouths of about 1622.[60]

While copying primarily exercised technical facility, Pacheco, following Italian precepts, recommended setting exemplary models of drawing, 'good things by skilled draughtsmen', which would sensitise students to quality.[61] An album of apprentices' ink drawings of varying levels of competence is known from a Sevillian workshop of the second half of the seventeenth century, and includes copies from master drawings and paintings, and life studies.[62] Copying could also benefit practising artists, and Pacheco noted that the sculptor Jerónimo Hernández, himself a skilled draughtsman, learned from copying works by Pedro de Campaña.[63] Francisco de Herrera's series of signed drawings of Apostles [fig 7.2] could have served as models for his more advanced students, as the wear and tear of the sheets might suggest.[64] In these, the figures are modelled with Herrera's distinctive hatched strokes of the reed pen, and a number of anonymous drawings from his circle are perhaps by students drilled in this style, foremost among whom was probably his son, also called Francisco de Herrera.[65] Most apprentices probably regarded drawing as a purely practical resource, rather than a medium for expressive purposes, and anonymous drawings which are closely related in style to those of Herrera and Pacheco suggest that many artists were content to continue using a uniform style of drawing which had been learned by rote in these important and influential workshops.

Copying was a prerequisite in a student and was probably the main activity of journeyman painters.[66] However, Pacheco was critical of artists who developed no further and consequently remained at an elementary level.[67] A further stage involved some selection, in which artists borrowed from different graphic sources to form a hybrid image in which the composition was their own.[68] Here the challenge lay in unifying the different parts, disguising sources and finding less well-known ones, a practice which Pacheco said was followed by many masters of his day.[69] Prints and drawings were a vital studio resource for Andalusian artists. In 1593, Pacheco already owned a collection of Italian prints and prints by Dürer and Lucas van Leyden, and his collection grew throughout his career.[70] The importance of graphic sources continued when the student left the workshop and began to amass his own collection, not only for his pupils, but also for his own use.[71] It is still surprising to see the habitual use mature artists of the calibre of Francisco de Zurbarán, Alonso Cano and Bartolomé Murillo made of these as aids in visualising and composing their own works.[72] Although in his youth, Pacheco did compose from prints in oil on canvas, he preferred to work out his compositions by drawing on paper, a procedure which allowed him to distance himself from his sources.[73] This was the method by which Cano and Murillo assimilated their sources. The ultimate grade of expertise of any artist lay in his independence from graphic models, where his own powers of invention and manual dexterity (*con solo su ingenio y mano*) allowed him to compose any *historia* without prompts but entirely from his creative imagination.[74]

In accordance with common studio practice in Italian academies, the student progressed from graphic sources to the representation of three-dimensional forms by drawing from sculpture and plaster casts.[75] These immobile objects in controlled light conditions allowed the student the time he needed to study the incidence of light and shade on the form, and create the illusion of volume on his sheet by modelling. Inventories of the studios of some Sevillian painters list a number of such props.[76] While prints were a studio commonplace, the use of sculptural models may have appealed more to artists schooled in the academic tradition, and were certainly of benefit to those with large teaching practices.[77] The most famous of these models in local artistic lore were casts of the hand of the Virgin which remained from a sculpture of the *Virgin and Child* made by Pietro Torrigiano in Seville and which he had hacked to pieces in a fit of pique over his insultingly low payment.[78] Drawing from casts of the body parts familiarised the student with anatomical forms as a prelude to his addressing the much more difficult subject of the live model.[79] This process is illustrated in García Hidalgo's *Drawing Academy* [fig 7.1], in which younger artists in a back room draw from a sculpture of Hercules, with other casts on a shelf, and more advanced students draw from a nude model, although they are, in fact, too close to the subject to represent the whole body. Two masters, wearing hats, are present, and one draws the most difficult view of the model from the front.

Pacheco also recommended drawing from 'some antique statue', by which he meant a nude figure, in order to study anatomy and to inculcate in the student an appreciation of the ideal beauty of ancient art.[80] This was a prerequisite for the idealised representation which he promoted in religious art. There was no shortage of ancient sculpture in Seville [see Lleó Cañal's essay pp.23–7] but few drawings after the Antique are known today. An anonymous pen drawing after an antique torso may be Sevillian [fig 7.3], its missing penis perhaps a reflection of 'Spanish' modesty, but it is not at all clear that this is taken from a real sculpture. The technique of cross-hatching, reminiscent of engraving, and some passages of fanciful anatomy suggest that it may be a free copy from a graphic source.[81] The range of marks in the drawing, including whorls and dots, would have made it an ideal model for students in the handling of the pen. Three drawings of a bust of 'Seneca', a strongly characterised head of the philosopher from Roman Córdoba, perhaps derive from a cast after the Antique and may have been produced in the circle of Herrera the Elder [fig 7.4].[82] These were evidently produced by a skilled draughtsman, who has resolved with ease the modelling and the foreshortened views he set himself.

As the ordinances of the painters' guild and exam certificates show, a painter was expected to be able to represent competently the human figure. Drawing from the live model was for advanced students only and was the core activity of Italian academies. This usually took place by night in order to maximise the contrasts of light and shade and facilitate modelling [fig 7.1]. Pacheco evidently drew from the model, as did Pablo de Céspedes and Antonio de Mohedano.[83] However, the lack of life drawings makes it difficult to assess the extent of this practice in Seville before the foundation of Murillo's drawing academy in 1660.[84] Pacheco, while fully aware of the advantages of the live model for naturalism, and the study of movement and flesh tones, in fact recommends drawing from sculptural models because the live

fig 7.2 Francisco de Herrera the Elder
St Bartholomew 1642
(British Museum, London)

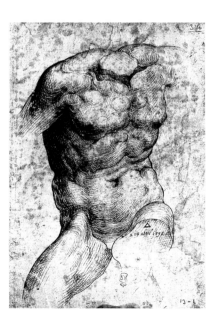

fig 7.3 Spanish School
Torso dated 14 April 1595
(Biblioteca Nacional, Madrid)

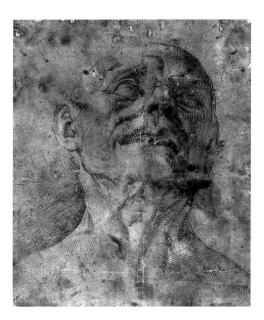

fig 7.4 Circle of Francisco de Herrera the Elder
Head of a Man ('Seneca')
(Biblioteca Nacional, Madrid)

fig 7.5 Pietro Torrigiano *Penitent St Jerome* (Museo de Bellas Artes, Seville)

model was not always available.[85] Drawing from the life invariably meant the male nude. Pacheco was well aware of the role female nudes played in religious paintings – Eve, Susanna and Mary Magdalen, for example – and was equally conscious of the moral dangers associated with their depiction, which he resolved practically by recommending drawing faces and hands from honest women and the rest from good paintings, drawings and prints, including the proportional studies of Dürer, as well as ancient sculpture.[86]

For Pacheco, proportion and anatomy were essential themes of drawing, and for which students and artists could refer to a number of well-known illustrated treatises.[87] One of these, Juan Valverde de Amusco's *Historia de la composición del cuerpo humano* (1556), was believed to have been illustrated by Gaspar Becerra, the Spanish follower of Michelangelo.[88] According to Pacheco, loose sheets of anatomical illustrations by Becerra were commonly to be found in the studios of artists.[89] He also admired the anatomical studies in low relief made by the learned painter Pedro de Campaña.[90] Michelangelo's figures, known from prints, were recommended for the artist's study of muscles and anatomy, along with a sculpture of the Crucified Christ which derived from a Michelangelo prototype, which Pacheco himself polychromed.[91] Ideally, Pacheco would also have artists draw from Michelangelo's beautiful figure of the *Resurrected Christ* (S. Maria sopra Minerva, Rome), which 'exceeded all its praise', and casts after its limbs circulated among artists.[92] Pacheco also noted that anatomical models by Giambologna and Prospero Antichi were well-known among Sevillian artists, which is supported by the fact that his colleague Juan de Uceda owned a bronze anatomical figure by the latter.[93] Once again, however, we should not overestimate the willingness and ability of the rank and file of Sevillian apprentices and painters to live up to Pacheco's ideal of the learned artist. Probably the vast majority were not intellectually-minded and were not able to work from artistic principles, but content to work from prints.

A model closer to home to which the most talented Sevillian artists referred for many years was the *Penitent St Jerome* by Pietro Torrigiano (Florence 1472–1528 Seville) from the high altar of the Hieronymite monastery of San Jerónimo de Buenavista [fig 7.5].[94] Not only was this the most important example of Italian sculpture in Seville, it was considered a touchstone of artistic excellence by nearly all local artists. It was admired as a great piece of devotional art, expressive, moving and intense, and was much imitated by Andalusian sculptors and, in one drawing, by Pacheco himself.[95] The figure is modelled in terracotta, a conventional medium for Sevillian polychrome sculpture, but its Renaissance naturalism broke completely with Gothic traditions of local sculpture. Indeed, the anatomical accuracy of the nude was the main attraction for artists. St Jerome is represented as an aged ascetic in which the musculature is so near the surface of the skin that the sculpture resembles an écorché figure.[96]

Some naturalistic Sevillian painters of Velázquez's generation, notably Zurbarán and Alonso Cano, painted the nude Christ directly from a live model. The study of anatomy was of greater concern to Sevillian sculptors, who regularly produced life-sized figures of the nude Christ in three dimensions and sculptors probably made the casts and copies from which painters drew, and also the lay figures they used in their studies.[97] Pacheco mentions Jerónimo Hernández's excellent sculptures of anatomy after Michelangelo, some of which Pacheco owned, and which Hernández's pupil Gaspar Núñez Delgado also made, particularly an exemplary arm and a leg in wax.[98] Other sculptural aids which practising artists used in their paintings included statuettes in order to study the disposition of light and dark in a composition and in foreshortening.[99] From the evidence of Pacheco, Sevillian painters made drapery studies from clothed manikins and from clay or wax figures draped with wet paper.[100] The acknowledged disadvantage of this method was that it produced crude, stiff and angular folds. Nor did the use of the draped manikin endow the painted figure with much life; although useful for studying a pose, the lay figure could not show the drapery clinging gracefully to the body underneath.[101] In some drawings [fig 7.2], the exaggerated massing of drapery on the figure, in disproportionately large swathes, may reflect the practice of working from a draped statuette or small manikin.[102] However, a number of drawings in charcoal and black lead from the circle

fig 7.6
Circle of Francisco de Zurbarán
Life Study for the Virgin (?) with a Book
(Kunsthalle, Hamburg)

fig 7.7
Francisco Pacheco *Mercedarian Friar*
1602 (Real Academia de San
Fernando, Madrid)

fig 7.8
Circle of Francisco de Zurbarán
Life study for The Mystic Marriage of St Catherine
(Kunsthalle, Hamburg)

of Francisco de Zurbarán are clearly studied from the draped live model, where the drapery is disposed in broader masses and simplified folds [fig 7.6].[103]

In describing his own drawing practice in his *Arte de la pintura*, Pacheco credited himself with having drawn from the model for forty years. He drew studies for poses required in his paintings, for the anatomy of limbs, hands and feet in drawings made with charcoal or lead with highlights on tinted paper, and for drapery, and stated that he also painted heads from nature.[104] Nearly all these drawings are lost today, although a study from the draped model for one of his early paintings for the cloister of the Convento de La Merced has survived, dated 1602 [fig 7.7].[105] However, such practice may always have been unusual among rank and file artists in Seville. Another drawing from the circle of Zurbarán shows a complex three-figure composition studied from dressed models [fig 7.8]. It is not surprising that an artist from the circle of Herrera the Elder should draw the head and hands of a real old man for the figure of a penitent saint [fig 7.9].[106]

Pacheco derived from Pablo de Céspedes his practice of painting heads from the life, which he would idealise in his religious paintings.[107] He recounts that when Velázquez was in his studio he used to bribe a country lad and fellow apprentice to pose. Velázquez made many drawings of him 'in different actions and poses', evidently to study the movement and foreshortening of the human figure, and also drew many heads from the life, with the boy 'sometimes crying and sometimes laughing, no matter how difficult' and 'by which he attained sureness in portraiture'.[108] Velázquez's drawings were in charcoal with white highlights on blue paper, in which the paper acted as a mid-tone. He learned this use of the medium and coloured paper from Pacheco, who probably derived the technique from Pedro de Campaña, among others.[109] Furthermore, a number of heads drawn in red chalk are known by Luis de Vargas and one of these depicts a young, smiling boy.[110] It is significant that the artists who Pacheco admired as skilled draughtsmen were also good portraitists: Luis de Vargas, Pedro de Campaña and Pablo de Céspedes. Pacheco was the equal of any of these in portraiture. It would

have been natural in the studio for Velázquez to train his eye and his hand by drawing from the life, to address the challenge of fixing difficult facial expressions, which helped to sharpen his powers to represent character in his portraiture.[111] Drawing the model in the extreme states of laughter and crying also helped any future painter of *historia* in the representation of emotion, the *affetti* in contemporary Italian artistic parlance. The expressions captured on the faces of the models of some of Velázquez's *bodegones* reflect this exercise.

Pacheco's emphasis on the importance of the study of nature must be understood in the context of the idealising style of representation he advocated and encouraged in his pupils. For artists of his generation, as for the masters of the Italian Renaissance they revered, a degree of naturalism resulted in a more skilful and affective representation of a religious subject. Thus, the greatest painters, like Michelangelo and Raphael, should seek to represent an 'improved' version of reality, one suited to their elevated subject-matter. For Pacheco 'perfection consists in passing from ideas to nature, and from nature to ideas, always seeking the best, most sure and perfect' and the process by which this synthesis was achieved was through drawing.[112]

The practice of drawing embodied a set of neo-platonic aesthetic values deriving from the sixteenth-century Italian theory of *disegno* to which Pacheco subscribed.[113] Drawing was the key to the artist's invention, the creative imagination by which he expressed in purest form the images and configurations conceived in his mind, and which ultimately derived from an ideal realm of perfection known to God. The corollary of this conceptual, idealising form of art was the knowledge of anatomy, proportion and perspective, for instance, which made for 'scientific' or 'learned painting' (*docta pintura*) which Pacheco opposed to direct painting from the model and the naturalistic works of Velázquez, Caravaggio and Ribera, which he also admired.[114]

Such ideas were well known in Spain through Federico Zuccaro, who had been employed in the decoration of the Escorial 1585–88.[115] His approach to drawing and techniques was continued in Madrid by Vicente Carducho and Eugenio Caxés.[116] Pacheco's own drawing style [cats 47 and 48] is close to that of

fig 7.9
Circle of Francisco de Herrera the Elder *Study of Head and Hands*
(Uffizi, Florence)

fig 7.10
Francisco de Herrera the Elder *St Matthew*
(Kunsthalle, Hamburg)

Luca Cambiaso, the Genoese painter who worked at the Escorial (1583–6). In Seville, however, the interpretation of Italian *disegno* was a little different. Pablo de Céspedes, an intimate of both Zuccaro and Pacheco, qualifies the abstract value of *disegno* by asserting the value of observation of nature and of colour in his *Poema de la pintura*.[117] Pacheco's own theoretical discussion of drawing in his *Arte de la pintura* is balanced by an equal emphasis on its practical applications in the training of artists and the production of paintings. Thus, Pacheco insisted on the value of drawing as a source of ideal inventions; practically speaking, drawing also fine-tuned the co-ordination of mind, eye and hand, and led students to progress from copying other artists' images to making their own.[118] In Andalusian artistic culture, in which artists depended so heavily upon the prompting of prints, 'invention' was not so pure a concept as it was in Italy and more often meant 'variation'.

In practice, Pacheco says he normally made two or three sketches (*rasguños*) in charcoal, pencil or pen to represent 'the first rough ideas for the movements, expressions and actions required for the lively expression of the subject to be painted'.[119] The best of these were chosen by the artist, or in consultation with learned men, to be worked up into finished drawings.[120] Although this notational method was also used by Francisco de Herrera in a number of drawings of apostles [fig 7.10], none of Pacheco's sketches have survived.[121] Perhaps there never were very many since Sevillian masters of the early seventeenth century did not consider drawing as an experimental creative medium to the same high degree as their Italian counterparts. Their loss may be purely fortuitous.[122] Or perhaps their destruction was deliberate; since rough sketches represented first stages in the pursuit of an idea, Pacheco may not have considered them worthy of preservation, if they served only as a means to an end in the development of final, definitive pen and wash drawings which are known today. Experimental drawing was more fully developed by younger artists, Alonso Cano and Bartolomé Murillo, whose works were also collected by artists and connoisseurs.

Pacheco adduced the Italian model for this procedure, citing the drawings of Gaspar Becerra and Federico Zuccaro, based on the techniques of Michelangelo and Raphael.[123] Highly resolved drawings reflect Pacheco's definition of 'finish' (*acabado*) as the prerequisite of the best art.[124] A number of these drawings are dated to the day they were finished, with the frames sketched in around the image. Pacheco painted from these *modelli*, rather than full-size cartoons, and ensured he preserved a stock of his own inventions in his studio, which he could re-use, show to patrons and, probably, allow students to copy.[125] He may have used these to make reproductions of his paintings throughout his career.[126] Perhaps Pacheco considered having some of his drawings of religious subjects engraved. He was proud of a drawing (*debuxo de invención*) on vellum he made in 1593 for a lost painting of the *Beheading of St Paul* and which he called 'his drawing of greatest renown'.[127] Pacheco himself made copies of his drawings *St Agnes* and *St Lucy*, set within classical egg and dart frames, which were probably presentation pieces.[128]

For Pacheco, drawing is synonymous with something he calls the 'good manner' (*buena manera*) or the 'Italian manner' (*manera italiana*), exemplified by the drawings of the masters of the Italian High Renaissance and antique sculpture. Michelangelo, then, was the 'light of drawing' (*luz del debuxo*) and among Pacheco's most prized possessions were a wash drawing of Ganymede, which he believed was an original by Michelangelo, and a wash

drawing by Raphael for the *School of Athens*.[129] Despite his admiration for the Brussels artist Pedro Campaña, Pacheco claims he never entirely lost a 'Flemish' particularness and 'dryness'.[130] Luis de Vargas (*c*.1506–1568), a painter who had also worked in Rome, was credited with bringing the Italian manner to Seville; his Italian sketchbook belonged to the Duke of Alcalá, and he was an indefatigable draughtsman in multiple techniques who was particularly noted for his pen sketches (*rasguños*), and who cultivated this faculty in many artists, including Pacheco's own master, Luis Fernández.[131] Pablo de Céspedes, an autodidact who worked in Rome (*c*.1570–7; 1583) is listed among the great Spanish artists who followed the path of Michelangelo and Raphael, with the added beauty of the colour of Correggio.[132] Pacheco himself aspired to the *buena manera* and claimed to imitate Michelangelo in the depiction of the nude and Raphael in composition and everything else.[133]

Despite Pacheco's reservations regarding the decorum of the nudes in Michelangelo's *Last Judgement* in the Sistine Chapel, this was for him 'the first and greatest work in the world'.[134] Although Pacheco had never seen the original, the work was widely known through those who had been in Rome, and through drawings and prints.[135] The presence of the Italian Matteo da Lecce in Seville in the 1580s should not be forgotten. He brought with him many of his Roman drawings, including one for his *Death of Moses* fresco in the Sistine Chapel, with its skilfully foreshortened nude and semi-nude figures in dynamic action and graceful contrappostos.[136]

Pacheco's own *Last Judgement* of 1611 was one of his most admired paintings, and for which he drew on the example of Michelangelo.[137] However, his most ambitious response to the challenge of Italian Renaissance *disegno* was his mythological paintings for the ceiling of the Casa de Pilatos [fig 7.11]. While Pacheco saw these as a vindication of his artistic methodology, they are too earnest, too studied.[138] His desire to display his knowledge of anatomy led him to a pedantic exaggeration of surface musculature, which falls short of looking natural; nor does it do justice to the revered ideal of Michelangelo's example.[139] The laboured foreshortening of the figures means the ceiling is not an entirely convincing illusion, which is ironic since Pacheco adduced such illusionism as the very artifice by which painting showed itself superior to sculpture.[140]

While credit is due to Pacheco for painting figures of his own invention, the difficulties he experienced may derive from inadequate technical training as much as his artistic limitations. It is perhaps telling that in his *Arte de la pintura* Pacheco has so little to contribute to the discussion of foreshortening in drawing, apart from recommending the Italian mechanical device of the squared transparent frame (*cuadrícula*), so praised by Céspedes, through which statuettes are drawn in different positions.[141] While Pacheco emphasises the importance of illusionistic perspective, and the expertise of Raphael in this field, his account relies totally on other authorities and he gives no clue as to how this skill might have been taught in practice.[142] No early seventeenth-century Sevillian drawings are known of perspective exercises, or even Italian-style compositions of figures on a reticulated pavement. Indeed, the ineptitude of the perspective in some of the paintings of Francisco de Zurbarán suggests that he, like many others, was not trained in this discipline and most probably did not understand the mathematical principles of perspective. Most Sevillian artists may have felt they could work without a knowledge of perspective, and it would appear to have been an interest and skill which Velázquez developed in Madrid. Indeed, Pacheco gives more emphasis to the value of relief or illusionistic three-dimensionality in paintings, the power of artists to represent things that appear 'round and alive' (*redondas y vivas*).[143] This 'sculptural' value in painting, linking works on canvas and the polychromy of wooden statues, is one which almost all Sevillian artists of this period sought.

Pacheco was highly critical of teachers who allowed pupils to follow their own inclination and did not train them in the *buena manera* by imitating the principles inherent in the works of the great masters of the Italian High Renaissance.[144] He lamented the loss of a long list of artistic values in the majority of his contemporaries, whom he cast as no more than vulgar copyists who did not draw.[145] But did not Pacheco's greatest pupil betray him most? Velázquez, as soon as he left Pacheco's studio, asserted his independence by painting less from drawings distilled from his creative imagination, but directly from posed studio models. A rebellious young naturalistic painter, did he not too, as later reported, reject Raphael and paint humble genre scenes?[146]

However, by the time Pacheco wrote his *Arte de la pintura* he was a nostalgic man in his eighties, the last of his generation of learned painters. When Velázquez's father had brought his son to his studio in 1611, Pacheco had been at the height of his career and had himself just returned from a study trip around Spain to broaden his artistic horizons. He surely instilled his heartfelt artistic convictions in the young Velázquez, both in his studio and in the academy at the Casa de Pilatos. Velázquez came to appreciate this training later when he was in Rome in 1630, drawing in the Sistine Chapel and Raphael's Stanze.

Like any intelligent teacher, who is also a practising painter, Pacheco was not narrowly doctrinaire and allowed the natural gifts of his best pupil full rein. Velázquez's youthful zeal may have urged him to make his mark in uncompromisingly modern terms, by working from the living model according to the controversial example of Caravaggio. Pacheco saw the astonishing results of Velázquez's 'imitation of nature' as a worthy reprise of the naturalism of fabled works of classical antiquity. After six years of education and teaching, and in the light of Velázquez's natural genius, it was only proper that pupil should have eclipsed master and that this should have redounded to the glory of both.

fig 7.11 Francisco Pacheco *The Fall of Phaeton* (Casa de Pilatos, Seville)

Enriqueta Harris

The Question of Velázquez's Assistants

ON 14 MARCH 1617, after six years' apprenticeship to Francisco Pacheco, Velázquez was examined and accepted as a 'master painter of religious images and in oils and in everything related thereto' (*maestro pintor de ymaginería y al olio y todo lo a ello anexo*). At the age of eighteen, he was licensed to practise his art in Seville or anywhere else in the kingdom, to set up shop and to employ assistants and apprentices (*poner y tener tienda pública y oficiales y aprendices*).[1] More than forty years later, in 1659, witnesses testifying in the application for his membership of the Order of Santiago swore that he had never had a shop or workshop and that he never sold his paintings but made them for pleasure (*por gusto*) or for the King's pleasure. Among the 148 witnesses were friends and colleagues of the artist in Madrid and Seville, who made these and other declarations about the purity of his blood and distinguished ancestry, in order to further his suit.[2] Many of their statements were patently false. As Painter to the King, Velázquez was paid for his works in addition to his salary, and he also sold some paintings to private patrons. In Madrid, he certainly had a workshop and several assistants to meet the demands for replicas of his royal portraits.[3]

In Seville, there is no documentary evidence that Velázquez had a shop, though this would not have been unusual. Francisco de Herrera, Velázquez's putative first teacher, was prosecuted by the painters' guild in 1619 for having a shop, workshop and apprentices, without having taken the guild's examination.[4] Was Velázquez perhaps one of his 'illegal' apprentices? Other painters, including Pacheco, sent paintings, usually of religious subjects, to the New World to be sold. But there is no evidence that Velázquez followed this practice or of how he disposed of his paintings. There is, however, good reason to believe that he had a workshop and assistants, judging from the number of versions known today of many of his Seville works. The religious paintings, with one special exception [cat 22], were not repeated, which means no doubt that they were commissions; so too, presumably, were the few portraits. Velázquez himself painted a replica of the famous nun *Mother Jerónima de la Fuente* [cats 42 and 43], which in turn was copied; copies of the portrait of the poet Góngora [cat 45] were probably made in Madrid, as was the engraving by Juan de Courbes [cat 46]. It was no doubt the novelty of the *bodegones* that made them so popular. Originals, copies, variants and pastiches of these that are still extant amount to nearly thirty pieces.[5] Those that had been lost sight of all bore the name of Velázquez when they were 'rediscovered' in the eighteenth and the nineteenth centuries.

Replicas of *The Waterseller* [cat 31] were probably made in Madrid as well as Seville. The painting must have been seen and admired in the collection of Juan de Fonseca, himself a painter, to whom Velázquez had taken it in 1622. One variant of the *Tavern Scene* [cat 30] includes two figures from *The Topers* and must therefore have been painted after 1628, possibly by a member of the artist's Madrid workshop: a late survivor of a popular genre. The two *Tavern Scenes* [cats 26, 28] and *The Musical Trio*

[cat 25], true *bodegones*, are the Sevillian subjects most often copied and imitated. Because of the poor quality of the copies, Peter Cherry doubted that they were produced in Velázquez's studio or under his supervision.[6] Their close dependence on the originals, however, both in composition and in detail argues for them having been painted in front of the originals and, presumably, in Velázquez's workshop. In one case, Velázquez appears to have had the collaboration of an assistant [cat 28]. Although the copies are evidently by several different hands, these hands are not easily identified.

So far, only one name of an apprentice engaged by Velázquez in Seville is known. Diego Melgar, aged between thirteen and fourteen 'more or less', was placed by his father as an apprentice for six years on 1 February 1620.[7] Nothing else is known of him, not even if he accompanied his master to Madrid, when he moved there in 1623, to complete his apprenticeship. Given his youth and lack of training in 1620, he can hardly have played a part of any consequence in Velázquez's studio in Seville. Pacheco's account of how Velázquez in his youth used to bribe 'a young country lad apprentice' (*un aldeanillo aprendiz*) to pose for him led Trapier to suggest that this 'apprentice' could have been Diego Melgar.[8] But López-Rey's argument that Pacheco was referring to the time when Velázquez himself was still an apprentice is more convincing.[9]

Until recently, Francisco López Caro was thought to have been a pupil of Velázquez in Seville because his only known work is a signed *bodegón* with a kitchen boy (*pícaro de cocina*) [fig 8.1]. The composition, figure, and details of still-life objects appear to be derived from Velázquez, as is the format.[10] Thanks to Peter Cherry, we now know that López Caro was not a pupil of Velázquez but a fellow pupil, apprenticed to Pacheco for six years on 1 October 1608.[11] Born a year before Velázquez, they were together in Pacheco's studio for three years. The simple, naive character of López Caro's *bodegón* and the poor quality of the painting raises the question of whether he made it when he was still a pupil of Pacheco. Were the ingredients of this and Velázquez's *bodegones* possibly studio property and the compositions set up by Pacheco for his pupils to copy? If so, we would expect Pacheco himself to have produced an example of a *bodegón*, which he only did for the first time when he was in Madrid in 1625. Possibly López Caro continued his studies with Velázquez; the two young men were known to have been closely connected. As one of the witnesses in 1659, López Caro declared that he had known Velázquez since he was nine years old. His name appears on documents together with that of Velázquez in Seville and Madrid. In 1622 he acted as witness when Velázquez assigned his power of attorney to Pacheco. The other witness was Velázquez's brother Juan who, like López Caro is described as *pintor de ymaginería*.[12] This is the first mention of Juan Velázquez as a painter. Two years younger than Diego, the oldest of his five brothers, he was apparently the only one to follow his brother's profession. Whether Velázquez played any part in his training or whether he too was apprenticed to Pacheco is not known. Possibly Juan or one of his brothers served Velázquez, if not as assistant or apprentice, as a model for the young men who appear in many of his Sevillian works. Later, in 1627, Juan, then resident in Madrid, led an appeal on behalf of the members of the painters' guild for the abolition of the *alcabala* (sales tax), with the support of Velázquez.[13] Nothing more is known of Juan and no painting by him is known.

The story told by Palomino that Juan de Pareja, Velázquez's mulatto slave, learnt to paint in his master's studio without his knowledge, whether it referred to his studio in Seville or Madrid, is no longer credible. It is now known that it was not because of a painting of his was seen by the King that he won his freedom. It was when he was in Rome in 1650 with his master that Velázquez freed him.[14] In fact, Pareja's paintings all date from after his term as a slave and show little dependence on Velázquez, although he was probably his teacher. In Seville, Pareja's duties were presumably the traditional duties of a slave: grinding colours and preparing canvases rather than learning to assist in painting them.

Velázquez's early maturity – he was a master painter at the age of eighteen and painting masterly works a year later – was exceptional. Alonso Cano's progress was more usual. Two years Velázquez's junior, he was apprenticed to Pacheco for five years in 1616, and was a fellow pupil of Velázquez for seven months. He was twenty-three years old when he painted his first known signed work in 1624 [cat 9] and that was four years before he qualified as a master painter.[15] It is hardly surprising, then, that the authors of the modest copies and variants of Velázquez's youthful works are difficult to identify. From the day he was licensed, in 1617, to employ assistants and apprentices until he left Seville for Madrid in 1623, there was hardly time to make any of them worthy of their master or to become known as master painters.

fig 8.1 Francisco López Caro *Bodegón with Kitchen Boy* (Private Collection)

Zahira Veliz

Velázquez's Early Technique

Increasingly, an understanding of how an artist created his paintings has come to be seen as essential to the study of his work. Perhaps this is because painting, unlike its fellow liberal arts of poetry or music is, of necessity, physically expressed by the artist's own hand. Is it the material uniqueness of the art-object that awakens our interest in knowing how it was created, or is it simply that the fascination lies in the colours and surface once manipulated by the hand of a great artist? Whatever the motivation might be, understanding a painter's method ultimately enhances our response to his work.

Technical study of working methods reveals information about inevitable changes in the original materials. One can examine the *pentimenti* which show major or subtle adjustments to the composition, the construction of the image in stages and how the artist exploited the colour, opacity or transparency of pigments. All of these factors, whether one is aware of them or not, strongly influence our perception of the finished work.

Velázquez's painting technique changed more dramatically during his career than that of almost any other seventeenth-century artist with the possible exceptions of Rembrandt and, perhaps, Guido Reni. After mastering the received practices of their teachers, these artists challenged and redefined the conventions of painting. An accurate understanding of Velázquez's pictorial methods can illuminate something ignored in the surviving documents on his life, and difficult to judge from the surface alone: the attraction which the process of painting held for him.[1]

The written sources for the early part of Velázquez's life offer only circumstantial information about how he painted. He was apprenticed to Francisco Pacheco, one of the most eminent masters in Seville, in 1611, for the standard period of six years.[2] By good fortune, Pacheco was also the author of the most important Spanish treatise on the practice and theory of painting in the first part of the seventeenth century, his *Arte de la pintura*,[3] from which much can be discovered about how Velázquez would have been taught to paint. Pacheco's writing shows a strong didactic bent, and his narrative tone suggests he was a very generous if slightly pompous teacher. Together with the technical information in *Arte de la pintura*, surviving inventories and contracts for commissions by Pacheco and others in his circle provide a reasonably complete view of painting practice in Seville, with which Velázquez's methods can be most fruitfully compared.

Velázquez's paintings have been studied with the aid of strong magnification, radiography, infra-red photography, and pigment identification. Some medium analysis has been published in recent studies, and it is hoped that further research in this area will soon be undertaken.[4]

The pictures known to have been painted by Velázquez in the years 1618–23 are invariably on stretched canvas. Of the paintings whose original canvases have been studied, *The Adoration of the Magi, St Ildefonso, Mother Jerónima de la Fuente* [cats 36, 39, 42] were all painted on canvases with a chequered weave [fig 9.1].[5] Linen canvas woven with simple chequered, or more complicated

damask patterns was generically termed *mantelillo* or *mantel*.[6] The ordinary tabby-weave linens were called *lienzos*. A 1623 contract for an altarpiece (*retablo*), signed jointly by Pacheco and Velázquez, distinguishes between the *mantel* required for the principal image, *The Immaculate Conception* which was to occupy the centre of the altarpiece, and the usual canvas (*lienzo*) on which the secondary subjects were to be painted.[7] There is no suggestion in this contract or elsewhere that the choice of *mantel* or *lienzo* had any practical significance. The patterned *mantel* was probably considered more attractive or precious, and therefore may have been deemed more fitting for subjects of iconographical importance, such as an Immaculate Conception.[8] Although a surprising number of later paintings by Velázquez have survived unlined, this is unhappily not the case with the early Sevillian works.

When Pacheco describes the preparation of canvases, he mentions that 'very large canvases are protected from humidity by stretching and nailing them over thick panels (*tableros*) where they last many years'.[9] In the contract for Pacheco's altarpiece for the Chapel in the church of San Lorenzo [cat 5], *tableros* again appear: *i es condicion que en el tablero principal de en medio se a de pintar sobre mantel una imagen ...* (and it is a condition that in the main panel at the centre is to be painted an image on patterned canvas ...).[10] This documented practice by Pacheco, was presumably familiar to his pupil Velázquez. A canvas backed by a solid wood panel would have been less yielding to the paintbrush and would have given the artist greater control.

The stretched canvas was made ready for painting by applying a sizing layer followed by a preparation of earth pigments ground in linseed oil. The ground or preparation layer provides an even surface for the application of paint, while impeding the medium from being absorbed into the canvas. By the seventeenth century artists everywhere had begun to exploit the optical possibilities of coloured or toned grounds. The use of a dark red or brown ground lends itself to the effective depiction of strongly contrasting light and shadow. The depth of the shadow is quickly achieved either by using the ground itself as the shadow, or by darkening it further with a transparent glaze. The light tones must have sufficient opacity to cover completely the dark ground. This method enables the artist to achieve a broad range of cool half-tones and warm highlights by varying the thickness of the paint applied over the ground. In these rigorously modelled compositions, the contrast between dark shadows and well-defined highlights heightens the plasticity of the forms. Velázquez's early paintings are all based on this kind of technique, which was well suited to the tenebrism so evident in his work at this time. Pacheco is specific in his recommendation: 'The best and smoothest priming is the clay used here in Seville, which is ground to a powder and tempered on the stone slab with linseed oil ... This is the best priming, and the one I would always use without further modifications, because I see my six canvases in the cloister of the Mercedarians conserved without having cracked nor shown any sign of flaking since the year 1600 when they were begun ...'.[11] This type of clay consisting of an heterogeneous mixture of iron oxides, silica and carbonates is probably the principal component of the dull-brown grounds found without exception in Velázquez's Sevillian paintings [fig 9.2]. Although a very similar ground is found constantly in seventeenth-century Sevillian paintings by Zurbarán, Herrera and others, preparations of this kind were by no means exclusive to Seville.[12] The tonality of a painting will inevitably be influenced by the preparation layer – whether dark or light, warm or cool – its colour will contribute to the characteristic palette of the painting, and will have, determined how Velázquez used his paints. It is interesting to observe that after leaving Seville, he soon abandoned the dull-brown ground and favoured increasingly lighter grounds as his technique became freer and more transparent.[13]

In the upper left background of *The Immaculate Conception* [cat 33] one sees on the preparation layer some arc-shaped indentations through the thinly painted, deteriorated sky. These are thought to be marks made by the palette knife used to apply the ground, as Pacheco recommends.[14] If the grounds were applied to the canvas stretched over the solid *tableros* it would have been possible to use considerable pressure in order to drive the size and ground into the weave of the canvas, thereby producing a smooth, compacted surface to receive the paint. Unfortunately, Pacheco's high hopes for the durability of this type of ground were not to be fulfilled. The calcite-rich grounds in the Seville paintings of Velázquez tend to be poorly bound and rather sensitive to moisture.[15]

It is intriguing to imagine the young Velázquez face-to-face with his canvas which was stretched and prepared with an even dull-brown ground – what was the next step? There is technical evidence to suggest that later in his career compositions were to some extent developed directly on the thinly prepared canvas using a brilliant *alla prima* method.[16] As a young artist, still to some degree influenced by Pacheco, Velázquez may possibly have worked from fully resolved drawings, none of which seem to have survived. Certainly this was the method advocated by Pacheco, who wrote: 'Cartoons for pictures to be painted in oil are rarely made the same size, so the figures or histories must be drawn onto the … canvases … from a small preparatory drawing by eye or by using a grid … The only difference in drawing onto the various surfaces to be painted is in the kind of crayon (*ocreón*) that is used … From an appropriate distance … block out all of the figure or history, stepping back to look at it often and erasing and redrawing until it agrees with the design. The sure and good grace of the entire work lies in the proper delineation of the figure or history, because it is certain that all the difficulty of painting consists in achieving the contours. After the entire picture is well-proportioned and outlined, the various figures are refined using smaller points … thus … all the details to be painted are perfected.'[17] He then advises that before beginning to paint 'everything to be painted has been drawn correctly with accurate profiles …'

Although the quest for preparatory drawings, or even the presence of underdrawing on the brown earth-coloured ground is frustrating with regard to Velázquez's Seville paintings, Pacheco's own drawings can give an idea of the small preparatory drawings with 'accurate profiles'. The finished drawings of *St John the Evangelist* [cat 35][18], and *St Jerome* [fig 9.3],[19] are typical of Pacheco's composition drawings, in which precise contours are given relief with white highlights and ink wash shadows.

Drawings of this kind were obviously kept as compositional references since the *St Jerome*, dated to 1605, was used again for an altarpiece in 1610–13. The drawing of *St John the Evangelist*, with an autograph date of 1632, is closely related to the Velázquez painting of this subject included in the exhibition. There is yet another drawing attributed to Pacheco of *St John on Patmos* [fig 9.4][20] which is closely related to a painting on panel by Pacheco, the early Velázquez painting of this subject, and the British Museum drawing. Recycling of iconographically orthodox compositions must have been inevitable in the close-knit milieu of Pacheco and Velázquez in Seville. Without any drawings firmly attributed to Velázquez for this period, it is difficult to say if Pacheco influenced Velázquez, or if the teacher took inspiration from his gifted pupil. Such features as the structure of drapery folds, the organisation of light and shadow, and the emphasis on contours in Pacheco's drawings are parallelled in Velázquez's Seville painting.

Pacheco's commentary on drawing onto the canvas assumes that a crayon (*ocreón*) in a cane holder would be used to establish the composition [see fig 9.5].[21] Velázquez employed a personal variation of this method. While still at the underdrawing stage, he 'drew' with a pointed, rather stiff small brush which produced a thin graphic line which stood in relief to the preparation layer [fig 9.6]. It is difficult to prove whether or not a sketchier drawing was laid down before the brush drawing; certainly it is possible, judging from Pacheco's instructions. In any event, the principal contours were carefully drawn with the pointed brush and sometimes, in areas such as hands or ears, an even finer line is evident, which might have been made by the drawing point (*clarión*).[22] These lines can be discerned in some of the radiographs, and occasionally in raking light on the picture surface. They contain pigments which are opaque to x-rays, producing white on the radiographic plate. Frequently these contour lines were later covered by a broader stroke of paint, the edges of which are very closely aligned with the graphic contour, thus doubling the radiographic opacity and making it difficult to distinguish the graphic line from the edge of the later brush-stroke. It is only in areas where the definitive paint layers contain very little radio-opaque material that the graphic lines are clearly visible and their interpretation reliable. Microscopic samples of the pigments from such areas in *The Immaculate Conception*, and in *St John the Evangelist*, show that the mixture could vary, but in both cases the opacity of the line results from the presence of lead white. In the foot of St John, a mixture of white lead, lamp black and yellow earth was used to indicate the edge of the shadow [fig 9.7].[23] In the carmine drapery at the feet of the Virgin in *The Immaculate Conception* a similar line contains lead white, red earth and a vegetable black pigment. In both cases, the tone of the line, olive-grey in the *St John*, opaque dark brown in *The Immaculate Conception*, would have had moderate contrast against the dull, flat brown preparation. Elsewhere, as in the contours of the Virgin in *The Immaculate Conception*, a much lighter line, possibly pure white, is evident even without the aid of radiographic examination [fig 9.8]. X-radiographs of the autograph early paintings display these characteristic graphic lines, and are especially noticeable in the radiographs of the *Kitchen Scene with Christ in the House of Martha and Mary* (straight lines describing the opening in the wall); *An Old Woman Cooking Eggs* (upper contour of the boy's head, lower contour of the old woman's extended arm, etc.) [fig 9.9]; *The Adoration of the Magi* (folds and contours of the drapery throughout, especially in the shadowed blue of the kneel-

fig 9.1 X-radiograph of Velázquez
The Adoration of the Magi [cat 36]

fig 9.2 Macrophotograph (3 × magnification) of Velázquez *Kitchen Scene with Christ in the House of Martha and Mary* [cat 21]. Detail of the left hand of Martha. The colour of the unpainted ground is visible to the left of the hand.

fig 9.5 (below) detail from Bartolomé Murillo *Self-portrait* (National Gallery, London) The lower left corner shows the cane holder or *toca lapiz* used to hold chalk, gesso or white lead points for drawing on the prepared canvas. The lower right corner shows brushes and palette similar to those Velázquez would have used. Note the relatively small size of the brushes.

fig 9.4 Pacheco *St John on Patmos* (Uffizi, Florence)

fig 9.3 Pacheco *St Jerome*
(Alcubierre Collection, Madrid)

Bart.ᵃ Murillo seipsum depin
gens pro filiorum votis acpreci
bus explendis

fig 9.6 Macrophotograph (3 × magnification) of Velázquez *Kitchen Scene with Christ in the House of Martha and Mary* [cat 21]. Detail of the graphic line describing the opening in the wall. The relief of this line and the way in which it stops and starts strongly suggest that it was made with a pointed, short, stiff brush rather than a rigid drawing point.

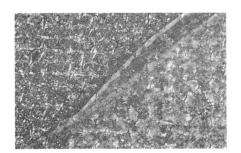

fig 9.7 Macrophotograph (3 × magnification) of Velázquez *St John the Evangelist on Patmos* [cat 34]. Detail of the graphic line describing the shadow edge in the saint's foot.

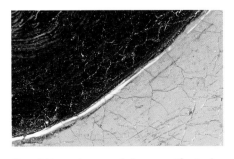

fig 9.8 Macrophotograph (3 × magnification) of Velázquez *The Immaculate Conception* [cat 32]. Detail showing a graphic line indicating the contour of the Virgin's cloak at the right side of the figure.

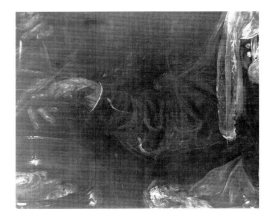

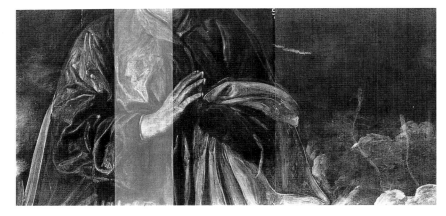

fig 9.9 X-radiograph of Velázquez *An Old Woman Cooking Eggs* [cat 16]. Detail showing fine graphic lines describing contours in the old woman's sleeve and adjustments of contour in the index finger at the far left.

fig 9.10 X-radiograph of Velázquez *The Immaculate Conception* [cat 33]. Detail showing graphic brush strokes in the dark area of the Virgin's cloak and also brush wipings in the background to the right of the Virgin's arm.

fig 9.11 (right) X-radiograph of Velázquez *St John the Evangelist on Patmos* [cat 34]. Detail showing the area of the saint's foot with the thin, radio-opaque line seen in fig 9.7.

fig 9.12 (far right) X-radiograph of Velázquez *Mother Jerónima de la Fuente* [cat 42]

fig 9.13 (lower right) X-radiograph of Velázquez *The Waterseller* [cat 31]. Detail showing a concentration of brush wipings below the painting of the goblet and hand. There are also fine graphic lines in the waterseller's hand.

fig 9.14 (lower far right) X-radiograph of Velázquez *The Immaculate Conception* [cat 33]. Note the major pentiment in the drapery near the Virgin's legs, where the arrangement of the cloak has been simplified.

fig 9.15 (below) Macrophotograph (2¼ × magnification) of Velázquez *The Immaculate Conception* [cat 33]. Detail showing the brush-work in the Virgin's tunic. The handling is noticeably deliberate when compared with the freer application typical of later paintings. This detail also shows the true colour of the organic red glaze which has faded far less where it accumulated in the texture of the underlying paint. The tunic would have had a rich, deep cherry red colour produced by the transparent organic red glaze, now very faded.

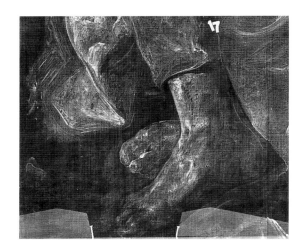

fig 9.16 (centre left) Macrophotograph (2¼ × magnification) of Velázquez *St John the Evangelist on Patmos* [cat 34]. Detail showing the delicate yet decisive wet-into-wet brushwork evident in the drapery of the saint's robe.

fig 9.17 (centre right) Macrophotograph (2¼ × magnification) of Velázquez *Christ in the House of Martha and Mary* [cat 21]. Detail showing well-blended paint applied wet-into-wet over the *bosquexo* of the ochre sleeve.

fig 9.18 (right) Macrophotograph (2¼ × magnification) of Velázquez *The Immaculate Conception* [cat 33]. Detail showing the blue cloak in which the broader strokes of the pale *bosquexo* are visible through the azurite blue glaze applied with a small brush in parallel strokes.

ing king's robe and in the dark areas of the Virgin's blue cloak); *The Immaculate Conception*, (in the landscape, contours of drapery of tunic and cloak) [fig 9.10]; *St John* (in the shadows of the ankles and feet) [fig 9.11]; *Mother Jerónima de la Fuente* (contours of the cloak and outline of the head; crucifix held in the hand) [fig 9.12]; *The Waterseller* (contour of waterseller's head, details of the ear, folds in the neck, outline of shadow area in waterseller's hand) [fig 9.13]; *St Ildefonso* (the typical opaque lines are visible throughout the blue cape of the saint).[24] Although these fine graphic strokes continue to be seen from time to time in the radiographs of paintings dating from the later 1620s, they become increasingly infrequent, suggesting perhaps that Velázquez's method had begun to bypass the stage of preparatory drawing.[25] An interesting comparison can be made between the drapery folds in the radiograph of *St Ildefonso*, and those of the figure kneeling at the far right in *The Feast of Bacchus*, c.1628–9, (Museo del Prado, Madrid), where almost no contour or fold lines are evident.[26]

Generally, the *pentimenti* in the Seville paintings were subtle in comparison with the major changes evident in works from the later 1620s, such as the royal portraits or *The Feast of Bacchus*.[27] For the most part *pentimenti* in these early works are limited to the adjustment of contours – altering the turn of a collar, narrowing the billow of a cape, or changing the lid of a jug – understandable if the composition was established beforehand in drawing. The important exception is the drapery around the legs of the Virgin in *The Immaculate Conception*. It seems probable that the relatively major change here was made by Velázquez after the laying-in (*bosquexo*) had been started, hence the highly opaque drapery folds seen in the radiograph [fig 9.14]. It seems that even some of the dark blue of the mantle had been applied in this area before the decision was taken to leave the vertical folds of the tunic uninterrupted. It looks very much as though the mantle once swept up and around from the lower part of the figure, to cover the lower part of the tunic, but still allowing the folds around the feet to be seen. Another possible exception is in the plate containing eggs at the lower right corner of *Christ in the House of Martha and Mary*. In the radiograph of this painting there is a suggestion of a carrot or parsnip in a lower layer of paint, which was supressed in favour of the eggs now visible.[28]

Close observation shows that in these early works the whole is built up from discrete, carefully studied parts. This impression accords well with Pacheco's accounts elsewhere of Velázquez making finished drawings from life, as well as the view that generally cartoons were not used, but rather small finished drawings.[29] Pacheco gives special prominence to the fact that Velázquez drew from life, which might imply that this was less common a practice than one might think. The carefully observed contours and artificial lighting of the painted compositions produced a charged stasis common to many figures and objects studied intently from nature. Nevertheless, the compositions are slightly disjointed. While the beautiful quality and accuracy of line does much to convince the eye that the compositional elements occupy a unified space, the treatment of colour, perspective and light serve to remind the viewer of their intriguing artificiality and skilful, slightly naive ingenuity.

Brush wipings which have begun to show as the paintings age are characteristic of Velázquez's work. Undoubtedly never intended to be seen, these strokes were made by Velázquez as he cleaned his brush on unpainted areas of the ground, ridding it of excess paint, or perhaps testing a hue. Such wipings do not

appear, however, in *The Adoration of the Magi*.[30] *The Waterseller* [fig 9.13] shows a flurry of vertical, white strokes, underlying the hands and goblet near the centre of the picture. Typically the brush wipings are seen in the background, or near the edges. In *The Waterseller*, their concentration in the area of the hands indicates that the painting was not only conceived from discrete elements, but that it was painted in sections, with the hands completed after the area to which the paint of the brush wipings corresponds.

This manner of painting presupposes that the principal elements of the composition are correctly placed on the canvas before painting, and that the application of paint can be undertaken almost object by object, filling-in, and giving volume to the delineated shapes. The broad planes of light and shadow which define the objects in Velázquez's paintings might suggest that they were painted in a vigorous, broad-brush technique. This is not the case, however, as close study of the surface will show: the broadest strokes are laid on with a brush of just under 2 cm in width, and a great deal of the painting was done with a very small brush, about 0.5 cm in width [fig 9.5]. Where an underlayer (*bosquexo*) exists, it seems to have been applied with the broader brush, and for the upper layers which give final relief to the form, the smaller brush was used. The paintings from the Seville period show a subtle progression from controlled, steady brushwork to a more vigorous, rather emphatic handling. This is especially evident when comparing *The Immaculate Conception* and *St John on Patmos* [figs 9.15 and 9.16].

The optical impact of these early compositions depends upon having a smooth, opaque paint mixture capable of maintaining its solid brightness when laid over a dark ground. One might expect these opaque paints to have been stiff and thick, yet Velázquez seems to have achieved the opacity required for painting over his flat brown grounds without making his paint stiff, which would have made it more difficult to manipulate with the delicate touch evident in even the earliest paintings. It is clear from studying the surface carefully that much of the painting was wet-into-wet, smoothly blending the opaque tones necessary for the representation of physical reality in this technique [fig 9.17]. In the few early paintings whose analyses have been published, it is evident that linseed oil was used. Into this medium, pigments of an unexpectedly limited range were mixed to achieve the tonalities typical of the early paintings: smalt, red ochre, yellow ochre, charcoal black, bone black, vegetable black, and lead white dominated the palette of the Seville years. Lead-tin yellow, red lake, azurite, and vermilion were also used, but far less frequently and usually in small quantities.[31] If this list of pigments is compared with those mentioned by Pacheco,[32] or with pigments listed in documents for this period,[33] it is possible to conjecture that although a wide range of native and imported pigments was available to artists in Spain, Velázquez seems intentionally to have limited his palette to inexpensive, abundantly available colours. Exceptionally, richer colours were used, notably in religious paintings, and particularly when the Virgin Mary was represented, probably as much for iconographical as for purely aesthetic motives.

In part, the tremendous contrast between light and shadow in paintings of this period may be the result of using selective underlayers, the *bosquexo* mentioned by Pacheco.[34] When certain areas of the precise drawing are developed in paint, or *bosquexados*, a greater thickness builds up thus reducing the role of the ground tone in the final appearance of the drapery or flesh colours. On the other hand, the ground tone plays a very important role in giving depth to the shadows and background in paintings like *The Adoration of the Magi*, or *The Waterseller*. In the latter one can see four examples of how Velázquez manipulated the ground tone with decreasing densities of paint as he moved into the deepest shadows, to achieve the notable chiaroscuro evident there. The shadow on the right side of the large water jug in the foreground is achieved by scumbling over the ground with a drab tone, allowing a delicate play of light and cool tones, from which the form of the jug is brought into relief by the finely graduated lead-white based colour of the highlight. The waterseller, seen in profile with the light striking fully upon his chest, is painted with a *bosquexo*, or firmly modelled underlayer, which is finished in thinner layers of ochre paint, in places worked wet-into-wet. The solid layer structure here has ensured that the cloak and white sleeve have preserved something of their original tonal relationship. The boy holding the goblet is painted less solidly, only the hands, collar and highlights on the face being sufficiently opaque to counteract the dark ground. Much of the boy's hair and his jacket are modelled by slightly altering the ground tone with a very thin, dark paint which has sunk considerably. Finally, in the figure drinking in the background, Velázquez has modelled form in the features, hair and jug with very thin, transparent paint, allowing the ground colour to play a large part in the tonalities of this area. From the technical point of view, this painting offers the full range of ways in which to work on a dark ground, a pithy essay on the aesthetics of tenebrism.

Paintings like *The Immaculate Conception*, *St John on Patmos*, and *The Adoration of the Magi*, contain rather more complex layer structures in some colours than do the 'earth-tone' works discussed above. In the blue mantle of the Virgin in *The Immaculate Conception*, a glazing technique was used. The *bosquexo* was made with white, lamp black and a very fine red earth.[35] When this was sufficiently dry, a layer of azurite was applied, producing the blue that is still quite well preserved today [fig 9.18].[36] Although the basic structure of the draperies was established in the *bosquexo*, the glaze was applied more thinly or thickly in relation to the light and shadow set in the *bosquexo*. So not only did the blue glaze layer give the mantle its rich hue, but it also provided the final subtle modelling of the folds. Had Velázquez simply painted a mixed blue over the ground, without the benefit of the intervening *bosquexo*, the colour might well have darkened similarly to the Virgin's cloak in *The Adoration of the Magi*. In that painting it is interesting to observe the darkening of the blue in the Virgin's cloak in comparison to the tunic of the king kneeling at the lower left, where it seems that a *bosquexo* was used [fig 9.1]. In the Virgin's cloak, the x-radiograph shows far less opacity because the blue was painted directly over the brown ground. Some glazing was used in the transparent reds of the Virgin's tunic in *The Immaculate Conception* and St John's cloak in *St John on Patmos*. Unhappily, the pigment carmine, an organic red, used to colour these deep reddish-pinks, is unstable and

fades in strong light. Perhaps the Virgin's red tunic in *The Adoration of the Magi* has fared best in this regard, the fading being less marked here than in *The Immaculate Conception* or *St John on Patmos*.

For all the mastery of his medium that Velázquez had already achieved in the Seville years, one thing that he could not have foreseen was the way in which his paintings would age. It is important to be aware of condition when looking at technique, and of such factors as the fading of pigments, increasing transparency of media, colour alteration in unstable pigments, texture changes caused by excessive pressure in old relinings, thinning of the paint layers from heavy lining and heavy cleaning in the past. Velázquez's early paintings have been susceptible to changes from many of the causes listed above, but perhaps the most problematic are the alteration of the smalt blue used in the skies from its original blue to a dark, grey-green, and the instability of the Seville ground, which has doubtless contributed to flake losses and the need for frequent relinings in the past. As in all dark ground paintings, with age and increasing transparency of the oil medium the darks become less distinct in comparison with the light areas, which remain optically stronger. The light passages come forward and the darks sink, which can cause an impression of imbalance in the picture.

Little by little, Velázquez's technique during the Seville years moved away from the strictures on correct methods of drawing and painting he undoubtedly received in Pacheco's studio. The compositions were established with fewer precise contour lines and the brushwork became freer and broader. The surfaces, however, were always closely worked and did not yet possess the transparency and delicate handling characteristic of his mature paintings. His palette in the early 1620s – in *Mother Jerónima de la Fuente*, *The Waterseller*, *Luis de Góngora* – was reduced to a minimum, yet his struggle to master and expand the optical potential of the oil medium was increasingly successful.

An anecdote recorded by Pacheco in his discussion of still life and genre painting springs to mind as one examines the intense, emphatic presence of the jugs in *The Waterseller*. Pacheco wrote that the artist Pablo de Céspedes painted a famous *Last Supper of Our Lord*,[37] and that, 'When he had it in his house, those who came to see it admired a certain glass vessel painted there, without attending to the artful ingenuity of the rest, and seeing that everyone's eyes went to that trifle, he became infuriated and called to his servant: "Andrés, come erase this jar and take it away from here! Is it possible that no one looks at the heads and hands into which I have put all my study and care, rather they indulge in this impertinence!"'[38] To this Pacheco adds, 'one should concentrate on the most difficult and important things in a painting, which are the figures, and avoid such diversions, always so despised by the great masters …'[39] It is tempting to see in *The Waterseller* a young man's rejection of the specific notions of orthodoxy and decorum propounded by his teacher in favour of a powerful new aesthetic based on the primacy of intensely observed reality.

Notes to the Essays

The Seville of Velázquez
John H. Elliott, pp.15–21

1 For population figures, and the description of Seville which follows, I have drawn in particular on Francisco Morales Padrón, 1977, who gives an account of the city in the sixteenth century, and the seventeenth-century section, by Antonio Domínguez Ortiz, of vol.4, *El barroco y la ilustración*, Seville, 1976, subsequently revised and amplified as a volume on its own under the title of *La Sevilla del siglo XVII*, 3rd ed., Seville, 1984.

I have also made use of Domínguez Ortiz's *Orto y ocaso de Sevilla*, 2nd ed., Seville, 1974. In English, useful accounts of different aspects of the city's social and commercial life can be found in Ruth Pike, 1966, and 1972.

2 Griffin, 1988; Morales Padrón, 1977, pp.317–20; Domínguez Ortiz, 1976, cited in note 1, p.120.

3 Domínguez Ortiz, 1976, cited in note 1, p.30.

4 See Lleó Cañal, 1979, p.9.

5 Lleó Cañal, 1979, p.74.

6 Morales Padrón, 1977, p.251.

7 Domínguez Ortiz, 1976, cited in note 1, p.104.

8 Victor Pérez Escolano, *Juan de Oviedo y de la Bandera (1565–1625). Escultor, arquitecto e ingeniero*, Seville, 1977, pp.45–9.

9 As translated in Melveena McKendrick, *Cervantes*, Boston, 1980, p.185.

10 Domínguez Ortiz, 1974, cited in note 1, p.109.

11 Elliott, 1989, p.24.

12 Cited in Julián Gállego, *Velázquez en Sevilla*, Seville, 1973, p.31.

13 Pike, 1972, p.132.

14 Pike, 1972, pp.203–4.

15 Brown, 1986, pp.60–1.

16 Domínguez Ortiz, 1976, cited in note 1, pp.45–6.

17 Domínguez Ortiz, 1974, cited in note 1, p.103; Pike, 1972, pp.170–92.

18 Brown, 1986, p.201.

19 Earl J. Hamilton, *American Treasure and the Price Revolution in Spain, 1501–1650*, Cambridge, Mass., 1934, appendix VI, p.392; Pike, 1972, p.117.

20 Domínguez Ortiz, 1976, cited in note 1, pp.116–18, Richard Kagan, *Students and Society in Early Modern Spain*, Baltimore and London, 1974, p.186.

21 See Martin Murphy, 1992.

22 See in particular Brown, 1978, ch.1.

23 See González Moreno, 1969. Also Brown and Kagan, 1987, pp.231–55.

24 For Olivares's Seville years, see Elliott, 1986, pp.19–27.

25 A phrase often used by the Count-Duke of Olivares.

The Cultivated Elite of Velázquez's Seville
Vicente Lleó Cañal, pp.23–7

1 See Lleó Cañal, 1979, especially p.205.

2 H. and P. Chaunu, *Seville et l'Atlantique (1504–1650)*, Paris, 1955–9.

3 For an overview of picaresque literature, see M. Bataillon, *Pícaro y picaresca*, Madrid, 1982.

4 This is the position adopted by Carl Justi, for example, in his *Velázquez and his Times*, London, 1889.

5 M. E. Perry, *Crime and Society in Early Modern Seville*, New England University Press, 1980.

6 J. Gestoso y Pérez, *Curiosidades antiguas sevillanas*, Seville, 1910, p.311.

7 For the memoirs of the Jesuit Pedro de León (died 1632), who was for many years Chaplain to the *Carcel Real* (Royal Prison) and an assiduous preacher in the *Mancebía*, the 'official' bordellos of Seville, see P. Herrera Puga (ed), *Grandeza y miseria en Andalucia; Testimonio de una encrucijada histórica (1578–1616)*, Granada, 1981.

8 A. Huerga, *Historia de los Alumbrados*, vol.IV, *Los Alumbrados de Sevilla (1605–30)*, Madrid, 1988, p.276.

9 See the documents relating to the familiars of Cardinal Castro published in F. Ariño, *Sucesos de Sevilla de 1592 a 1604*, Seville, 1873, p.183, and also the interesting material in F. Rodríguez Marín, *Perfiles de la Sevilla Cervantina; Discurso Preliminar a la Edición de Rinconete y Cortadillo*, Madrid, 1920 (new edition Seville, 1992).

10 The most amusing description of this deception, which took place in 1616, is in the *Cartas de D. Juan de la Sal, Obispo de Bona*, in vol.36 of the *Biblioteca de Autores Españoles*, Madrid, 1855, p.539. The majority of these pseudo-religious frauds are part of the phenomenon of *Alumbradismo* in the city.

11 V. Lleó Cañal, 'La conjoncture classique dans la sculpture sevillaine: les années 1570', *La Revue de l'Art*, 70, 1985.

12 Kubler, for example, in discussing architecture, speaks of the 'Italianised south', G. Kubler, *Arquitectura de los siglos XVII y XVIII, Ars Hispaniae*, vol.14, Madrid, 1957, p.26. Wethey thought that Alonso Cano must have studied the Roman sculptures of nearby Itálica. This is historically improbable since the town was only excavated in the eighteenth century but it constitutes an accurate critical assessment of Cano's work, see Wethey, 1983, p.17. On Velázquez and classicism, see F. J. Sánchez Cantón, *Velázquez y lo clásico*, Madrid, 1961. Brown has studied the 'academy' of Pacheco in which artists and humanists came together in a common devotion to antiquity, see Brown, 1978, p.21.

13 For Caro, see the recent biography by L. Gómez Canseco, *Rodrigo Caro, un humanista en la Sevilla del Seicientos*, Seville, 1986; see also the introduction by J. P. Etienvre to his edition of Caro's *Días Geniales o Lúdricros*, Madrid, 1978. In the Biblioteca Capitular y Colombina of Seville Cathedral, there is an important group of letters, drafts and miscellaneous papers by Caro, Ms.84–8–5, 83–6–33, 83–7–25, etc.

14 J. Beltrán Fortes, 'Entre la erudición y el coleccionismo: anticuarios andaluces de los siglos XVI al XVIII', in J. Beltrán and F. Gascó (eds.), *La Antigüedad como argumento. Historiografía de Arqueología e Historia Antigua en Andalucía*, Seville, 1993.

15 Biblioteca Capitular y Colombina, Ms.63–9–83. This is a volume containing miscellaneous material relating to archeology and includes a text by the Licenciado Francisco Porras de la Cámera, a friend of Canon Pacheco, entitled *Sobre varias antigüedades de España*, as well as correspondence between the archeologists referred to above.

16 For this erudite collecting tendency, see K. Pomian, *Collectionneurs, amateurs et curieux; Paris, Venise XVI–XVIII*, Paris, 1987, p.143.

17 López Martínez, 1929, p.205. J. M. Serrera, *Pedro de Villegas Marmolejo*, Seville, 1976, p.23. For other examples of artists who collected antiquities, see Lleó Cañal, 'Orígen y función de las primeras colecciones renacentistas de antigüedades en Andalucia', in J. Beltrán and F. Gasco (eds.), *La Antigüedad como argumento, II; Historiografía de Arqueología e Historia Antigua en Andalucía*, Seville, 1995.

18 For Pacheco's relations with the Duke of Alcalá, see Pacheco, 1990.

19 For Alcalá's collection, see Lleó Cañal, 'El jardin arqueológico del primer Duque de Alcalá', *Fragmentos*, 11, 1987.

20 Lleó Cañal, 'La obra sevillana de Benvenuto Tortello', *Napoli Nobilissima*, XXIII, 5–6, 1984.

21 For Pacheco's relations with the third Duke, see Pacheco, 1990. The posthumous inventory of Alcalá's collection (1637) shows that he owned two *bodegones* by Velázquez, see Brown and Kagan, 1987, pp.231–55.

22 The secretary of the Spanish embassy in Rome, for example, does not hesitate in regarding Alcalá the collector as the equal of the Grand Duke Cosimo de'Medici and Cardinal Farnese, see J. López Toro (ed.), *Epistolas de Juan de Verzosa*, Madrid, 1945, p.133. See also Diego de Villalta, 'De las estatuas antiguas' in F. J. Sánchez Cantón, *Fuentes literarias para la Historia del Arte español*, vol.I, Madrid, 1923, p.292.

23 Part of the collection was displayed in another Alcalá property, the Castle of Bornos (Cádiz) in the grounds of which Tortello built loggie on the model of the Vatican Belvedere, see Lleó Cañal, cited in note 20.

24 R. Caro, *Antigüedades y Principado de la Ilustrissima Ciudad de Sevilla…*, Seville, 1634, *passim*.

25 Pacheco, 1990, p.348.

26 There is a large bibliography on this subject; it ranges from those who claim that academies did exist, like J. Sánchez, *Academias literarias del Siglo de Oro Español*, Madrid, 1961, to those who dismiss the notion like B. Bassegoda i Hugas in his introduction to Pacheco, 1990, to those who adopt an intermediate position like Brown, 1978.

27 A picture of what these informal meetings were like may be found in the dialogues which form the *Días Geniales o Lúdicros* by Rodrigo Caro, see the edition cited in note 13.

28 Brown and Kagan, 1987.

29 González Moreno, 1969, p.87.

30 In addition to the role he played in guiding Alcalá as a collector, Pacheco was also consulted over the drawing up of the inventory of 1637, see Brown and Kagan, 1987. For Pacheco's restoration of a work by Campaña in the Ducal collection, see Pacheco, 1990, p.549.

31 C. López Martínez, *Arquitectos, escultores y pintores vecinos de Sevilla*, Seville, 1928, p.56. At this time Gracht took on an apprentice for six years, which suggests that he had undertaken a lengthy commitment. Perhaps the ceiling

decorated with the gods of Olympus, modelled on the ceiling painted by Ottavio Semino in the Palazzo Pallavicino in Genoa, is by him. Gracht had resided in Genoa for many years.

32 One part is still *in situ* in the Casa de Pilatos, although some pieces were given to the Museo Arqueológico. Another important part passed to the Duquesa de Cardona and is not accessible.

33 The bibliography on the activities of the Casa de la Contratación is very small, perhaps because many of the undertakings were secret. The standard works are: M. de la Puente y Olea, *Los trabajos geográficos de la Casa de Contratación*, Seville, 1900, and J. Pulido Rubio, *El Piloto Mayor de la Casa de Contratación*, Seville, 1923. There is some interesting material in J. M. López Piñero, *Ciencia y Técnica en la Sociedad Española de los siglos XVI y XVII*, Barcelona, 1979.

34 This was pointed out by F. J. Sánchez Cantón in his article on 'La librería de Velázquez', in *Homenaje a Menéndez Pidal*, Madrid, 1925.

35 F. M. Quílez Corella, 'La cultura artística de Pablo de Céspedes', *Boletín del Museo e Instituto Camón Aznar*, 39, 1990.

36 Including, for example, Vasco Pereira, in whose inventory of goods there is an entry referring to 'his books of architecture and perspective and one on anatomy' (*sus libros de arquitectura y perspectiba y uno de notomía*), although these are not individually identified, Archivo de protocolos Notariales de Sevilla. Oficio 1°, Lib.3° de 1609, fol.1294.

37 P. E. Pérez-Mallaina, 'La eclosión de la ciencia', in *Sevilla, siglo XVI; El corazón de las riquezas del mundo*, Madrid, 1993.

38 On this subject, see B. Reckers, *Arias Montano*, Madrid, 1973. It should be noted that among the group of intellectuals and scientists whom Montano put into contact with Flemish and Dutch colleagues was Canon Francisco Pacheco, uncle of the eponymous painter.

39 J. Vernet, *Historia de la Ciencia Española*, Madrid, 1975; J. M. López Piñero, *Ciencia y Técnica en la Sociedad Española de los siglos XVI y XVII*, Barcelona, 1979, *passim*.

40 Licenciado Alfonso Sáez, *Relación de las fiestas que el Colegio Mayor de Santa María de Jesús Universidad de Sevilla hizo en la publicación de un Estatuto en que se juró la Concepción Limpísima de Nra. Señora…*, Seville, 1617. There is a modern edition, Seville, 1947.

41 Pacheco, 1990, p.385. It is also mentioned by Céspedes himself in the list of his own works included in his *Libro de Instrumentos Nuevos* where it appears as no.6, 'Una perspectiva teórica y práctica'. J. Pulido Rubio, *El Piloto Mayor de la Casa de la Contratación de Sevilla*, Seville, 1923. Pacheco also mentions that he owned a translation of a manuscript by Leonardo da Vinci, which had been made for him by Juan de Jáuregui.

42 B. Daza, *Arte y uso de los antojos*, Seville, 1623.

43 The correspondence between them is published in J. M. Asensio y Toledo, *Francisco Pacheco; Sus obras artísticas y literaria*, Seville, 1886, p.81.

44 In the eulogy which accompanies his portrait in the *Libro de Retratos*, Facsimile edition, Madrid, 1983, p.83.

45 Biblioteca Capitular y Colombina Ms.82–4–13. These were made known by A. Morales Martínez, 'Arte y ciencia en la Sevilla del siglo XVI. Los manuscritos del cosmógrafo Rodrigo Zamorano', in *Actas del X Congreso del Comité Español de Historia del Art; Los Clasicismos en el Arte Español*, Madrid, 1994.

46 There is a modern edition with an introduction by M. Márquez published as part of the series entitled *Biblioteca Clásica de la Medicina Española*, Madrid, 1923.

47 J. Vernet, cited in note 39, p.117.

48 In the library of Seville University there is a copy of Copernicus's *De Revolutionibus Orbium Coelestium*, Nuremberg, 1543, which belonged to the cosmographer Jerónimo de Chaves, see *Universitas Hispalense*, exh. cat., Seville, 1995, no.120.

49 There is a modern edition by V. Infantes de Miguel, Madrid, 1979, who dates it to about 1620–5.

50 It is quoted by F. Rodríguez Marín in his *Pedro Espinosa; Estudio biográfico, bibliográfico y crítico*, Madrid, 1907, p.117.

51 Pacheco states that he was 'an admirer of his painting', see Pacheco, 1990, p.203. It is possible that *The Waterseller of Seville* was given as a present by Velázquez to the influential cleric. When Velázquez valued Fonseca's collection of paintings at his death in 1627, he gave the highest valuation to his own painting, see J. López Navío, 'Velázquez tasa los cuadros de su protector, don Juan de Fonseca', *Archivo Español de Arte*, 34, 1961.

52 D. T. Kinkead, 'Tres bodegones de Velázquez en una colección sevillana del siglo XVII', *Archivo Español de Arte*, 52, 1979.

53 …*Lástima tenga Vm. de los que vivimos en esta última Bética que, siendo madre en todas las edades de tan ilustres ingenios, se halla en este infelice tiempo tan postrada, que en esta gran ciudad, lumbrera del mundo nuevo y viejo, no sé si se hallarán tres que traten estos estudios, y si alguno lo trata, es, o con vana ostentación y sin provecho público, o con ignorancia de los verdaderos principios, que es ejercitarse en el glorioso polvo de la Antigüedad…*, quoted from S. Montoto, *El Ldo. Rodrigo Caro. Varones Insignes en Letras Naturales de la Ilustrisima Ciudad de Sevilla. Epistolario*, Seville, 1915, p.121.

Politics, Religion and Piety in Seville
Ronald Cueto, pp.29–33

I should like to thank Margaret Kay and Anthony D. Wright for their help.

1 Carlos Martínez Shaw, (ed.), *Sevilla, siglo XVI; El corazón de las riquezas del mundo*, Madrid, 1993, pp.15–16.

2 Stephen N. Orso, *Art and Death at the Spanish Habsburg Court; The Royal Exequies for Philip IV*, New York, 1989, p.13.

3 Francisco Morales Padrón, (ed.), *Memorias de Sevilla (1600–1678)*, Córdoba, 1981, pp.37–8.

4 Morales Padrón, cited in note 3, p.62.

5 Carlos Alvarez Santaló, 'Dios, el diablo y la Inquisición', in Martínez Shaw, cited in note 1, pp.170–181: 180.

6 Antonio Domínguez Ortiz, *Orto y ocaso de Sevilla*, Seville, 1946, p.54. According to Pike, 1972, p.60, in the sixteenth century the Sevillian Chapter consisted of eleven dignitaries, forty canons and forty prebendaries.

7 Paul Bairoch, Jean Batou, Pierre Chèvre, *La population des villes européennes*, Geneva, 1988, pp.19, 45, 57.

8 José Antonio Ruiz Hernando, 'El monasterio y la arquitectura jerónima', in *El monasterio de Nuestra Señora de Prado*, Salamanca, 1995, pp.269–91.

9 Antonio Domínguez Ortiz, 'Murillo's Seville', in *Bartolomé Esteban Murillo 1617–1682*, Royal Academy, London, 1983, pp.29–39: 31.

10 For the Trinitarian connection in the Court of Philip III, see Ronald Cueto, 'Patronage, Politics, Religion and Cervantes's *Novelas ejemplares*', in J. J. Macklin, (ed.), *After Cervantes*, Leeds, 1993, pp.43–90: 49–54. For the special relationship between Philip III and the Augustinians in the convent of the Encarnación in Madrid, see Luis Muñoz, *Vida y virtvdes de la Venerable Madre Mariana de S. Ioseph*, Madrid, 1643, p.300.

11 Guillermo Vázquez Núñez, O. de M., *Mercedarios ilustres*, Madrid, 1966, p.7.

12 Ronald Cueto, 'La piedad y la política en la pintura de Zurbarán; analectas iconográficas', *Estudios Segovianos*, vol.XXXIV, 1994, pp.665–710: 670–2, 676–8, 680–1.

13 Domínguez Ortiz, cited in note 6, p.57.

14 Domínguez Ortiz, cited in note 6, p.68.

15 Morales Padrón, cited in note 3, p.48.

16 Morales Padrón, cited in note 3, p.58.

17 Cueto, cited in note 10, p.56.

18 José Angel López Lanusse, Ronald Cueto, 'Martín Muñoz de las Posadas: Politics, Religion and Art in Hapsburg Old Castile', in Rees, 1994, pp.103–49: 128.

19 Cristóbal Moreno, O.F.M., *Iornadas para el Cielo*, Madrid, 1616, sees sins as sores (f.5r), confessors as physicians (f.82r), and the Blessed Sacrament as infallible heavenly medicine (f.265v).

20 Stephen N. Orso, *Philip IV and the Decoration of the Alcázar of Madrid*, Princeton, 1986, p.133.

21 Diego de Villalobos, O.P., *Apologia por el estado eclesiastica especialmente religioso*, Valladolid, 1641, p.148. Diego Matute de Peñafiel Contreras, *Prosapia de Cristo*, Baza, 1614, p.2, claims that Philip III is directly descended through the House of Habsburg from Adam and Eve.

22 Orso, cited in note 2, p.9.

23 Sancho Dávila, *De la Veneracion qve se deve a los cverpos de los Sanctos y a svs Reliqvias*, Madrid, 1611, p.287.

24 Morales Padrón, 1977, p.271.

25 Morales Padrón, cited in note 3, p.49. The same predicament awaited thirty-six Englishmen in 1616, see Antonio Domínguez Ortiz, *Crisis y decadencia de la España de los Austrias*, Barcelona, 1969, p.18. More resolute, after a certain amount of understandable vacillation, was the Scotsman James Bolen, who died affirming his Protestant faith, Pedro de León, S.J., *Grandeza y miseria en Andalucía*, (ed.) Pedro Herrera Puga, S.J., Granada, 1981, pp.490–5.

26 Antonio de la Banda y Vargas, 'La espiritualidad y la cultura en la Sevilla seiscentista', in VV.AA., *Sevilla en el siglo XVII*, Seville, 1983, pp.39–48: 41–2.

27 Brown, 1978, p.1.

28 Morales Padrón, cited in note 3, p.35.

29 Martin Murphy, 1992.

30 Enrique Valdivieso, 'Una serie de santos reyes de Inglaterra de Francisco Pacheco', *Boletín del Seminario de Estudios de Arte y Arqueología*, vol.LX, 1994, pp.463–70, quoting Michael E. Williams, 'Portraits of English Royal Saints at Valladolid and Oscott', paper presented at Catholic Record Society Conference, July 1993.

31 Diego Ortiz de Zúñiga, *Anales eclesiásticos y seculares de la muy noble y muy leal ciudad de Sevilla, metrópoli de la Andalucía*, 8 vols., Madrid, 1795–6, vol.IV, pp.255–256.

32 Antonio de Quintanadueñas, S.J., *Santos de la civdad de Sevilla, y sv arcobispado: fiestas qve sv santa iglesia Metropolitana celebra*, Seville, 1637, pp.118–40: 131–2.

33 Morales Padrón, cited in note 3, p.29.

34 Martín de Roa, S.J., *Antigvedad, Veneracion i Frvto de las Sagradas Imagenes, i Reliqvias*, Seville, 1623, ff. 43v, 44r.

35 Hilary Dansey Smith, *Preaching in the Spanish Golden Age; A study of some preachers of the reign of Philip III*, Oxford, 1978, pp.90–1.

36 Enriqueta Harris, 'Velázquez, Sevillian Painter of Sacred Subjects', in Rees, 1994, pp.9–49.

37 Ortiz de Zúñiga, cited in note 31, p.141.

38 Ortiz de Zúñiga, cited in note 31, p.251.

39 Ortiz de Zúñiga, cited in note 31, pp.234–8.

40 Francisco de Pereda, O.P., *Libro Intitvlado la Patrona de Madrid y Venidas de Nuestra Señora a España*, Valladolid, 1604, ff.229v–230r.

41 Juan de Tamayo Salazar, *Trivnfos de las Armas Catolicas por intercession de Maria S.N.*, 2 vols., Madrid, 1648, vol.I, Preface, no pagination.

42 See cat.33.

43 Cueto, 1991, pp.63–104.

44 For Franciscan involvement, see J. L. Phelan, *The Millennial Kingdom of the Franciscans in the New World*, Berkeley, 1956. For Luis de León, O.S., Sandalio Diego, S.J., 'Fray Luis de León y Francisco de Ribera en el comentario de Abdías', *Estudios Eclesiásticos*, vol.8, 1929, pp.5–22: 19, 21.

45 For learned academies in Seville, see Brown, 1978, pp.21–43. For the Congregation of the Pomegranate, see Alvaro Huerga, O.P., *Historia de los alumbrados*, 4 vols., Madrid, 1978–1988, vol.IV, pp.218–9. Eschatological motifs were present in the Jesuit Novitiate in Seville. According to an Oratorian petition of 17 May 1784, the paintings and ornaments of San Luis had been taken over by the Discalced Franciscans after the suppression of the Society of Jesus. A series of paintings on the Four Last Things used to hang in the Spiritual Exercises Chapel, Archivo Histórico Nacional, Madrid, *Clero*, Jesuitas, legajo 484. Many believed at the time that it was the Society of Jesus that was destined to lead the onslaught against the Antichrist, see Cueto, cited in note 43, p.81. The Adoration of the Magi also has eucharistic associations. It is one of the three scriptural references quoted by the Tridentine Fathers in their defence of Catholic adoration of the Eucharist, H.J. Schroeder, O.P., (ed.), *Canons and Decrees of the Council of Trent*, St Louis, 1960, p.76, quoted Matthew II:11, Matthew 28:17, as well as Luke XXIV:52.

46 For the significance of the subject of the painting in relation to the missionary ideals of the Jesuit Order, see cat.36.

47 See cat.21.

48 For the Tridentine quoting of St James 2:24, see Schroeder, cited in note 45, p.36.

49 Marcel Bataillon, *Erasmo y España*, Mexico and Buenos Aires, 1966, p.69.

50 Alonso de Andrade, S.J., *Libro de la Gvia de la Virtvd, y de la imitacion de Nuestra Señora para todos los estados*, 3 vols., Madrid, 1642–1646, vol.I, p.176.

51 Roa, cited in note 34, p.137.

52 María Teresa López Díaz, 'Hambrunas, pestes e inundaciones', in Martínez Shaw, cited in note 1, pp.157–69: 163–6. Domínguez Ortiz, cited in note 25, p.27, quoting the Jesuit Pedro de León, notes that pimps used to pawn their women in Sevillian brothels for between ten and twenty ducats. See also Pike, 1972, pp.204–6.

53 One of the first measures taken by Olivares when he came to power was to establish a *Junta de Reformación* against all forms of vice in the Catholic Monarchy.

54 Huerga, cited in note 45, 155–75. Antonio Domínguez Ortiz, *Autos de la Inquisición de Sevilla (Siglo XVII)*, Seville, 1981, p.80, also mentions this case.

55 Jean-Michel Sallmann, *Naples et ses saints à l'âge baroque (1540–1750)*, Paris, 1994, p.97.

56 Schroeder, cited in note 45, p.26, and *Catechismus, ex decreto concilii tridentini ad parochos*, Paris, 1567, p.4.

57 Schroeder, cited in note 45, p.13.

58 Jean Delumeau, *Reassurer et protéger; Le sentiment de sécurité dans l'occident d'autrefois*, Paris, 1989, p.570.

59 *Sumptuosas fiestas que la villa de Madrid celebro a XIX de Iunio de 1622. En la canonizacion de San Isidro, San Ignacio, San Francisco Xauier, San Felipe Neri Presbitero Florentino, y Santa Teresa de Iesus*, Seville, 1622, Biblioteca Nacional Madrid, V–226–18.

60 Morales Padrón, cited in note 3, pp.40,59.

61 Louis Chatellier, *The Europe of the Devout. The Catholic Reformation and the Formation of a New Society*, Cambridge, 1989, p.173. To this very day the Sacramental Confraternities in Seville combine a deep devotion to the Eucharist with an abiding commitment to the Immaculate Conception. See José Roda Peña, 'La devoción inmaculista en la Hermandad Sacramental de la Colegial de San Salvador de Sevilla', in *La Orden Concepcionista; Actas del I Congreso Internacional*, 2 vols., León, 1990, vol.II, pp.91–105:91.

Velázquez and Sevillian Painting
Juan Miguel Serrera, pp.37–43

1 For Seville as the 'New Rome', see Lleó Cañal, 1979.

2 S. B. Vranich, *Ensayos sevillanos del Siglo de Oro*, Valencia, 1981.

3 A good overview of Sevillian painting in the sixteenth and seventeenth centuries is provided by E. Valdivieso, *Historia de la pintura sevillana; Siglos XIII al XX*, Seville, 1986. For Sevillian sixteenth-century painters, see J. M. Serrera, 'Pinturas y pintores del siglo XVI en la catedral de Sevilla', in *La Catedral de Sevilla*, Seville, 1984, pp.353–404. For Sevillian painters in the first third of the seventeenth century, see Valdivieso and Serrera, 1985.

4 On Esturmio (Ferdinand Sturm), see J. M. Serrera, *Hernando de Esturmio*, Seville, 1983.

5 For the fraught question of the chronology of Pedro de Campaña, see J. M. Serrera, 'Pedro de Campaña; Obra dispersa', *Archivo Español de Arte*, LXII (245), Madrid, 1989, pp.1–33.

6 For Alonso Vázquez, see J. M. Serrera, 'Alonso Vázquez: el retablo mayor del Hospital de las Cinco Llagas', *Archivo Hispalense*, LXXIV (227), Seville, 1991, pp.139–72, and *Alonso Vázquez en México*, Mexico City, 1991.

7 For the poem by Baltasar de Cepeda, see W. L. Fichter, 'Un poesía contemporánea inédita sobre las bodas de Velázquez', *Varia Velazqueña*, vol.I, Madrid, 1960, pp.636–9.

8 On Herrera and Mal Lara, see Vranich, cited in note 2. *Aunque esto no se usa en Hespaña, es loable costumbre de otras naciones ayudar todos los hombres doctos al que escrive, y aun leer los autores sus obras en las Academias para ellos concertadas, y todos dar sus pareceres y dezir cosas notables, y con cierta sencilles dárselo todo al autor, sin publicar que ellos hizieron mercedes. Sale el libro emendado y acabado, por approbación común de los varones doctos de aquel tiempo. Pero, en fin, passaremos assí, donde la invidia y sobervia pueden tanto, que a unos tienen ocupados en alabar sus obras y a otros en murmurar de la agenas.*

9 On the relationship between painting and literature in Seville during Velázquez's early years, see M. Pérez Lozano, 'Velázquez en el entorno de Pacheco. Las primeras obras', *Ars Longa*, no.3, Valencia, 1991, pp.89–102. For a study of the career of Vasco Pereira, see Serrera, 1987, pp.197–239.

10 The best work on Alejo Fernández is still D. Angulo Iñiguez, *Alejo Fernández*, Seville, 1946.

11 At present the panels of this triptych are undergoing restoration in the Instituto Andaluz del Patrimonio Histórico. The panels bear the mark of the city of Antwerp which confirms the provenance of the triptych.

12 On the portraits by Jan van Hemessen in Seville, see J. M. Serrera, 'Nuevas obras de Jan van Hemessen', *Boletín del Seminario de Estudios de Arte y arqueología*, vol.LIII, Valladolid, 1987, pp.363–8.

13 Ministerio de Asuntos Exteriores, Madrid. Archivo Embajada Española ante la Santa Sede. Legajo núm.17, fols.166–76.

14 The ceiling paintings in the house of the poet Arguijo and in the Casa de Pilatos are discussed in: D. Angulo Iñiguez, *La Mitología y el Arte Español del Renacimiento*, Madrid, 1952; Lleó Cañal, 1979; and R. López Torrijos, *La mitología en la pintura española del Siglo de Oro*, Madrid, 1985. For the ceilings in the Archbishop's Palace, see E. Valdivieso and J. M. Serrera, *Catálogo de las pinturas del Palacio Arzobispal de Sevilla*, Seville, 1979; A. E. Pérez Sánchez, *Pintura española de bodegones y floreros de 1600 a Goya*, Museo del Prado, Madrid, 1983; and Jordan and Cherry, 1995.

15 For the attribution to Ribera of the Caravaggio copy in Seville, see C. Fernández, *El oratorio de San Felipe Neri de Sevilla; Su historia, instituciones, particularidades y biblioteca oratoriana*, Seville, 1894. For the Caravaggio copy in Bolivia, see L. de Moura Sobral, 'Una copia de Caravaggio en Bolivia', *Arte y Arqueología*, nos.5 and 6, La Paz, 1978, pp.175–80.

Velázquez, Painter of Sacred Subjects
Enriqueta Harris, pp.45–9

I am grateful to David Davies for helpful discussions in the preparation of this essay.

1 For the quotations of Pacheco on Velázquez in English, see Harris, 1982, Appendix I, pp.191–5. Other references are to the recent annotated edition of Pacheco, 1990.

2 For references to Palomino's *Parnaso Español*, see Harris, 1982, Appendix II, pp.196ff.

3 E. Tormo, *La Inmaculada y el Arte Español*, Madrid, 1915, p.32.

4 On Pacheco's 'Academy', see Brown, 1978, Part I; for the *romance* on the wedding feast, W. L. Fichter, 'Una poesia inédita ... sobre las bodas de Velázquez', *Varia Velazqueña*, vol.I, Madrid, 1960, pp.636–9.

5 The documents concerning Velázquez in Seville are printed in *Varia Velazqueña*, vol.II, 1960, pp.213–22.

6 On the polychroming of wood sculpture that Pacheco claimed to have revived in Spain, see Pacheco, 1990, pp.494ff; Z. Véliz, 1986, pp.81ff.

7 For Pacheco's career and production as painter, see Valdivieso and Serrera, 1985. Of the portrait drawings, less than half the 160 or more sheets are known today. See Angulo and Pérez Sánchez, 1985, pp.132–95.

8 A. Valbuena Prat, *La Vida española en la Edad de Oro*, 1943, p.140.

9 On the 'Marian War' and Seville's devotion to the mystery, see T. D. Kendrick, *Saint James in Spain*, London, 1960, pp.88–103, 207; for the festivals, J. Alenda y Mira, *Relaciones de Solemnidades y Fiestas públicas de España*, Madrid, 1903, pp.188–91.

10 For a description of this complicated 'allegory', see Valdivieso, 1978, pp.55–60, 91; see also Valdivieso and Serrera, 1985, p.126, pls.110–12.

11 On the iconography of the subject in Spanish art, see Tormo, cited in note 3, and S. Stratton, *La Inmaculada Concepción en el Arte Español*, Cuadernos de Arte e Iconografía, vol.I, 2, Madrid, 1988. English edition, *The Immaculate Conception in Spanish Art*, Cambridge, 1994.

12 See Valdivieso and Serrera, 1985, especially pp.65–9, for his many versions of the subject.

13 On the sculptor and his many versions of the subject, see the major monograph by Proske, 1967; for fig.5, pp.47–9, figs.27–8.

14 Pacheco, 1990, pp.575–7. For the history and iconography of Velázquez's paintings, see MacLaren and Braham, 1970, pp.129–33.

15 Pacheco, 1990, pp.670–73. On St John's likeness to an early portrait, possibly a self-portrait, see Harris, 1982, pp.10–11.

16 *Vestigatio arcani sensus in Apocalypsi*, Antwerp, 1614, p.614. As a plausible source for Velázquez's composition, Martínez Ripoll suggests an engraving by Sadeler after M. de Vos 'El "San Juan Evangelista en la isla de Patmos" de Velázquez, y sus fuentes iconográficas', *Areas*, Revista de Ciencias sociales, Murcia, 1983, nos.3, 4, pp.199–208.

17 F. Portocarrero, *Libro de la Descensión de Nuestra Señora*, Madrid, 1616. El Doctor Salazar de Mendoza, *El Glorioso Doctor San Ildefonso*, Toledo, 1618.

18 R. López Torrijos, *Iconografía de San Ildefonso desde sus orígenes hasta el siglo XVIII*, Cuadernos de Arte e Iconografía, 1, 2, Madrid, 1988.

19 Kendrick, cited in note 9, p.102. Castro was a zealous believer in the 'lead books of Granada' and other spurious relics that were purported to provide early evidence of the mystery.

20 Pacheco, 1990, pp.612–27.

21 *Bodegón*, the name given to a novel type of genre subject, a kitchen or tavern scene with prominent still-life. The rival at court was presumably the Italian-born Vicente Carducho, author of *Diálogos de la Pintura*, 1633, (ed.) Calvo Serraller, Madrid, 1979, where, pp.350–1, he inveighs against secular subjects disguised as religious ones, mentioning in particular a Christ in the House of Martha and Mary surrounded by so much food and many kitchen utensils 'que más me parecía hostería de la gula, que hospicio de santidad'. His attack on the naturalism of Caravaggio whom he calls the anti-Christ, pp.270–2, is taken as an attack on Velázquez.

22 Pacheco, 1990, p.519 (Pliny, *Nat. Hist.*XXXV, 112). Palomino: Harris, p.197, cited in note 2. Gracián cited in *Varia Velazqueña*, vol.II, 1960, pp.52–3.

23 Inventory of the artist's books, etc., *Varia Velazqueña*, vol.II, pp.397–9, nos.416, 552.

24 The fullest and most balanced discussion is that of MacLaren and Braham, 1970, pp.121–5.

25 Ruth Fainlight, 'Velázquez's *Christ in the House of Martha and Mary*', *Selected Poems*, 1987, p.22. Reprinted in 'Picture Choice', *The Independent*, 4 July, 1989.

26 Valdivieso and Serrera, 1985, pp.101–2. The scene of martyrdom is based on an engraving by Jan Muller.

27 M.S. Soria, 'An unknown early painting by Velázquez', *The Burlington Magazine*, 91, 1949, p.127.

Velázquez's Bodegones
David Davies, pp.51–65

28 On the types of local pottery still made, see N. Seseña, 'Los barros y lozas que pintó Velázquez', *Archivo Español de Arte*, 254, 1991, pp.171–9.

29 See Mulcahy, 1988, pp.79–82.

30 J. Ainaud de Lasarte, 'Francisco Ribalta', *Goya*, 20, 1957, pp.86–9, first drew attention to the similarity of pose suggesting the engraving was a possible source for Velázquez's figure of the nun.

31 First published (with inscriptions) by J. E[zquerra] del B[ayo], 'La Exposición Franciscana', *Arte Español*, 8, 1926–7, pp.246–8.

32 As 'St Geronima' in A. B. C. Dunbar, *Dictionary of Sacred Women*, London, 1904, vol.I, p.341. As 'Girolama' in Bibliotheca Sanctorum, vol.VI, 1965, p.1107, with bibliography. See also P. Ruano Teresa O.F.M., *La V. M. Sor Jerónima de la Asunción*, Madrid, 1993.

33 See sources cited in note 7. Luis de Granada died in 1588.

1 Palomino, 1947, vol.3, Harris, 1982, p.197 (for translation).

2 Sebastián de Cobarruvias Orozco, *Tesoro de la Lengua Castellana o Española*, Madrid, 1611, 1977 ed., p.224: 'El sótano o portal baxo, dentro del qual está la bodega, a donde el que no tiene quien le guise la comida la halla allí adereçada y juntamente la bevida, de manera que se dixo de bodega.' For a discussion of the terminology of genre subjects, especially the *bodegón* and still-life, see Pérez Sánchez, 1983, pp.18–19.

3 See note 2.

4 Real Academia Española, *Diccionario de Autoridades*, 3 vols., Madrid, 1726, (1990 ed.), vol.I, p.634.

5 Cobarruvias, cited in note 2, p.949; *Autoridades*, cited in note 4, vol.3, p.203.

6 Cobarruvias, cited in note 2, pp.224, 949.

7 J. Zarco Cuevas, *Inventario de las alhajas, relicarios, estatuas, pinturas, tapices y otros objetos de valor y curiosidad donados por el rey don Felipe II al Monasterio de El Escorial. Años de 1571 a 1588*, Madrid, 1930, p.93, nos.1494 and 1496. Jordan and Cherry, 1995, p.189, n.2.

8 M. Kusche, *Juan Pantoja de la Cruz*, Madrid, 1964, p.231. Pérez Sánchez, 1983, p.18.

9 See the seminal essay by Sarah Schroth, 'Early Collectors of Still-Life Painting in Castile', in Jordan, 1985, p.32.

10 Jordan, 1985, p.32.

11 Jordan, 1985, p.34.

12 Pacheco, 1990, p.517.

13 Pacheco, 1990, p.519; Harris, 1982, p.194 (for translation).

14 Pérez Sánchez rightly stressed the importance of this basic belief. See Pérez Sánchez, 1983, p.15.

15 Cobarruvias, cited in note 2, f.1.r.

16 Pacheco, 1990, pp.75–6, 134, 238–44.

17 Émile Mâle, *The Gothic Image*, London and Glasgow, 1961, p.65.

18 E. H. Gombrich, *Symbolic Images; Studies in the Art of the Renaissance*, London, 1972, p.53. See, also, the same author's 'The Renaissance Theory of Art and the Rise of Landscape', *Norm and Form*, London, 1966, pp.107–21.

19 Pliny, *Natural History* (Loeb ed.), 10 vols., London and Cambridge, Mass., vol.IX, p.345.

20 *Parable of the Blind*, Capodimonte Museum, Naples.

21 F. Grossmann, *The Paintings of Brueghel*, London, 1955, pp.201–3.

22 Grossmann, cited in note 21, p.21.

23 See also P. K. F. Moxey, 'Erasmus and the Iconography of Pieter Aertsen's *Christ in the House of Martha and Mary* in the Boymans-Van Beuningen Museum', *Journal of the Warburg and Courtauld Institutes*, 34, 1971, pp.335–6.

24 S. J. Freedberg, *Painting in Italy 1500–1600* (2nd ed.), Harmondsworth, 1983, p.589.

25 For a discussion of these different forms of nourishment in relation to Velázquez's *bodegones*, see Ronald Cueto's essay, pp.27–31.

26 Fernand Braudel, *The Mediterranean and the Mediterranean World in the Age of Philip II*, 2 vols., London, 1972–3, vol.II, p.734.

27 *Meditations on the Life of Christ*, I. Ragusa and R. B. Green (ed.), Princeton, 1961, p.367.

28 Ainaud, 1947, p.371. Ainaud compares the description to the painting by Caravaggio in the National Gallery, London.

29 For a discussion of the influence of Caravaggio and the Caravaggisti on Spanish painting and on Velázquez in particular, see, especially, Ainaud, 1947, pp.345–413; Pérez Sánchez, 1973; Harris, 1982, pp.53–4.

30 Ainaud, 1947, pp.366, 380, 406; Anna Tzeutschler Lurie, in collaboration with Denis Mahon, 'Caravaggio's Crucifixion of St Andrew from Valladolid', *The Bulletin of The Cleveland Museum of Art*, January, 1977, pp.3–24.

31 Ainaud, 1947, pp.368, 408.

32 F. Benito Domenech, *Los Ribalta y la Pintura Valenciana de su tiempo*, Madrid, 1987–8, pp.122–3.

33 Pacheco, 1990, p.443; Harris, 1982, p.194 (for translation).

34 Ainaud, 1947, p.380.

35 Harris, 1982, p.54.

36 Ainaud, 1947, pp.400–1.

37 Pérez Sánchez, 1973, nos.31–3.

38 José Milicua, 'Ribera en Roma', *Archivo Español de Arte*, 1952, p.309; Pérez Sánchez and Spinosa, 1991, p.166.

39 Pérez Sánchez and Spinosa, 1991, p.174.

40 I am grateful to Gabriele Finaldi for clarifying this point.

41 Harris, 1982, p.54; Pérez Sánchez and Spinosa, 1991, pp.26–8, 81,166.

42 Benito Domenech, cited in note 32, p.122.

43 E. Harris, 'Aportaciones para el estudio de Juan Bautista Maino', *Revista Español de Arte*, XII, 1934–5, pp.333–9.

44 Ainaud, 1947, pp.367–8, 408.

45 Pacheco, 1990, pp.534, 546.

46 Ainaud, 1947, p.372.

47 Pacheco,1990, p.15.

48 Pacheco, 1990, p.443; Harris, 1982, p.194 (for translation).

49 Pacheco, 1990, p.404; E. Holt, *A Documentary History of Art*, 2 vols., New York, 1958, vol.II, p.216 (for translation).

50 Harris, 1982, p.198 (for translation).

51 F. J. Cummings, *The Conversion of the Magdalene* (The Alzaga Caravaggio), Detroit, 1973.

52 Pike, 1966; Griffin, 1988, p.27.

53 For the publication and illustration of this important scheme, see Pérez Sánchez, 1983, pp.79–82.

54 Pérez Sánchez, 1983, p.80. Since Góngora refers to the paintings and relics as in the gallery of Niño de Guevara, it is likely that the latter commissioned the decoration. It is also likely that he had seen *bodegones* in Madrid and Toledo prior to his arrival in Seville.

55 Jordan and Cherry, 1995, p.16; Pliny, cited in note 19, Book XXXV, p.311.

56 Jordan and Cherry, 1995, pp.19–20.

57 Jordan and Cherry, 1995, p.20.

58 Pacheco, 1990, p.519; Harris, 1982, p.194 (for translation).

59 Harris, 1982, p.197.

60 Murphy, 1992, p.140.

61 J. López Navío, 'Velázquez tasa los cuadros de su protector D. Juan de Fonseca', A.E.A., 34, 1961, pp.53–84.

62 Brown and Kagan, 1987, pp.238, 249, 251.

63 Valdivieso and Serrera, 1985, pp.104–6.

64 Diego Ortiz de Zúñiga, *Anales Eclesiasticos y Seculares de la muy noble y muy leal Ciudad de Sevilla*, 5 vols., 1795–6, vol.IV, pp.361–2. See also Brown and Kagan, 1987, p.233.

65 Pacheco, 1990, p.217.

66 José Sánchez, *Academias literarias del siglo de oro Esapañol*, Madrid, 1961, pp.207–8; Brown, 1978, pp.38–9.

67 *Velázquez; Homenaje en el tercer centenario de su muerte*, Madrid, 1960, p.291.

68 M. J. Woods, *The Poet and the Natural World in the Age of Góngora*, Oxford, 1978, p.20.

69 Pacheco, 1990, p.519. Harris, 1982, p.194 (for translation).

70 J. Bialostocki, 'Puer Sufflans Ignes', *Arte in Europa; Scritti di Storia dell' Arte in onore di Eduardo Arslan*, 1966, vol.I, pp.591–5.

71 D. Davies, *El Greco; Mystery and Illumination*, National Gallery of Scotland, Edinburgh, 1989.

72 R. Robres Lluch, 'El Beato Ribera y El Greco', *Archivo Español de Arte*, vol.XXVII, 1954, p.254.

73 J. M. Pita Andrade, 'Sobre la presencia del Greco en Madrid y de sus obras en las colecciones madrileñas del siglo XVII', *Archivo Español de Arte*, vol.LVIII, 1985, p.330. For the identification of Juan de Borja with San Francisco de Borja, see C. Pérez Pastor, *Bibliografía Madrileña de los siglos XVI y XVII*, 3 vols., Madrid, 1891–1907, vol.3, pp.336–7. The son of Juan de Borja, Francisco de Borja, refers to the saint as his grandfather.

74 See, for example, the versions in the National Gallery of Scotland (no.2491) and in the Earl of Harewood's collection.

75 See Davies, cited in note 71.

76 Robres Lluch, cited in note 72. In the inventory of García de Loaisa, the painting is desribed as: 'otro quadro de una figura con un animal a manera de bicho y otro allí soplando'. The name of the artist is not given, but the authorship of El Greco can be presumed because of the unique subject and the association of García de Loaisa with both El Greco and his friends. I am most grateful to Fernando J. Bouza Álvarez for generously giving me this reference.

77 C. Pérez Pastor, cited in note 73, vol.I, no.564, pp.291–3.

78 *Velázquez; Homenaje en el tercer centenario de su muerte*, Madrid, 1960, p.243.

79 Brown, 1978, p.59.

80 Harris, 1982, p.196 (for translation).

81 G. A. Davies, *Recognitions: essays presented to Edmund Fryde* (ed. C. Richmond and I. Harvey), Aberystwyth, 1996, pp.375–410. Indeed these ideas were embedded in the fabric of contemporary Christian thought. In his famous *Introducción del símbolo de la fe* (chapter X, Salamanca, 1583), Fra Luis de Granada wrote that the variety, colour and perfume of flowers, for example, had been created for man's pleasure or recreation and especially as a means of awakening his mind to the contemplation of the beauty of the Creator.

82 *Velázquez; Homenaje en el tercer centenario de su muerte*, Madrid, 1960, pp.313 (no.416), 314b (no.522), 314c (no.552).

83 John Collins, *A Dictionary of Spanish Proverbs*, London, n.d., pp.15, 179, 261.

84 A. A.Parker, *Literature and the Delinquent; The Picaresque Novel in Spain and Europe, 1599–1753*, Edinburgh, 1967. R. O. Jones, *A Literary History of Spain. The Golden Age: Prose and Poetry*, London, 1971, ch.6.

85 S. Resnick and J. Pasmantier, *An Anthology of Spanish Literature in English Translation*, London, 1958, p.129.

86 Mateo Alemán, *Guzmán de Alfarache*, 2 vols., Madrid, 1962, (ed. S. Gili y Gaya). E. Moreno Baez, 'Lección y Sentido del Guzmán de Alfarache', *Revista de Filología Española*, XL, Madrid, 1948.

87 Jones, cited in note 84, p.130.

88 Jones, cited in note 84, p.127–8.

89 A. A. Parker, *The Allegorical Drama of Calderón*, Oxford, 1968, p.124. I am grateful to Ángel García for drawing my attention to this text.

90 Indeed, in this context, it is surely significant that in the *Kitchen Maid with the Supper at Emmaus* [cat 22], the maid not only has a dawning realisation of the presence of Christ but also is of negroid origin and probably one of the many slaves in Seville. They, like converted Jews and Moors, were labelled 'new' christians, that is recent converts. As such they were deemed to have 'impure blood' and were ostracised. In that society, purity of faith was identified with purity of blood. Nevertheless, in Velázquez's painting, the implication is that salvation is possible for all those who have faith, irrespective of their social status or ethnic origin.

91 *The Colloquies of Erasmus* (transl. Craig R. Thompson), Chicago and London, 1965, pp.248–50, 253–4. See also Mary Elizabeth Perry, *Gender and Disorder in Early Modern Seville*, Princeton, 1990, pp.157–8.

92 The philosophical observation on beggars happy in rags may well have inspired later images of beggar philosophers, such as those by Ribera and Velázquez.

93 *Elizabethan-Jacobean Drama* (ed. Blakemore Evans), London, 1989, fig.22.

94 Mary Elizabeth Perry, cited in note 91, pp.159–60.

95 Pike, 1972, pp.150–3.

96 *Dios te libre de la enfermedad que baxa de Castilla, y de la hambre que sube de Andalucía.* Quoted and translated in David E. Vassburg, *Land and Society in Golden Age Castile*, Cambridge, 1984, p.227.

97 For a list of his publications, see C. Pérez Pastor, cited in note 73, vol.I, pp.253–4, 267–8, 282–3, 312–16.

98 El Greco's magnificent portrait of Ceballos is in the Museo del Prado, Madrid.

99 *Arte real para el buen govierno de los Reyes, y Principes, y de sus vassallos*, Toledo, 1623, f.2r and v.

100 Mulcahy, 1988, p.81–2, n.12.

101 See Montañés's image [cat 7].

102 Florentino del Valle, S.I. 'Sentido Social en San Ignacio', *Razón y Fe*, Madrid, T.153, 1956, p.150.

103 For a classic study of this concept in English literature, see E. M. W. Tillyard, *The Elizabethan World Picture*, London, 1943.

ARTISTIC TRAINING IN SEVILLE
Peter Cherry, pp.67–75

1 For this document, see *Varia Velazqueña*, vol.II, Madrid, 1960, pp.215–16. The apprenticeship was for six years, but the contract was backdated to December 1610, probably because Velázquez had already served a year with Francisco de Herrera. Pacheco may have been referring to him in saying that another master had sought to take the credit for Velázquez's career, 'stealing from me the crown of my later years'. Pacheco, 1990, p.202.

2 Pacheco also agreed to pay any medical attention for minor illnesses, lasting up to fifteen days, and at the end of his apprenticeship to furnish him with a new suit of clothes. Pacheco's payment to Velázquez is unspecified, although normally a small monthly allowance was given to the apprentice and a lump sum at the end of the contract. For apprenticeships, see J. J. Martín González, *El artista en la sociedad española del siglo XVII*, Madrid, 1984, pp.17–24; María del Carmen Heredia, *Estudio de los contratos de aprendizaje artístico en Sevilla a comienzos del siglo XVIII*, Seville, 1974.

3 For Velázquez's certificate of examination (*carta de examen*), *Varia Velazqueña*, vol.II, 1960, p.217. Velázquez was given a notarised copy of this document. In accordance with the norm, no details were given here of the examination's contents.

4 The election of the two *alcaldes veedores* for the year took place at the guild's annual assemblies on the day of Corpus Christi in their chapel of the Hospital of San Martín, who were then sworn into office before the Seville town council (*Cabildo*). In July 1599, Pacheco and six other painters were expressly asked by the *Cabildo* to elect *alcaldes veedores* of the guild. Francisco Bravo was elected on 2 August 1599, but opposed by the majority of the twenty-seven master painters of Seville in the convocation. On 5 October, Vasco Pereira and Juan de Saucedo were elected. See Valdivieso and Serrera, 1985, p.36, p.370, n.3. In 1614, Pacheco led a lawsuit against the tax assessment made by the *alcaldes* of the guild. C. López Martínez, *Desde Martínez Montañés hasta Pedro Roldán*, Seville, 1932, p.195.

5 The papers of the guild have not been found. José Gestoso y Pérez (*Ensayo de un diccionario de los artífices que florecieron en Sevilla desde el siglo XIII al XVIII*, 2 vols., Seville, 1899–1900; vol.I, p.xlix) looked for the archive, but found only papers pertaining to the Seville guild of silversmiths.

6 The Seville civic ordinances (*Ordenanzas*, p.162) are unspecific in this regard. They refer to the compulsory inspection of images for export, and the right of the guild to seal good paintings and burn those painted on old canvases. In Córdoba, the guild could denounce works 'which were not perfect and good … in their workmanship and their colours' (*lo que no fuere perfecto e bueno … asi de la obra como de los colores*). For the ordinances of Córdoba in 1493 and 1543, see Rafael Ramírez de Arellano, 'Ordenanzas de pintores (Córdoba)', *Boletín de la Real Academia de Bellas Artes de San Fernando*, 35, 1915, pp.29–47.

7 Pablo A. Sole, 'El gremio gaditano de pintores en la segunda mitad del siglo XVII', *Archivo Hispalense*, LVII, no.175 (1974), pp.171–7. The guild thought this a *grabisimo scandalo, maiormente en esta siudad* (sic) *donde ai tantos erejes e infieles*.

8 Pacheco, 1990, p.561.

9 *Ordenanzas de Sevilla*, reissued by Andrés Grande, Seville, 1632, pp.162–3 for Pintores. For an analysis of these, see Okada, 1991, pp.233–8.

10 Within the last two *oficios*, there was a distinction between those painters who included figurative details in their compositions and purely decorative work. For the statutes of the *Pintores de sargería* in Madrid in 1543, see M. Agulló Cobo, *Noticias sobre pintores madrileños de los siglos XVI y XVII*, Granada, 1978, pp.193–4.

11 *Ordenanzas de Sevilla: los mas sabios y mas artizados, y aquellos q mas estudiaro(n) y trabajaro(n) en la dicha arte.*

12 Gestoso, cited in note 5, 1899–1900, pp.8, 46.

13 For Pacheco's tract of 16 July 1622, see F. Calvo Serraller, *Teoría de la pintura del Siglo de Oro*, Madrid, 1981, pp.180–91; R. Enggass and J. Brown, *Italian and Spanish Art, 1600–1750*. Evanston, 1992, pp.221–6. The documentation for this lawsuit, led by Miguel Güelles, *alcalde* of the painters guild, is not known. However, copies of Montañés's Santa Clara contract were ordered on 27 May, 1623, along with copies of two further contracts signed by him in 1610 and 1617. See *Documentos*, vol.I, 1927, pp.170–5; C. López Martínez, *Retablos y esculturas de traza sevillana*, Seville, 1928 (2), pp.54–5. On 3 August 1623, the painter Baltasar Quintero signed a contract with the sculptor for the work of painting at Santa Clara. *Idem.*, p.55.

14 In his tract of 1622, Pacheco (Enggass & Brown, cited in note 13, pp.222–3) stressed the dependence of the sculptor on the painter to bring his figures to life, adducing the precedent of classical antiquity. On flesh painting (*encarnaciones*) and drapery painting (*estofado*) of wood sculptures, see Pacheco, 1990, pp.494–503, 462–3; Veliz, 1986, pp.56–63, 79–85; R. Kasl, 'Painters, Polychromy and the Perfection of Images' in *Spanish Polychrome Sculpture, 1500–1800, in United States Collections*, New York, 1993, pp.33–8.

15 One of the main arguments of the *paragone* in favour of the superiority of painting rested on its universality and illusionism. Pacheco published his *Breve tratado sobre la antigüedad y honores del arte de la pintura y su comparación con la escultura* in 1622, which later formed part of his lengthy rehearsal of the *paragone* in Pacheco, 1990, pp.94–142.

16 One exception is the retablo of the convent of Santa Paula, the ensemble and ten paintings commissioned from Cano in 1635. Wethey, 1983, pp.113–5; Kasl, cited in note 14, pp.33–8.

17 One of the most famous was the company formed at the end of the sixteenth century by Vasco Pereira and his son-in-law Antón Pérez. For this, see Serrera, 1987, pp.219–223. In turn, the daughter of Pérez was the first wife of the painter Juan del Castillo, the master of Murillo; see Valdivieso and Serrera, 1985, pp.11, 303. On artists' companies, see also Martín González, cited in note 2, p.40; Kasl, cited in note 14, pp.43–6.

18 *Documentos*, vol.II, 1928, p.188.

19 For Camprobín, see most recently Jordan and Cherry, 1995, pp.110–15. Camprobin signed the receipt of his dowry of his wife María de Encalada on 5 November, 1628 (Archivo protocolos de Sevilla, Oficio 18, 1628, libro 4, fols.467–71) and two weeks later rented five rooms by a rental agreement witnessed by the painter Sebastián de Arteaga (Archivo protocolos de Sevilla, Oficio 19, 1628, libro 6, fol.836). Arnos's younger daughter Ignacia was married to the painter Ignacio de Ries in 1641. Archivo protocolos de Sevilla, Oficio 19, 1641, libro I, fols.579–81,for Ries's receipt of dowry, dated 17 February 1641.

20 Camprobín, for example, was a lifelong member of the Hermandad Sacramental del Sagrario, for whom he also painted. See E. Valdivieso, 'Nuevos datos y obras de Pedro de Camprobín', *Revista de Arte Sevillano*, 3, 1983, pp.72–5. He also joined the Jesuit Congregación del Santísimo y Doctrina Cristiana. Gestoso, cited in note 5, vol.II, p.23. Other painter members of this brotherhood included Juan del Castillo (1611), Diego de Ahedo Calderón (1613) and Francisco Varela (1613). For artist members of another brotherhood, the Hermandad del Traspaso, see Heliodoro Sancho Corbacho, 'Artífices sevillanos del siglo XVII', in *Homenaje al Profesor Dr Hernández Diáz*, Seville University, 1982. Later in the seventeenth century, Murillo and Juan de Valdés Leal were famous painter members of the Hermandad de la Caridad.

21 For this, see Vicente Lleó Cañal, *Arte y espectáculo; la fiesta del Corpus Christi en la Sevilla de los siglos XVI y XVII*, Seville, 1975.

22 See José Guerrero Lovillo, 'La capilla de los Pintores de la Hermandad de San Lucas de Sevilla', *Archivo Hispalense*, vol.XVII, 1952, pp.123–33; María Jesús Sanz and María del Carmen Heredia, 'Los pintores en la iglesia de San Andrés', *Archivo Hispalense*, nos.177–9, 1975, pp.71–81. The painting, now lost, was said to depict the Virgin with many attributes of the art of painting, from the school of Murillo. The collection also included a portrait of Philip IV as protector of painting by Juan Martínez de Gradilla, now at Pollok House, Glasgow.

23 The examination certificate allowed a master to work legitimately in Seville, the kingdom of Spain and throughout South America, as well as opening a workshop (*tienda pública*) and to take apprentices. Failure to comply with the regulation incurred fines, closure of the practice and eventual imprisonment.

24 It may not have been unusual that older apprentices were allowed to work for themselves at specified times. The apprenticeship agreement of Francisco de Zurbarán, aged sixteen when apprenticed to Pedro Díaz de Villanueva for three years, stipulated that he could work for himself *los días de fiesta*, as noted by Okada, 1991, p.235. The guild ordinances prohibited an apprentice from working for any other master before finishing his contract of apprenticeship and one apprentice of Montañés was imprisoned for this infraction in 1614. See López Martínez, cited in note 4, p.252.

25 Gestoso, cited in note 5, p.22. The *alcades veedores* in this year were Gonzalo de Campos Guerrero and Diego de Campos.

26 Gestoso, cited in note 5, p.232.

27 In 1661, Juan Rodríguez Mejía, petitioned the municipality for a licence to practice his art, given the stringency of the times (*estrecha de los tiempos*) and his 'great poverty'. Gestoso, cited in note 5, p.87. In 1676, Luis de Silva claimed he was too poor to pay the examination fee, and applied for a licence to continue painting small pictures and flowerpieces in order to maintain his family, in the face of threats from the guild to close him down. Gestoso, cited in note 5, p.105.

28 The notarised *cartas de examen* generally follow the same notarial formulae. This normally included giving the age and a description of any distinguishing features of the examinee, something which is omitted from Velázquez's. Alonso Cano's certificate, for example, describes him as twenty-four years old, of sound body, with three scars above his left eyebrow. *Documentos*, vol.II, 1928, pp.184–5. For an extensive sample of these documents, see López Martínez, *Arquitectos, escultores y pintores vecinos de Sevilla*, Seville, 1928 (1), (2), cited in note 13; *Documentos*, vols.II, III, VIII, 1927–46.

29 Ramírez de Arellano, cited in note 6. The need to maintain good prices and good quality of workmanship were the reasons given by the Seville painters in 1480 who moved to form a corporation of painters with its own statutes, including the need to hold examinations. Gestoso, cited in note 5, pp.xlv–xlix.

30 *Ordenanzas de Sevilla: sean artizados y muy buenos debuxadores*.

31 *Ordenanzas*, 1632: *y sepa relatar el dicho debuxo, y dar cuenta, que ha menester un hombre desnudo, y el trapo y pliegues que faze la ropa, y labrar los rostros y cabellos muy bien labrados, de manera que ... ha de saber hazer una Imagen perfectamente, y dar buena cuenta, asi de platica como de obra a los dichos examinadores. Asimimo sea platico el que fuere examinado en la imagineria de lexos y verduras, y sepa quebrar un trapo ....*

32 The Córdoban ordinances (1493) stipulate that the examinee for the title of *Maestro de imaginería* should show from his drawing that he is a 'good draughtsman for the composing of istorias' (*buen debuxador para saber ordenar estorias*) and knows how to paint a sculpture (*e que de una pieza labrada de imagineria de colores en lo que lo puedan ver si es maestor para lo labrar*). He should also know how to prepare and paint an altarpiece, to gild and to use oil paint. Ramírez de Arellano, cited in note 6, pp.29–46. In the revised ordinances of 1543, a statute was introduced requiring a *carta de examen* to be held by any practitioner of gilding and *estofado* of sculpture. *Idem*, p.43. In the ordinances of Zaragoza's Cofradía de San Lucas (1517), the candidate who aspired to paint altarpieces (*retablos*) had to draw on a panel an historia of the examiners' choice (*debuxar en una table una ystoria*), which the assembled masters judged as to its being 'good and well finished' (*buena y bien acabada*). See Vicente González Hernández, 'Cofradías y gremios zaragozanos en los siglos XVI y XVII', *Cuadernos de Aragón*, vol.II, 1967, pp.132–239.

33 Pedro de Camprobín, mentioned above, had been trained in Toledo and in order to pass his guild examination as *pintor de ymaginería* in 1630, must have acquired the rudiments of the art of painting sculpture in Seville. *Documentos*, vol.II, 1930, p.270.

34 The *carta de examen* of Martínez Montañés as a sculptor and architect on 1 December 1588, states that the inspectors questioned him according to the guild ordinances 'to see, know and understand whether ... (he) ... was a good artist' (*buen artífice*), and, for the sculptural part of the exam, in their presence he made two figures, one nude and the other dressed. See López Martínez, 1929, p.267 and p.38, for a similar certificate of 1587 for the sculptor architect Juan Bautista.

35 Pacheco, 1990, p.273; *Qué sea diligencia, ya se ve: saber dibujar y pintar un hombre de todas edades, una mujer, un caballo, un león, un edificio, un país, y componer y adornar estas cosas, en lo general, con buena proporción, manera y práctica: que es de muy pocos.*

36 *Documentos*, vol.VIII, 1935, p.38.

37 In 1553, the examinee Alonso de Lara responded to questions concerning painting on canvas and on walls. López Martínez, 1929, p.203. In 1591, painters competing for the polychromy of a carved altarpiece in Pamplona were examined by means of a practical exercise – to gild and paint (*estofar*) a panel following a print model – and by answering questions on the preparation of pigments and panels, and *estofado* techniques. Kasl, cited in note 14, p.46.

38 See J. Brown, 'Academies of Painting in seventeenth-century Spain' in *Leids Kunsthistorisch Jaarboek*, 5–6, 1986–7, pp.177–85.

39 For Uceda, see Valdivieso and Serrera, 1985, pp.188–227 and for Varela, see pp.228–59.

40 Gestoso, cited in note 5, p.8. Güelles was elected along with Diego de Ahedo Calderón.

41 For Güelles' apprentices between 1618–31, see Sancho Corbacho, cited in note 20, pp.636–7, and between 1632–3, C. López Martínez, 1928 (1) cited in note 28, p.58.

42 Archivo protocolos de Sevilla, Oficio 18, 1638, libro 2, fols.442–445 for the posthumous valuation of some 190 pictures in Güelles' studio by the painters Juan de León Salcedo and Juan del Castillo on 26 May 1638. Most of the paintings were listed as 'devotional pictures' and paintings of unspecified saints. The document specifies that five of the devotional paintings and three of the saints 'served as originals'. Other subjects described in this manner comprised a picture of Christ, a set of twelve worn paintings of the Sibyls in Flemish frames, and an old painting of some pagan goddesses (*de unas diosas*). The inventory also included three paintings of *bodegones*. For Güelles' contracts for lots of 22 and 41 religious paintings in 1607 and 1608 respectively, see López Martínez, 1932, cited in note 4, pp.184–5, and for his shipments of pictures of hermit saints to South America, see Sancho Corbacho, cited in note 20, pp.636–7, nos.17, 24, 26; Okada, 1991, p.237.

43 See *Documentos*, vol.II, 1928, pp.95, 184–5, for Cano's apprenticeship to Pacheco for five years in 1616, and his *carta de examen* of 1626. In 1630, Cano was also the artist chosen to design and paint the altarpiece in the chapel leased by the Brotherhood of St Luke in the church of San Antonio Abad. *Documentos*, vol.II, 1928, pp.291–5. He also enjoyed a high status among the community of sculptors and in 1638 was designated to represent them in a lawsuit against paying the same tax as carpenters. López Martínez, cited in note 4, p.264.

44 *Documentos*, vol.VIII, 1935, p.86.

45 In 1616, Herrera frescoed a chapel in the convent of San Francisco in Seville, Conde de Viñaza, *Adiciones al diccionario histórico de … Ceán Bermúdez*, vol.II, Madrid, 1889, pp.264–71, and painted five pictures for the Convento de la Merced in Huelva in 1617, *Documentos*, vol.II, 1928, pp.88–9.

46 Sancho Corbacho, cited in note 20, pp.638–9. The document states that Pacheco undertook the examination in the absence of the two elected *alcaldes* of the guild, but that he himself had occupied this office many times (*de muchas y diversas veses*) and was the most qualified person to be found at the time (*es la persona mas benemerita y esperta que oy se halla del dicho arte*).

47 *Documentos*, vol.II, Seville, 1928, p.267. The *carta de examen* is dated 14 August 1619, and the examiners were the incoming *alcaldes veedores* Juan de Uceda Castroverde and Miguel Güelles, and the outgoing *alcaldes* Blas Martín and Pedro Calderón. On this occasion, Herrera is described as a prisoner (*reo acusado*). See Sancho Corbacho, 1982, pp.637, no.23, p.669, for Herrera's payment of 118 *reales* costs for the lawsuit taken out against him by the guild, dated 15 July 1620.

48 In 1616, Herrera had been awarded a prize for a shield he painted (*la tarja valiente, bizarra y vistosa*) in celebrations in honour of the Immaculate Conception by the Cofradía de Sacerdotes de San Pedro ad Víncula. F.J. Sánchez Cantón, *Fuentes literarias para la historia del arte español*, vol.V, Madrid, 1941, p.438.

49 It is worth noting that the statutes of the Seville Academy of drawing in the 1660s stipulated that at the opening sessions all members swear allegiance to the Holy Sacrament and the Virgin of the Immaculate Conception.

50 Gestoso, cited in note 5, pp.124–6 for the decision of the *Cabildo*, dated 27 June 1629.

51 For this documentation, see Gestoso, cited in note 5, pp.125–6. However, in an analogous case in 1635, Cano and Francisco Varela, as *alcaldes veedores* of the guild, examined a twenty-three year old Córdoban painter Gaspar Fernández de Rivas, who, like Zurbarán, had earlier undergone his apprenticeship in Seville. López Martínez, cited in note 4, pp.129–30.

52 Although the *Cabildo* had the power to issue special licences for artists to practice without sitting the guild exam, Zurbarán did not humble himself by asking for one of these.

53 In 1602, for instance, Gonzalo de Campos Guerrero petitioned the *Cabildo* to allow him to be entitled municipal painter (*Pintor del cabildo*), without salary, in recognition of his past services, as did Alonso de Llea in 1628. Gestoso, cited in note 5, pp.22, 57. In support of his claim, Campos Guerrero adduced the custom of princes giving titles to artists who served them so that they are 'esteemed and honoured'. In the 1560s, for instance, Pedro de Alcázar adopted the title *Pintor de la Audiencia*, Gestoso, cited in note 5, pp.9–10.

54 For translations of the technical sections of Spanish art treatises, see Veliz, 1986.

55 For López Caro's apprenticeship, Archivo protocolos de Sevilla, Oficio 4, 1608, libro 4, fols.599–600.

56 *Varia Velazqueña*, vol.II, 1960, pp.219–20. Melgar, who was about fourteen, came from a relatively more distinguished background than most, his father a professional person described as an *escribiente*.

57 For the best discussion of Spanish drawing, see A. E. Pérez Sánchez, *Historia del dibujo en España de la edad media a Goya*, Madrid, 1986 and Pérez Sánchez, 1995.

58 Pacheco, 1990, pp.265–6, speaks of the most common (*lo más usado*) practice of students, subject to the drawing style of their master (*sujetos al debuxo del maestro*), aiming to copy as closely as possible drawings he gives them as a model (*dechado*). For common aspects of artistic training in Europe of this period, see *Children of Mercury; The Education of Artists in the 16th and 17th Centuries*, Providence, 1984.

59 Pacheco, 1990, pp.266–9.

60 For the *Cartillas de dibujo*, see Pérez Sánchez, cited in note 57, pp.54–61; Jesusa Vega, 'Los inicios del artista; El dibujo, base de las Artes' in *La Formación del artista de Leonardo a Picasso*, Madrid, 1989, pp.2–5.

61 Pacheco, 1990, pp.267–9. He lamented the predicament of apprentices who were forced to copy poor quality images (*lienzos ordinarios por perfiles perdidos*). In 1593, Pacheco already owned a collection of drawings, and one book contained forty-three leaves of drawings 'by good masters' (*de buenos maestros*). López Martínez, 1929, p.182.

62 On the Jaffé album of 315 sheets, see J. Brown, *Murillo and His Drawings*, Princeton 1976, pp.46–8; Pérez Sánchez, 1995, pp.42–3.

63 See Pacheco's eulogy of Campaña in his *Libro de retratos* 1599, in Sánchez Cantón, *Fuentes literarias para la Historia del Arte Español*, vol.II, Madrid, 1933, pp.55–7.

64 Angulo and Pérez Sánchez, 1985, nos.1–9; Pérez Sánchez, 1995, pp.24–5, nos.26–9.

65 Angulo and Pérez Sánchez, 1985, nos.49, 51–69, 73–4, 77–89. The same point could be made about Herrera's drawings in pen and wash.

66 See López Martínez, cited in note 4, p.188, for instance, for Gabriel Jiménez's 1591 contract to work for one and a half years in the studio of the painter Diego Esquivel for a monthly salary and to paint from drawings supplied by Esquivel.

67 Pacheco, 1990, pp.98, 269, 434.

68 Pacheco, 1990, pp.269–70, 434.

69 Thus, Pacheco, 1990, pp.269, 272, says that the artist, *haciendo un compuesto, viene a disimular algunas veces de manera esta disposición, que … se recibe por suyo propio lo que en realidad de verdad es ageno. Y esto, tanto más, cuanto mejor ingenio tiene el que lo compone, para saberlo disimular, valiéndose de cosas menos ordinarias y comunes.* In Pacheco's inventory of 1593, there were 'five canvases of many trifles from good authors' (*sinco lienços de munchas menudencias que bienen de buenos autores*), which were possibly for recycling in other pictures.

70 López Martínez, cited in note 34, p.182. The largest holding of prints recorded in a Sevillian painter's studio numbered nearly 2,500 in the posthumous inventory of Vasco Pereira in 1609.

71 In 1587, for instance, Matteo da Lecce bought in Seville a lot of prints and drawings, including the complete works of Dürer. López Martínez, 1929, pp.192–3. In 1611, Diego de Esquivel, father of the painter Miguel de Esquivel, bought a lot of Flemish and Italian prints, probably for his son at the beginning of his career. Valdivieso and Serrera, 1985, p.378. Pacheco, 1990, p.127 on the use Sevillian sculptors made of print sources.

72 See A. Pérez Sánchez *De pintura y pintores*, Madrid, 1993; B. Navarrete Prieto 'Otras fuentes grabadas utilizadas por Francisco de Zurbarán' *Archivo Español de Arte*, 268 (1994) pp.359–76.

73 Pacheco, 1990, pp.269, 434–5. Pacheco directly copied Northern prints in two early works, Valdivieso and Serrera, 1985, pp.24, 26, 72, no.117; p.75, no.127 and for the martyrdom scene in his *St Sebastian Attended by St Irene* of 1616, p.101, no.239, and for a *Crucifixion* of the same year B. Navarrete Prieto 'Los grabados de Cornelis Cort en la pintura sevillana de fines del siglo XVI' *Lecturas de Historia del Arte*, vol.4, Vitoria, 1994, p.204.

74 Pacheco, 1990, pp.272–3. Pacheco gives the examples of the inventiveness of Pedro de Campaña's work on a triumphal arch of Charles V, and his own improvisation of a figure for the catafalque of Philip II in Seville in 1598. He also (p.273) mentions the famous ability of Michelangelo to sketch from his imagination and the sculptor Jerónimo Hernández's skill for resolving artistic difficulties through drawings.

75 Pacheco, 1990, pp.101, 126, 267, 346–7.

76 In 1593, Pacheco himself owned a collection of thirteen wax models, and eighty plaster ones, as well as a lead anatomical figure. López Martínez, 1929, p.181. In his testament in 1639, he ordered that all of his studio resources be auctioned. In 1596, Pedro de Villegas Marmolejo willed all of his models and moulds to his assistant Alonso Rodríguez, and his wax and bronze figures, with his library, paintings and antiquities to the humanist Benito Ariás Montano. López Martínez, 1929, pp.204–5. In an earlier testament of 1563, he willed three marble figures and two marble faces of children to the Cathedral for the benefit of its artists.

77 No sculptural models or books were listed in the studio inventories of Francisco López Caro in 1629, Archivo protocolos de Sevilla, Oficio 16, libro 1, fols.256–8, Miguel Güelles in 1638, see note 42, or Juan de Barreda in 1651, Archivo protocolos de Sevilla, Oficio 5, 1651, libro 3, fols.224–6.

78 Antonio Palomino, *Vida del Torrigiano* in *Vidas*, (ed.) N. Ayala Mallory, Madrid, 1986, p.25. The heads of the Virgin and Christ Child apparently also survived.

79 See Vega, cited in note 60, pp.19–20.

80 Pacheco, 1990, p.126.

81 The source for this drawing has not been traced. It may be a free version of the famous fragment of a seated Hercules in the Vatican, the *Belvedere Torso*. It even resembles, in reverse and in fragmentary form, the father figure of the equally famous *Laocoön* group in the Vatican collections. However, it is also close to a mutilated torso of a Myronian Discobolos which is now restored as a gladiator in the Capitoline Museums, Rome. The fragment was well known in the sixteenth century, and the fact that the drawing resembles this but is in reverse might reflect the mediation of a print.

82 Angulo and Sánchez, 1985, nos.84–86. Pacheco recounts the Córdoban artist Céspedes's celebrated restoration in Rome of an ancient torso with a head of Seneca, which he brought to Spain. Sánchez Cantón, cited in note 63, p.48.

83 Pacheco, 1990, p.440.

84 Pacheco, 1990, p.126, describes the practice of an academy, in which artist members pay a live model (*un hombre*) to pose for a number of hours during the night, with the pose changed weekly. However, this may be based on Pacheco's experience during his visit to Madrid in 1625.

85 Pacheco, 1990, p.127.

86 Pacheco, 1990, p.377.

87 For Pacheco on proportion and anatomy, for him the second and third parts of drawing respectively, see Pacheco, 1990, pp.350–84, 384–5. His account of proportion is based on citations from other authorities, including Albrecht Dürer and the important work of Juan de Arfe Villafañe, *De varia commensuración para la escultura y arquitectura*, Seville, 1585. For knowledge of the working of the body he recommends Juan Valverde de Amusco's *Historia de la composición del cuerpo humano* (1556), based on Andrea Vesalio's *De humanis corpori fabrica libri septem* (1543).

88 Pacheco, 1990, pp.122, 350, 384.

89 Pacheco, 1990, pp.384–5. See Palomino, cited in note 78, p.36 for Becerra's expertise in anatomy and anatomical models made by him. Angulo and Pérez Sánchez, 1975, nos.31, 52–5 for écorché and anatomical studies by Becerra.

90 Cited in his eulogy from the *Libro de retratos* (1599), in Sánchez Cantón, cited in note 63, pp.55–7.

91 Pacheco, 1990, p.385.

92 Pacheco, 1990, pp.126–7 for this sculpture which *excede todo lo que se puede encarecer*. It was drawn and eulogised in Diego de Villalta's treatise on sculpture (1590), who said that it was celebrated among connoisseurs of sculpture and that the whole world was full of casts of its arms, legs and other members made by sculptors to copy. Sánchez Cantón, *Fuentes literarias para la Historia del Arte Español*, vol.I, Madrid, 1923, p.290.

93 Pacheco, 1990, p.350. In the testament codicil of Juan de Uceda in 1631, he willed that all of his prints, drawings and models be divided between his brother Juan Bautista de Uceda Castroverde and his partner (*compadre*) Gonzalo Nuñez, living in his house, and that the latter keep *la anatomía de prospero ... de bronce con su peaña* which he had already given him. López Martínez, 1928 (1), p.199.

94 Vasari mentioned the lost Crucifixion at San Jerónimo as Torrigiano's most famous work in Spain. There was also a *Virgin and Child* (Seville, Museo de Bellas Artes) at the same place. A variant of the St Jerome by Torrigiano, with the saint kneeling on both knees, was taken to the royal Hieronymite monastery church at Guadalupe and placed in the central niche of the high altar in 1526. It is now in the sacristy. No documents have been found for Torrigiano's Spanish career (*c*.1525–8). See Alan P. Darr, *Pietro Torrigiano and his Sculpture for the Henry VII Chapel, Westminster Abbey*, Ph.D. diss., New York University, 1980, pp.61–6, 426–7.

95 Pacheco, 1990, p.105 cited this 'famous' sculpture in terracotta in the context of the *paragone* debate between painting and sculpture. For his variant in a drawing of 1602, see Angulo and Sánchez, 1985, no.104. Imitations in sculpture include Jerónimo Hernández's relief of the altarpiece of the Visitation in Seville Cathedral (1565–6) and the central relief of the high altar of the church of San Jerónimo in Granada by a number of hands (1570). Martínez Montañés carved two penitent St Jeromes kneeling on two knees for the convent of Sta. Clara, Llerena (1603–4) and the high altar of the monastery church of San Isidoro del Campo, Santiponce, Seville (1611), in which the later sculpture shows a fuller assimilation of the Torrigiano prototype. In 1585, for instance, Juan Bautista Vázquez the Elder was commissioned to make a copy in polychromed wood for Jerónimo de Aliaga, a citizen of Los Reyes, Peru. López Martínez, 1929, p.113.

96 Ceán Bermúdez, 1800, pp.68–9 for praise of the sculpture as the best in Spain and for Goya's fascination with it. After the secularisation act (1835) and before it entered the Seville Museum, in the 1840s the sculpture was used as an anatomical model for students of the Real Academia de Nobles Artes de Santa Isabel, when a number of casts of the whole figure and parts were taken. See Jesús M. Palomero, 'La colección escultórico' in Seville, Hospital de los Venerables, *Obras maestras del Museo de Bellas Artes de Seville*, Seville, 1992, pp.50–1.

97 For a three-month apprenticeship in 1574 of Cristóbal Gómez to the painter and *ynpresor* Francisco Ramos to learn casting techniques, see López Martínez, 1929, pp.195–6. The posthumous studio inventory of the sculptor Andrés de Ocampo in 1623, for instance, listed Dürer's book on proportion, treatises on perspective, many prints, drawings

and sketches (*rasguños*) and 122 models in wax, clay and plaster. *Documentos*, vol.II, 1928, pp.43–9. In the sale of goods from the studio of the sculptor José de Arce in 1666, the painter Juan de Valdés Leal bought models of wax, plaster and terracotta and a box of hands and feet, some of which were unfinished. *Documentos*, vol.III, 1931, pp.88–90.

98 Pacheco, 1990, p.385. For an accomplished study of a right foot in pen and ink by Jerónimo Hernández, Angulo and Pérez Sánchez, 1985, no.9. Jerónimo Hernández's studio inventory of 1586 included a library, a collection of 350 prints, two dozen wax models and two dozen plaster ones. López Martínez, 1929, pp.252–3.

99 Pacheco, 1990, pp.127, 436, recommended the use of small clay or wax figures on a surface to study lighting and to give the painting 'more ... force and relief'.

100 Pacheco, 1990, p.440 for Antonio de Mohedano's use of the manikin. Also, p.443, for the practice of Sevillian sculptors and the Italian artist in Seville Matteo da Lecce using wet paper.

101 Pacheco, 1990, p.443.

102 It is not clear from the study of a draped sleeve from the circle of Francisco de Herrera whether a manikin or a model has been used. See Angulo and Pérez Sánchez, 1985, no.89.

103 Angulo and Pérez Sánchez, 1985, no.89, nos.230–9, 240–4, 248–250.

104 Pacheco, 1990, pp.443–4. A. E. Pérez Sánchez, 1986, cited in note 57, p.178, suggests that at the end of the eighteenth century J.A. Ceán Bermúdez knew anatomical studies by Pacheco, whereas the latter author *Diccionario histórico ... de las Bellas Artes en España*, 1800, vol.IV, p.13, paraphrases Pacheco himself on this point.

105 See Angulo and Pérez Sánchez, London, 1985, no.119. See also the preparatory drawing for *St Sebastian Attended by St Irene* (1615), which may also be studied from the life. *Idem*, no.118. Pacheco, 1990, p.444, cited the cycle at La Merced (1600–1611), painted with Alonso Vázquez, as the result of a creative process based on drawing and studies from the life, which he himself described. In this context, he also mentioned the Casa de Pilatos ceiling (1604), the *Last Judgement* for Santa Isabel (1611) and *St Michael* for the church of San Alberto (1637).

106 Angulo and Pérez Sánchez, 1985, no.83. The right hand clutches a stone, in the manner of a nude, penitent saint, perhaps St Jerome, but the artist has drawn in the sleeve of the left arm.

107 For the practice of Céspedes, from Pacheco's eulogy of Céspedes in his *Libro de retratos* (1599), see Sánchez Cantón, cited in note 63, pp.47–53; also Pacheco, 1990, pp.440–4.

108 Pacheco, 1990, pp.527–8. Also, p.127 on the value of drawing from the moving live model.

109 Pérez Sánchez, 1995, nos.5, 7. In this context, Pacheco also cited the portrait drawings of the Roman artist Ottavio Leoni (*c*.1587–1630).

110 Pérez Sánchez, 1995, nos.2, 3.

111 A number of drawings of character heads are known by Herrera the Elder and his studio. Angulo and Sánchez, 1985, nos.44–6, 48, 51, 81–3.

112 Pacheco, 1990, pp.274–5, speaks of the ideal manner of Michelangelo and Raphael, whose figures are perfected by imitating the best of nature (*que las invenciones de las figuras o historias se ajusten y perfecionen conla imitación de las cosas mejores de la naturaleza*) and p.275, *De manera, que la perfeción consiste en pasar de las ideas o a lo natural, y de lo natural a las ideas; buscando seimpre lo mejor y más seguro y perfecto*. Pablo de Céspedes, in his *Poem on Painting*, also spoke of the artist having to 'know' what to look for in nature and of drawing selectively. Pacheco, 1990, p.403. The artist's powers of discrimination are to be based on the example of antiquity and the Italian masters of the High Renaissance.

113 For Italian theories of drawing with reference to Spain, see Pérez Sánchez, cited in note 104, pp.19–23. For Carducho, see pp.29–31. Carducho, who was a friend of Pacheco, emphasised sixteenth-century Italian *disegno* in his *Diálogos de la pintura* (1633), in which he urged the student to 'draw, speculate and draw more'.

114 Pacheco, 1990, pp.443. Drawing was also a fundamental of the belief in the higher status of the painter practising a liberal art; those who merely copied were cast as artisans who reduced painting to the level of a common trade. Pacheco, 1990, pp.274–5, 346.

115 For Zuccaro's drawings for his work at the Escorial, see Rosemarie Mulcahy, 'Federico Zuccaro' in *Dibujos Italianos para El Escorial*, (ed.) Mario di Giampaolo, Madrid, 1995. Zuccaro published his treatise, *Idea dei pittori, scultori ed architecti* in 1607.

116 Angulo and Pérez Sánchez, 1977.

117 Pérez Sánchez, cited in note 104, pp.27–8.

118 Pacheco, 1990, p.435.

119 Pacheco, 1990, p.435, *hacen los primeros intentos, los movimientos, los semblantes y acciones pertenecientes a la vida de aquella pintura*; Veliz, 1986, p.36. Speaking of his own practice for over forty years, Pacheco, p.444, said he made two or three sketches to 'try out the idea' (*de intentar la invención*).

120 Pacheco, 1990, p.436. Pacheco also says here that Luis de Vargas and Pedro Campaña, active in Seville made wash drawings in the manner of Raphael and Polidoro da Caravaggio. Two *modelli* in bistre for *The Three Maries and the Magdalen* were drawn by Herrera the Elder and the more expressive one of these is squared for transfer, which suggests that of the two alternatives, this was the image to be painted. See Pérez Sánchez, 1995, nos.34, 35.

121 Many sheets of experimental sketches for compositions and figure studies are known from the Madrid school. Angulo and Pérez Sánchez, 1977.

122 See Pérez Sánchez, 1986, cited in note 57, pp.81–106, on collecting drawings in Spain. Among Spanish artists, drawings by Cano and Murillo have survived in comparatively large numbers.

123 Pacheco, 1990, p.436.

124 Pacheco, 1990, pp.412–14, 416–19. He did not like the sketchy painting (*borrones*) associated with Venetian art, which only made visual sense from a distance, but promoted a type of finished painting which is a convincing illusion from both near and far.

125 Pacheco, 1990, p.444, said he used such small drawings for his paintings without the need of squaring for enlargement, because of a certain facility he had for doing this. In 1635, Pacheco made a copy of his drawing for *The Funeral of St Albert* (1610–12), perhaps wishing to preserve his invention if the original sheet was worn.

126 See, for instance, the catalogue of Pacheco's works in Valdivieso and Serrera, 1985, pp.46–116; nos.44 and 107; 107/108 and 109/110; 24 and 28; 25 and 30; 135 and 136; 22 and 183; 23 and 188; 62 and 186.

127 Pacheco, 1990, p.286.

128 Angulo and Pérez Sánchez, 1985, nos.109–110 (1612), 102–103 (1614). See also nos.94–95 (1632).

129 Pacheco, 1990, pp.348–9, 456.

130 Pacheco, 1990, p.348; … *cuando una pintura es seca y sin fuerza y brío, decimos que es flamenca; que se huya de aquella manera, porque tiene poca fuerza y muncha simpleza*. While Flemings had good finish in their paintings, they lacked the *buena manera* of the Italians based on drawing. *Idem*, pp.417–18. Campaña had lived in Italy and was seen as a follower of the example of Michelangelo and Raphael, and had also made drawings of antiquities, one of which Pacheco owned. See also his eulogy of Campaña from his *Libro de retratos* (1599) in Sánchez Cantón, cited in note 63, pp.55–7.

131 See Pacheco's eulogy of Vargas from his *Libro de Retratos* (1599), in Sánchez Cantón, cited in note 63, pp.51–3.

132 Céspedes was said to have made a particular study of Michelangelo's *Last Judgement*. Pacheco, 1990, p.440; Sánchez Cantón, cited in note 63, p.48. See Angulo and Pérez Sánchez, 1975, no.125, for a drawing after one of the damned attributed to Céspedes. Pacheco, 1990, p.403, 415–16, 420 for Correggio and Céspedes's colour.

133 Pacheco, 1990, p.349.

134 Pacheco, 1990, p.337. For Céspedes's praise of it, see pp.345–6.

135 For instance, Ambrogio Brambilla's print of 1588 reproduced the *Last Judgement* surrounded by Michelangelo's ceiling frescoes. Gaspar Becerra's Michelangelism is praised in Pacheco, 1990, pp.349, 438–9, and Pacheco may have known his drawn copies of the *Last Judgement*. In 1596, the testament of the painter Diego de Zamora ordered Juan Martínez Montañés to be paid for two papers he held in pawn, one of the *Last Judgement* of Becerra and another of a Bacchus by Taddeo Zuccaro. López Martínez, 1929, p.211. For fragments of drawings copied from the *Last Judgement* and attributed to Becerra, see Angulo and Pérez Sánchez, 1975, nos.28–29.

136 Pacheco, 1990, p.439.

137 Pacheco, 1990, p.309.

138 Pacheco, 1990, p.444.

139 The musculature of the figure of Phaeton is far more exaggerated in the final painting than in the drawn modello. See Angulo and Pérez Sánchez, 1985, no.128.

140 Pacheco, 1990, p.108, and pp.121–3, where he speaks of the 'terrible difficulty' of foreshortening flying figures.

141 Pacheco, 1990, pp.390–3. Pellegrino Tibaldi also followed this method for foreshortened figures in his frescoes at the Escorial. Pacheco, 1990, pp.391, 437–8.

142 Pacheco, 1990, pp.385–90.

143 Pacheco, 1990, pp.404–7.

144 Pacheco, 1990, p.414.

145 Pacheco, 1990, p.414.

146 Palomino, 1986, p.156.

VELÁZQUEZ'S ASSISTANTS
Enriqueta Harris, pp.77–8

1 For the *carta de examen*, see *Varia Velazqueña*, vol.II, Madrid, 1960, p.217, Doc.10. On the Painters' Guild in Seville, see H. Okada, 1991, pp.233–238. *Oficiales* are taken to mean (trained) assistants who have not taken the exam.

2 See *Varia Velazqueña*, vol.II, pp.335–63.

3 Few of his assistants in Madrid are documented, but several are named by Palomino. See the chapter 'Velázquez's Workshop', López-Rey, 1979, pp.121–4, reprinted from his *Velázquez's Work and World*, London, 1968, pp.121–4.

4 A. Martínez Ripoll, *Francisco de Herrera 'el Viejo'*, Seville, 1978, p.21.

5 Most are listed among the 'Bodegones and other Genre Pictures' in López-Rey, 1963, pp.152–67, (which include many items not related and also some lost works).

6 Cherry, 1991., vol.I, p.180

7 *Varia Velazqueña*, vol.II, p.219, Doc.14.

8 Trapier, 1948, p.57.

9 López-Rey, 1963, p.24.

10 The boy recalls the boy in cat.24; the mortar and pestle are very like, if not the same, as those in cat.22; the jugs similar to those in cats.21 and 22, as is the format.

11 Cherry is the source of most of our present information about López Caro (1598–1661); Cherry, 1991, vol.II, pp.473–80.

12 *Varia Velazqueña*, vol.II, p.221. Doc.18.

13 A. Matilla Tascón, 'Comercio de pinturas y alcabalas', *Goya*, 178, 1984, pp.180–82.

14 J. Montagu, 'Velázquez Marginalia: his slave Juan de Pareja and his illegitimate son Antonio', *The Burlington Magazine*, 125, 1983, pp.683–5.

15 H. E. Wethey, *Alonso Cano*, Princeton, 1955, p.205.

Velázquez's Early Technique
Zahira Veliz, pp.79–84

I wish to thank the following colleagues for their generous collaboration, without which this study could not have been completed: Martin Wyld, Gabriele Finaldi, Ashok Roy and David Bomford from the National Gallery, London. I must also acknowledge the most important contribution of published research by Gridley McKim-Smith, and by Carmen Garrido Pérez on the technical examination of paintings by Velázquez. Their valuable work is a firm foundation which has made possible the study of the Seville period in greater depth. Translations from the Spanish are my own.

1 Recent research on technical aspects and scientific examination of Velázquez's paintings in the Prado has been published by G. McKim-Smith, *Examining Velázquez*, New Haven and London, 1988; M. C. Garrido Pérez, 1992; and G. McKim-Smith and R. Newman, *Ciencia e Historia del Arte: Velázquez en el Prado*, Madrid, 1993. McKim-Smith's work has integrated the study of technique with the consideration of art historical questions, while the publication of excellent technical documents and commentary on these by Garrido Pérez has contributed invaluably to the primary material which must inform our understanding of Velázquez's technique.

2 The contract for Velázquez's apprenticeship was first published in *Varia Velazqueña*, vol.II, Madrid, 1960, document 8, pp.215–16.

3 Pacheco, 1990.

4 The most complete medium analysis to date is found in McKim-Smith and Newman, cited in note 1, 1993, pp.139–41.

5 Garrido Pérez, 1992, pp.53–63, gives ample attention to the canvases used by Velázquez. The radiographs published show the chequered pattern of the canvas used in *Mother Jerónima de la Fuente*, and in *The Immaculate Conception*. Important commissions by El Greco from 1570–90 were frequently painted on an elaborate *mantelillo*. This can be seen in photographs published in *Informes y trabajos del Instituto de Conservación y Restauración de Obras de Arte*, vol.13, 'El Entierro del Conde de Orgaz: Nueva instalación, estudio científico y tratamiento', Madrid, 1977. I have also observed the use by El Greco of beautifully patterned canvas for *The Expolio* (Toledo Cathedral), and the paintings for the high altar of Santo Domingo el Antiguo in Toledo. Some paintings by Zurbarán were painted on a chequered pattern canvas similar to those seen in the early works by Velázquez, see for example, *The Holy House of Nazareth* (Cleveland Museum of Art), and the paintings made for the Monastery of Guadalupe. Some paintings by Juan Bautista Maíno dating 1600–20, such as the *Adoration of the Shepherds* (Museo del Prado), are also painted on chequered linens.

6 Both terms are related to *mantel* (tablecloth), suggesting that these canvases were manufactured principally as table linens.

7 *Documentos*, vol.VIII, 1935, pp.65–6, *i es condicion que en el tablero principal de en medio se a de pintar sobre mantel una imajen de nuestra Señora de la pura i limpia Concepcion.*

8 Garrido Pérez, 1992, p.86, suggests that canvases with a complex weave may have been used to provide a textured surface.

9 Pacheco, 1990, p.481, records that large canvases were stretched over solid panels in order to protect them from humidity and conserve them for many years. *muy grandes lienzos se aseguran de la humedad estirados y clavados sobre tablas gruesas, donde se conservan muchos años.* This method was used by El Greco in Toledo, and by painters elsewhere in Castille, so it was not an exclusively Sevillian method. In any event, the role of the thick panels was more likely to stabilise moisture content rather than to 'protect' the canvas from humidity.

10 *Documentos*, cited in note 7, 1935, p.65.

11 Pacheco, 1990, pp.481–2.

12 Very similar grounds have been identified in Neapolitan paintings from this period, (Ashok Roy, personal communication).

13 The change to red, and eventually beige or cream-coloured grounds has been observed and documented by McKim-Smith, 1988, 1993, cited in note 1, and by Garrido Pérez, 1992, who also illustrates numerous cross-sections in which the changing grounds are clearly evident.

14 Pacheco, 1990, p.481.

15 Specific research into the characteristics of the grounds used by Velázquez has not yet been undertaken. It is evident, however, that the paintings on the Seville grounds seem to suffer more dramatic pigment alteration than later paintings. Perhaps the high carbonate content noted by Garrido Pérez, 1992, and McKim-Smith and Newman, 1994, cited in note 1, has contributed to instability because of the intrinsic hygroscopicity of carbonates. I am grateful to Ashok Roy for insightful discussions on the nature of the Seville grounds.

16 See the technical studies of McKim-Smith, 1988 and 1993, cited in note 1, on paintings such as *The Surrender of Breda* or *Las Meninas*.

17 Pacheco, 1990, p.482, *...pocas veces se hacen cartones iguales del mesmo tamaño de los cuadros que se han de pintar al olio; y, así, por los dibuxos pequeños, o por cuadrícula, o a ojo teniéndolos delante, se podrán debuxar las figuras, o historias sobre pared, tablas o lienzos, láminas o piedras (que en esto no hay diferencia más que en los ocreones). ...desviándose la distancia conveniente, se vaya abultando el todo de la figura, o historia, apartándose a menudo, quitando y poniendo hasta ajustarse con el patrón, o disegno que esté presente. Y en esto de compartir el todo de la historia, o figura, que satisfaga, está el acierto y buena gracia de toda la obra; porque, es cosa cierta que, en los perfiles de afuera consiste toda la dificultad de la pintura. Después de estar bien compartida en el todo, con las demás puntas se van afinando y llegando las partes de las figuras, con perfección. ...Hagamos cuenta que tenemos ya debuxado y puesto en razón, con perfiles ciertos, todo lo que pretendemos pintar...*

18 Angulo and Pérez Sánchez, 1985, no.107, p.35.

19 Angulo and Pérez Sánchez, 1985, no.105, p.35.

20 Angulo and Pérez Sánchez, 1985, no.106, p.35.

21 Pacheco, 1990, pp.482–83.

22 A. Palomino de Castro y Velasco, *El Museo Pictórico y Escala Optica*, 1724, vol.II, Madrid, 1988, p.199. Palomino provides circumstantial evidence for the use of drawing chalks (*clarión*) containing white lead in this phrase which, in fact, discourages their use: *Y para tocar de luz las figuras, prevengo, que nunca use del albayalde, porque con el tiempo se toma y vuelve negro...* Lead-containing drawing strokes would have definite opacity in an x-radiograph, while it is possible that drawing made with white chalk would not be detectable.

23 These pigments were identified through optical microscopy, (Ashok Roy, personal communication).

24 Garrido Pérez, 1992, p.104, fig.2, shows the x-radiograph of *St Ildefonso*.

25 It is interesting that in two works whose attribution to Velázquez is not unanimous, the half-length *Mother Jerónima de la Fuente*, (Private collection, now on view at Pollok House, Glasgow), and *The Immaculate Conception*, (Sotheby's Old Master Paintings, London, 6 July, 1994), which I have had the opportunity to study closely, graphic lines of the kind described are visible in the x-rays. Until there is comparative technical study of other painters working in Seville, and indeed, of Pacheco's method, it is impossible to say if these x-rays are unique to Velázquez, or if Velázquez was simply employing a method common to his immediate contemporaries or collaborators.

26 Garrido Pérez, 1992, p.168, shows the x-radiograph of *The Feast of Bacchus*.

27 Garrido Pérez, 1992, pp.120, 128, 168.

28 Conservation Record, National Gallery, London.

29 Pacheco, 1990, see pp.443, 527–8.

30 McKim-Smith and Newman, 1993, cited in note 1, p.140.

31 McKim-Smith and Newman, 1993, cited in note 1, and Garrido Pérez, 1992, identify and discuss the pigments used in a number of paintings. From the samples that have been analysed, it can be asserted that Velázquez used these more expensive pigments in approximately a third of his early paintings.

32 Pacheco, 1990, pp.483–8. The following pigments are mentioned by Pacheco for use in oil for painting on canvas or panel: white lead, orpiment, lead-tin yellow, verdigris, malachite, lamp black, bone black, azurite (*azul de Santo Domingo*), yellow lake (*ancorca*), carmine, vermilion, ochre, smalt, umber.

33 The inventory of the contents of the royal painter, Vicente Carducho's, Madrid studio after his death in 1638, included lead-tin yellow, artificial copper blue (*azul de costras*), red earth, yellow lake, azurite, various grades of carmine, malachite, verdaccio, verdigris, smalt, ultramarine, white lead. See Maria Luisa Caturla, 'Documentos en torno a Vicencio Carducho', *Arte Español; Revista de la Sociedad española de amigos del arte*, vol.XXVI, 1968, pp.184–5.

34 Pacheco, 1990, pp.482–7, *passim*.

35 Personal communication, Ashok Roy.

36 Pacheco, 1990, pp.485–7. In painting blues, Velázquez seems to follow Pacheco in adding smalt to the darkest, purest blues *...los azules se labren claros y que lo más oscuro sea el mismo azul puro, y cuando mucho, se añade...un poco de buen esmalte delgado, y de lindo color...,* (personal communication, Ashok Roy). Yet he ignores the advice given by Pacheco against glazing blues, *Los azules bañados no los abruebo, si no es con ultramarino...*

37 Pacheco, 1990, p.521.

38 Pacheco, 1990, p.521.

39 Pacheco, 1990, p.521.

Authors of the
Catalogue Entries

David Davies & Enriqueta Harris
*Cats 1, 2, 8, 14, 15, 16, 21–31, 33, 34, 36, 37, 38, 39,
41, 42, 43, 44, 45, 46*

Gabriele Finaldi
Cats 11, 12, 13

Enrique Pareja López
Cat 9

Marjorie Trusted
Cats 7, 32, 40

Enrique Valdivieso
Cats 4, 5, 6, 35, 47, 48

Aidan Weston-Lewis
Cats 3, 10, 17–20

James Yorke
Cat 49

Velázquez in Seville · III
CATALOGUE

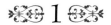

1

UNKNOWN ARTIST *c.*1600
VIEW OF SEVILLE

Oil on canvas · 146 × 295cm
Museo del Prado, Madrid
On loan to the Museo de América, Madrid

The view is taken from the district of Triana on the west bank of the River Guadalquivir. The artist has focused on the port, showing the bustling activity on the river and the waterfront. Ships are being tarred, galleons are at berth and galleys with slaves at the oar ply the water. All are testimony to the maritime importance of Seville as the centre of trade with the Indies. In the foreground, the artist has portrayed the social life of the city in a series of vignettes. The city, dominated by the Giralda, the old Moorish tower adjoining the Cathedral, serves as a dramatic backcloth.

The scale, the high viewpoint and the human activity in the foreground point to a Netherlandish tradition of topographical views. The style and costume suggest a date in the late sixteenth or early seventeenth century.

REFERENCE
Splendeurs D'Espagne, Palais des Beaux-Arts, Brussels, 1985, vol.II, A2, pp.368–9.

2

SIMON WYNHOUTSZ FRISIUS *c.*1580–1628

PANORAMIC VIEW OF SEVILLE

Originally titled: HISPALIS VULGO SIVILIAE URBIS TOTO ORBE CELEBERRIMAE HISPANIAEQUE PRIMARIAE EFFIGIES
Engraving · 50.5 × 227.5cm · Assembled from four plates, one of which was a proof as indicated by the blank half of the cartouche
The British Library, London

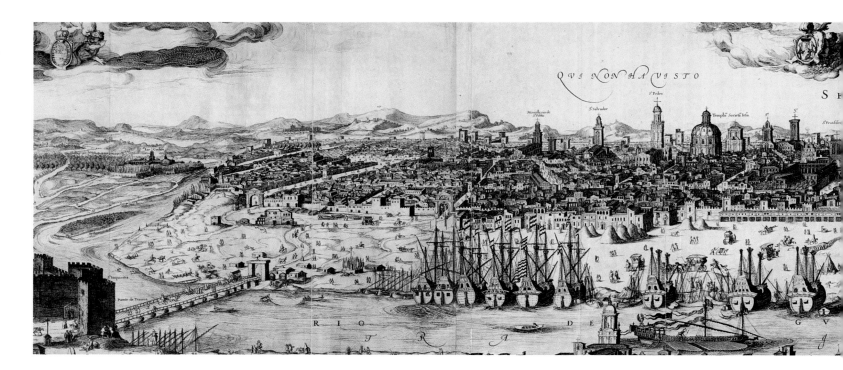

The patent to print and publish the engraving in large or in small, in whole or in part, was issued by the States-General to Frisius and Jan Janssen van Aernhem, a printer-publisher in Amsterdam, on 19 August 1617.[1]

The present engraving is cropped at top and bottom and is thought to have been assembled in Amsterdam *c.*1700 because of the dating of the maps that form the backing. It is one of only two known examples; the other is in the Royal Library, Stockholm. The latter is complete with Latin title above and explanatory text in French below. The place of publication and the name of the printer, but not the engraver, are given at the end of the text. The inscription in the sky is an inaccurate version of the Spanish saying: *Quien no ha visto Sevilla no ha visto maravilla* (He who has not seen Seville has not seen a marvel).

In contrast to the painted *View of Seville* [cat 1] in which the port and daily life of the city predominate, here its religious importance as well as its maritime significance are celebrated. The order and harmony of the composition underline the elegance of the ecclesiastical and civic buildings that made Seville a 'marvel' to see.

The year 1617, the date of the engraving, was propitious. It was the year in which Velázquez was to become a master painter and add lustre to the city of Seville.

[1] I. A. Welcker, 'Simon Wynhoutsz Frisius Konstryck Plaetsnyder', *Oud-Holland*, 53, 1936, pp. 232–5.

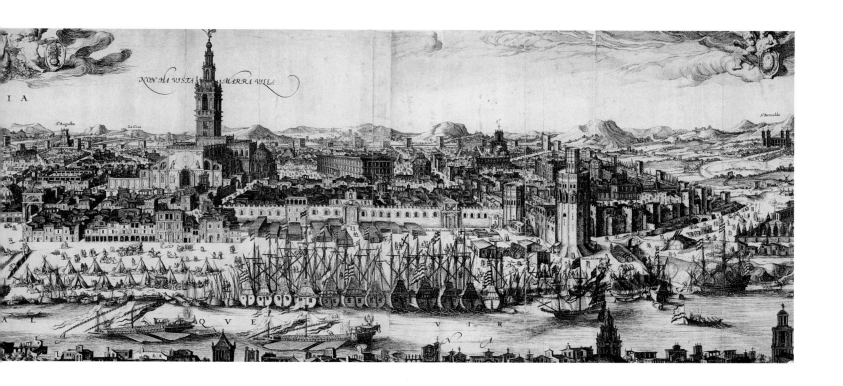

3

SPANISH SCHOOL, MID-SEVENTEENTH CENTURY
A VIEW OF THE ALAMEDA DE HÉRCULES, SEVILLE

Oil on canvas · 106.7 × 162.5cm

Private Collection, Scotland[1]

Although clearly a compilation of separate incidents and typical characters rather than a faithful record of a specific moment or event, this view of one of Seville's most popular open spaces gives an excellent flavour of what the city was like in Velázquez's day, albeit dating from a couple of decades after he had left for Madrid. The creation during the 1570s of the Alameda de Hércules, a broad avenue lined with poplar trees, from an area of marshy waste ground in the northern part of Seville was the initiative of the Conde de Barajas, mayor of Seville. At one end, two classical columns transferred from an ancient building in the city were set up and surmounted with statues by Diego de Pesquera of Hercules, the legendary founder of ancient Seville (Hispalis), and of Julius Caesar. Inscriptions on the bases of the columns draw symbolic parallels between Hercules and Charles V and Julius Caesar and Philip II respectively, and liken the Conde de Barajas's efforts in creating the Alameda to one of the labours of Hercules. The classical pedigree of Seville was the subject of intensive research by the city's antiquarians and humanist scholars at just this time, and one guaranteed to engender strong civic feelings.[2]

A broad cross-section of Sevillian society is represented in the picture. Young *caballeros* attend to the ladies in the shade of the trees. A distressed waterseller raises his arms in exasperation as his earthenware flasks are smashed in a squabble between his donkeys. Two pairs of fencers face up, watched by a group of figures behind (to judge from the threatened intervention of a third party, the duel between the foremost pair is in earnest). A fist-fight involving a black man near the well serves as further evidence of the underlying violence and social tension in the city. Wealthier citizens sit closeted in their carriages, or parade on horseback, several of their mounts rearing in a manner blatantly borrowed from royal equestrian portraiture. One sombrely dressed *hidalgo* is identified by the red insignia embroidered on his cloak as a knight of the military order of Calatrava. Two clerics converse at the left and a small crowd has gathered to listen to a preacher in the middle-distance. Stall-holders tempt passersby with their wares along the avenue. This wealth of incidental detail recalls the contractual instructions given to the Sevillian

painter Miguel de Esquivel in 1620, which required him to include in three views of the city he was commissioned to paint a staffage of people going about their daily business and as many incidents and 'curiosities' as possible.[3]

When it was in Louis-Philippe's Galerie espagnole this painting was catalogued as a work of Velázquez himself and more recently it has been ascribed to his pupil and son-in-law Juan Bautista Martínez del Mazo, but neither attribution is tenable. The treatment of the foliage, in particular, suggests that it may be the work of the one of the Flemish artists resident in Seville, or by a local painter influenced by Northern landscape paintings. A very similar view now owned by the Hispanic Society of America in New York [fig 1.7], dated 1645, was presumably painted in the same studio, although it is rather weaker in execution.[4] Several other more or less contemporary paintings of the Alameda survive,[5] and their evident popularity reflects strong civic pride on the part of Sevillians in this recently established urban space which reasserted the city's ancient roots. The view would have been especially well-known to Velázquez since he owned property on the Alameda, facing the columns.

[1] Provenance: King Louis-Philippe, Paris, 1837 (letter of 1 September records its purchase in Seville, with three other pictures, from Aniceto Bravo); Galerie espagnole, Louvre, 1838–48 (as Velázquez); Louis-Philippe sale, Christie's London, 21 May 1853 (lot 492, as Velázquez), bought by G. A. Hoskins for £66; his posthumous sale, Christie's, London, 18 June 1864 (lot 224), bought by Kibble for £65; London, Sir William Farrer (by 1895). For the provenance and bibliography of this picture see J. Baticle and C. Marinas, *La Galerie espagnole de Louis-Philippe au Louvre 1838–1848 (Notes et Documents des musées de France 4)*, Paris, 1981, pp.194–5, no.301.

[2] See the essay by V. Lleó Cañal (pp.23–7) and Lleó Cañal, 1979.

[3] López Martínez, *Desde Martínez Montañés hasta Pedro Roldán,* Seville, 1932, pp.181–2. (I am grateful to Peter Cherry for this reference.)

[4] I am grateful to Marcus Burke for supplying information about this picture. The last digit of the date is partly obliterated and could be read differently.

[5] See, for example, *Velázquez y lo Velázqueño,* 1960, cat.104 (with references to other versions, although that to a similar picture in the Louvre is incorrect); and Baticle and Marinas, cited in note 1. The mention in the 1925 edition of the *Klassiker der Kunst* volume (p.259) that the exhibited painting was then in the Philadelphia Museum of Art is erroneous and presumably refers to another version, no longer there.

4

JUAN DE ROELAS 1558/60–1625

THE TRIUMPH OF ST GREGORY

Oil on canvas · 440 × 257cm
Ushaw College, Durham

Roelas was born in Seville where he studied and was ordained for the priesthood. He is assumed to have trained as a painter in Venice during his stay in Italy, which probably took place between 1585 and 1595. In 1597 he is recorded in Valladolid, which at that time was the residence of the court. He must have left there by 1603, since in that year he was serving as chaplain to the collegiate church of Olivares. From 1604 he was in Seville where he executed several very important works and quickly became the most admired painter in the city. In 1616 Roelas moved to Madrid where he sought to obtain the post of Painter to the King. On failing to be appointed he returned to Olivares, taking up his post as chaplain again until his death in 1625.

In the context of Sevillian painting of the period Roelas's activity is innovative and impressive, combining qualities of spiritual grandeur with the imagery of popular life. His handling is free and light, indebted to the Venetian tradition, and his palette is warm and vibrant. He exerted a great influence on later painting in Seville, which is especially apparent in the early work of Murillo.

When the Prior of the English College in Seville, Padre Juan, made the first payment to Roelas for this altarpiece in 1608, the artist referred to it as: 'the picture of Saint Gregory which I am painting'. More recently, in 1935, Diego Angulo called it 'The Triumph of St Gregory', a title it has retained. The composition of the painting is simple and schematic. It is divided into two registers, a lower earthly register and a higher heavenly one. The lower zone is dominated by the seated figure of St Gregory the Great as Pope who is flanked by two groups of bishops. In the foreground are two students of the College and two children dressed as acolytes. In the upper register are portrayed the Virgin and Child accompanied by angels who scatter flowers. The backdrop of solemn architecture with an arcaded patio recalls the appearance of the College.

According to the interpretation of Father Romano Ríos, the painting was intended by the Fathers of the English College in Seville to reflect the part played by the College in bringing to an end the dispute between the Benedictines and the diocesan clergy of Seville concerning their respective roles in the religious life of the city. St Gregory's association with the Benedictine order and the dedication of the English College of Seville to this saint contributed towards reconciling the divergent parties. The painting thus illustrates the links between the English and Sevillian churches and the need for the clergy to enjoy concord under the protection of the Virgin, as well as the exaltation and defence of the Faith.

English Catholics had a great devotion to St Gregory since it was he who in 590AD, shortly after his election to the papacy, undertook the evangelisation of England. This accounts for why the English priests resident in Seville decided to place their college under his protection. It is also significant that many of the students of the college went on to enter the Benedictine order.

The figure kneeling in front of St Gregory is St Hermenegild, one of the patron saints of Seville [see cat 40]. He offers his royal crown to the Pope as a sign of his intention not to succeed his father Leovigildo who was king of an Arian kingdom. His refusal to wear the crown in order that he might defend the Christian faith led to his imprisonment and subsequent martyrdom. In the right foreground is San Leandro, the friend of St Gregory. The figures on the left and right are ten great Spanish bishops of the seventh century who had studied in Seville in the school founded by San Leandro. They are San Isidoro of Seville, San Fulgencio of Cartagena, San Eladio, San Eugenio I, San Eugenio II, San Ildefonso, San Julián of Toledo, San Braulio and San Tajo of Zaragoza. The English College of St Gregory in Seville is thus presented in this picture as the seventeenth-century equivalent of the brilliant ecclesiastical school founded in the sixth century by San Leandro.

From 1608, the date of its execution, the painting stood above the high altar in the English College in Seville. In about 1767 it passed to the Colegio de San Albano in Valladolid whence it came, in the mid-nineteenth century, to its present location.

REFERENCES

J. M. Carriazo, 'Correspondencia de don Antonio Ponz con el Conde de Aguila', *Archivo Español de Arte*, 1929, pp.162–3.

D. Angulo Iñiguez, 'El cuadro de San Gregorio de Roelas', *Boletín del Seminario de Arte y Arqueología*, Valladolid, 1935–6, pp.51–7.

J. A. Gaya Nuño, *La pintura española fuera de España*, Madrid, 1958, p.290.

R. Ríos, 'College Notes', *The Ushaw Magazine*, July 1965, pp.72–4.

D. Angulo Iñiguez, *Pintura del siglo XVII; Ars Hispaniae*, vol.xv, Madrid, 1971, p.80.

Valdivieso, 1978, p.48.

Valdivieso and Serrera, 1985, pp.124, 165.

M. Murphy, 1992, pp.viii and 20.

5

FRANCISCO PACHECO 1564–1644
THE VIRGIN OF THE IMMACULATE CONCEPTION

Oil on canvas · 305 × 195cm · Signed: O.F.P. [Opus Francisco Pacheco]
Arzobispado de Sevilla
Parroquia de San Lorenzo

Pacheco was born in Sanlúcar de Barrameda in 1564. From about 1580 he was in Seville with his uncle, also called Francisco Pacheco, a canon of Seville Cathedral. He was apprenticed to a now unknown painter called Luis Fernández until about 1585 when he became a master painter. From his youth Pacheco was associated with Seville's intellectuals and with influential churchmen who enabled him to obtain important commissions. In 1611 he travelled to Castile and visited the Escorial, Madrid and Toledo. The art and artists with whom he came into contact increased his understanding of painting and led to an improvement in the quality of his own works. In 1624 he spent a long period in Madrid in an effort to be nominated Painter to the King but, despite the support of his former pupil and son-in-law Diego Velázquez, was unsuccessful.

In his later years he reacted to the new style of his younger contemporaries like Zurbarán and Herrera by retreating to a more rigorous and conceptualised kind of painting. It is characterised by a reliance on fixed formulas, resulting in a cold and unimaginative art based on a firm outline and conventionalised colouring. His artistic writings, like the *Arte de la pintura*, and his *Libro de retratos*, and his important role as an art theorist make Pacheco one of the most interesting painters of the period.

This is the central part of an altarpiece that was commissioned in 1623 by Don Diego López de Porras and his wife Doña Isabel de Montemayor for their chapel in the parish church of San Lorenzo, Seville. It is one of Pacheco's most beautiful representations of the Immaculate Conception. The figure of the Virgin is solemn and ecstatic; she stands on a half-moon with her arms crossed over her breast. The Holy Trinity appears above and she is surrounded by angels who carry the Marian attributes of lily and mirror which derive from the Old Testament and Apocryphal books of the *Song of Songs* (II, 2) and *Wisdom* (VII, 26) respectively. In the lower right part of the picture there are several other symbols which allude to the Virgin. The city is the 'civitatis Dei' mentioned in *Psalms* (LXXXVI, 3); it resembles Seville since it includes the Giralda, or Cathedral tower, and parts of the city walls. In the foreground is a tower which recalls Seville's Torre del Oro on the bank of the Guadalquivir. This is the 'Tower of David' referred to in the *Song of Songs* (IV, 4). There is a door in the walls beyond the tower which appears to be open, an allusion to the 'porta Coeli' mentioned in *Genesis* (XXVIII, 17). The ship crossing the sea is a reference to the Virgin as the 'help of mariners'. At lower left are symbols from the Marian litanies drawn from the Book of *Ecclesiasticus*: the roses, 'plantatio rosae' (XXIV, 18); the cypress, 'cypressus in monte Sion' (XXIV, 17); the palm tree, 'palma exaltata' (XXIV, 18); and the cedar, 'cedrus exaltata', (XXIV, 17). There is also a fountain, the 'fons hortorum' of the *Song of Songs* (IV, 15).

REFERENCES

Ceán Bermúdez, 1800, vol.IV, p.21.

F. González de León, *Noticia artística, histórica ... de Sevilla*, Seville, 1884, p.91.

J. M. Asensio, *Francisco Pacheco; Sus obras artísticas y literarias*, Seville, 1886, p.8.

J. Gestoso, *Sevilla monumental y artística*, Seville, 1889, p.243.

A. L. Mayer, *Die Sevillaner Malerschule*, Leipzig, 1911, p.93.

A. Muro Orejón, *Documentos*, vol.VIII, 1935, p.65.

Ponz, 1947, p.781.

P. Muller, 'Francisco Pacheco as a Painter', *Marsyas*, 10, 1960–1, p.40.

J. Camón Aznar, *La pintura española del siglo XVII*, Madrid, 1978, p.168.

A. Morales, *La iglesia de San Lorenzo de Sevilla*, Seville, 1981, p.56.

Valdivieso and Serrera, 1985, pp.54–6.

Valdivieso 1990, pp.28–9.

6

FRANCISCO PACHECO 1564–1644
ST RICHARD

Oil on canvas · 104 × 86.5cm

English College, Valladolid

This painting is part of a series of the kings of England which belongs to the Colegio Inglés de San Albano (English College of St Alban) in Valladolid. The series originally comes from Seville and was painted by Pacheco in 1610. He had already painted a series of kings and queens of England, probably for the Colegio de San Gregorio, the English College in Seville.

Like the other paintings in the series, the image is shown in an oval surround of elegant mannerist design. At the top of the surround is the Tudor coat of arms and at the bottom there is a rectangular panel with some biographical details written in Latin. In the oval frame there are Latin phrases from the Old Testament which allude metaphorically to the life of the king.

St Richard is dressed as a pilgrim with staff and hat. He had undertaken a pilgrimage with his family to the Holy Land but died *en route* in the Italian city of Lucca and was buried there. The inscription in the oval frame is: EGREDERE DE TERRA TUA. GENES 12 (Depart from your land; *Genesis* XII, 1). On the panel is written: S. RICHARDUS ANGLIÆ REX PATER SANCTORUM WILEBALDIE WINEBALDI E SANCTÆ WALBURGIS VIRGINIS OBIIT DIE V FEBRUARII ANNO DOMINI 750 (St Richard, King of England, father of Sts Willebald and Winnebald and of St Walburga Virgin. He died on 5 February in the Year of Our Lord 750).

REFERENCE

E. Valdivieso, 'Una serie de santos reyes de Inglaterra de Francisco Pacheco', *Boletín del Seminario de Arte y Arqueología*, Valladolid, 1994, p.466.

S. RICHARDVS ANGLIÆ REX PATER SANCTORVM
WILEBALDI E WINEBALDI E SANCTÆ WALBVRG IS
VIRGINIS OBIIT DIE V FEBRVARII ANNO DOMINI 750.

✻ 7 ✻

JUAN MARTÍNEZ MONTAÑÉS 1568–1649
AND FRANCISCO PACHECO 1564–1644
St Ignatius Loyola

Polychromed wood and fabric · 167cm high
Church of the Annunciation, Seville University

Ignatius of Loyola (1491–1556) was the founder and first General of the Society of Jesus (the Jesuits), and was canonised in 1622. This statue was recorded soon after its completion in a contemporary account of the celebrations of the beatification of Ignatius in Seville in February 1610, having been commissioned from Montañés by the Congregation of the Holy Trinity. The sculptor carved the head and hands, but the rest of the life-size manikin was to be dressed (an *imagen de vestir*). When it was first made, the figure was apparently clothed in a black velvet soutane embroidered by the nuns of the Convent of La Encarnación, and adorned with jewels brought by residents of the city. In the eighteenth century it was dressed in black velvet with gold and silver trimmings. The soutane is now represented in stiffened fabric soaked in glue. This probably dates from 1836, during the renovation of the chapel, when the statue and its pendant, St Francis Borgia, also by Montañés (on the other side of the high altar in the University Chapel, Seville) were rediscovered, having been relegated to storage. The painter Francisco Pacheco, who frequently collaborated with Montañés, recorded that he undertook the polychromy of the heads of both figures in matt colours. Guild regulations in Seville prescribed that painters rather than the sculptors themselves were responsible for the polychromy of wooden sculpture, and we know that such work formed part of Velázquez's training.

By the time Montañés was given this commission he was established as the leading sculptor in Seville. Here the portrait of Ignatius is derived from the death-mask preserved in Rome, of which Pacheco owned a plaster copy. As well as idealising the features of the subject, Montañés added traces of tears on the cheeks. According to the 1610 account, the figure originally held a framed monogram of Christ (IHS, the symbol of the Jesuit Order), at which he was gazing 'as if in a mirror'. This is now replaced by a cross, at which the saint gazes intently.

REFERENCES

F. de Luque Fajardo, *Relación de la fiesta qve se hizo en Sevilla a la beatificacion del glorioso S. Ignacio*, Seville, 1610, *verso* f4–f5; *verso* f6, *verso* f4, *tr.* (cited in Proske, p.155, note 233).

Pacheco, 1956, p.316.

Proske, 1967, pp.76–8, p.155 and figs.86 and 88.

W. Braunfels (ed.), *Lexikon der Christlichen Ikonographie*, vol.6, Freiburg im Breisgau, 1974, p.571.

Hernández Díaz, 1987, pp.167–68, and figs.176 and 177.

La Iglesia en América: Evangelización y Cultura, Seville, 1992, p.142 (entry on St Francis Borgia by J. M. Palomero Páramo).

Francisco Pacheco. 350 Aniversario de su Muerte, Seville, 1994, no.19.

Universitas Hispalensis, Seville, 1995, p.46 (entry by J. M. González Gómez).

FRANCISCO DE HERRERA THE ELDER *c.1590–c.1656*

ST IGNATIUS LOYOLA

Engraving · 17.8 × 12.3cm · Signed *franᶜᵒ de herrera f.* · and dated 1610

Biblioteca Nacional, Madrid

The engraving is the frontispiece to Francisco de Luque Fajardo, *Relación de la Fiesta que se hizo en Sevilla a la Beatificación del Glorioso S. Ignacio fundador de la Compañía de Jesus* (Account of the Festival in Seville on the occasion of the Beatification of the Glorious St Ignatius, founder of the Company of Jesus), published in Seville in 1610 and dedicated to Sancho Dávila y Toledo, Bishop of Jaén.

The portrait of Loyola (1491–1556) appears to be based on an engraving by Pedro Perret (1597), who had as his model a plaster cast of a death mask of Loyola belonging to Pacheco.[1] The inscription in the surround of Perret's print is similar but abbreviated. Herrera mistakenly gives Loyola's age at his death as sixty-nine instead of sixty-five.

In the inscription in Perret's engraving Loyola is referred to as 'Blessed', anticipating his beatification in 1609; similarly, in Herrera's frontispiece, Loyola is given the title of Saint although he was not canonised until 1622. A contemporary Jesuit biographer, Pedro de Ribadeneyra, described Loyola's countenance in detail:

His face was distinguished, the forehead broad and unwrinkled, the eyes deep set, the lids contracted and scored with the tears that he continually shed, the ears of average size, the nose prominent and aquiline, the fair complexion florid. What with his baldness, his appearance was very venerable. The expression of his face was gladly grave and gravely glad, so that by his serenity he cheered those who looked at him and by his seriousness he calmed them.[2]

Juan Martínez Montañés, whose statue of Loyola was finished in time for the festivities in February 1610, may also have used this description and the cast in Pacheco's possession [see cat 7].[3]

Herrera, a native of Seville, although better known as a painter, produced some accomplished engravings, of which the present example is one of the earliest, and earlier than any known painting by the artist. He appears to have studied engraving with his father, a *pintor iluminador*, who was also probably a printmaker. Herrera is reputed to have been Velázquez's first master but there is no firm evidence to support this.

[1] Pacheco, 1990, pp.708–9.

[2] Pedro de Ribadeneyra, 'Vida del Padre Ignacio de Loyola', *Obras escogidas*, Madrid, 1868, pp.117–8. Proske, 1967, p.77 (for translation).

[3] Proske, 1967.

REFERENCES

A. Martínez Ripoll, 'Francisco de Herrera el Viejo, Grabador', *Actas del XXIII Congreso Internacional de Historia del Arte*, Granada, [1973], 1978, vol.III, pp.145–154.

A. Martínez Ripoll, *Francisco de Herrera el Viejo*, Seville, 1978, pp.50–1, 247:G2, fig 105.

RELACION DELA FIESTA QVE
se hizo en Sevilla a la Beatificacion del Glorioso
.S. IGNACIO fundador de la Compañia de IESVS.

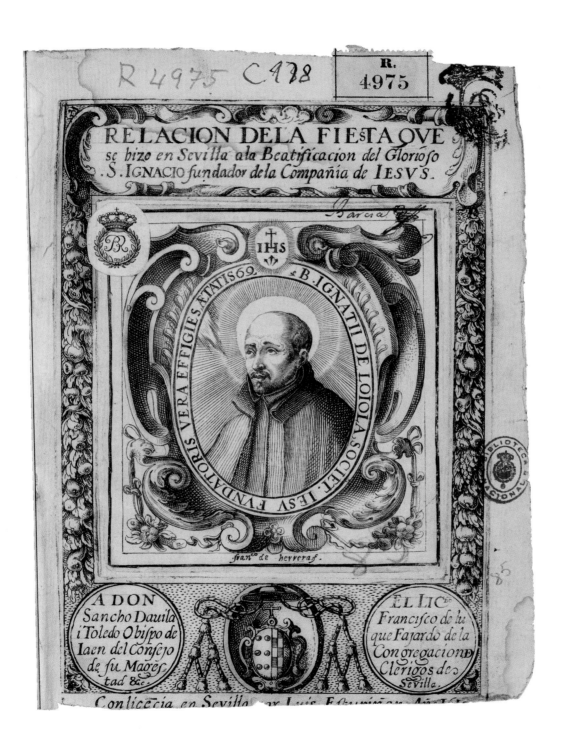

B. IGNATII DE LOIOLA SOCIET. IESV FVNDATORIS VERA EFFIGIES ÆTATIS 69.

IHS

fran.co de herrera f.

A DON
Sancho Dauila
i Toledo Obispo de
Iaen del Consejo
de su Mages-
tad &c.

EL LIC.
Francisco de lu
que Fajardo de la
Congregacion D
Clerigos de
Sevilla.

Con licécia en Sevilla por Luis Estupiñan Año

❋❦ 9 ❦❋

ALONSO CANO 1601–1667

ST FRANCIS BORGIA

Oil on canvas · 129 × 123cm · Signed and dated, lower left: … VS CANO | AN 1624
Museo de Bellas Artes, Seville

Although born in Granada in 1601, Alonso Cano may be considered a Sevillian, at least as regards his training. He settled in Seville when he was thirteen and first studied with his father Miguel Cano, an altarpiece joiner, before passing to Francisco Pacheco's workshop in 1616, where he was a fellow pupil of Velázquez. There he absorbed his master's mannerist and tenebrist tendencies, although these were quickly modified by the impact of the naturalism and warm colour of, among others, Juan del Castillo, a close collaborator of his father. A master painter in 1626 and master sculptor in 1629, Cano collaborated with Juan Martínez Montañés on numerous sculptures for Sevillian convents.

In 1638 he went to Madrid where his style evolved through direct contact with Velázquez and with the Venetian paintings in the royal collection. He enjoyed the patronage of the court of Philip IV and was appointed Painter and Usher of the Bedchamber to the Count-Duke Olivares. He returned to his native Granada in 1652 where he was appointed Prebendary and Chief Architect of the Cathedral. There he was able to combine his skills as an architect, sculptor and painter, achieving a dynamic baroque synthesis of great quality and laying the foundations for what would become the baroque school of Granada. He died in Granada in 1667 having achieved the status, like Velázquez, of a great master, admired for his abilities and the flamboyancy of his style.

Among Cano's Sevillian works the *St Francis Borgia*, restored by the Seville Museum for this exhibition, is one of the finest. The restoration has permitted the recovery of several centimetres along the left edge so that more of the signature can be seen and the three cardinal's hats are now visible.

Francisco de Borja (Francis Borgia), Marquis of Lombay and Duke of Gandía, was born in 1510 and entered the service of the Emperor Charles V and Isabel of Portugal. After the latter's death he was entrusted with delivering her remains to Granada and on opening the coffin and seeing her decomposed face he is said to have declared: 'Never again shall I serve a master who is subject to corruption'. This event took place in 1539; in 1546 he entered the Jesuit order becoming General Superior in 1565. He died in Rome in 1572, was beatified in 1624 and canonised in 1671 (Bull of 1724).

Although the present work is undocumented, Cano must have painted it for the church of the Casa Profesa of the Jesuits in Seville and the date 1624 suggests that it was commissioned to mark Francis Borgia's beatification. The date of its entry into the Seville Museum is not recorded but it is first referred to in the inventory of 1897 as a work by Francisco de Zurbarán, an attribution which was only corrected in 1946 with the discovery of the signature.

The saint is shown full length wearing the black Jesuit habit and contemplating, with a mystical expression, a skull with an imperial crown. This, his attribute, is an allusion to his renunciation of earthly glories. At his feet there are three Cardinal's hats, signifying his repeated refusal to accept the distinction. The monogram of the Jesuits, IHS with three nails, appears in the upper left in a cloud of glory.

The work is Cano's earliest known painting and demonstrates the precocious tenebrism inherited from his master Francisco Pacheco and shared with Velázquez during his Sevillian years. It also betrays the influence of Zurbarán, however, and a certain debt to the sculptures of Juan Martínez Montañés, particularly those he made for the church of the Casa Profesa.

Blacks and dark greens dominate the chromatic range of the picture. The light falls dramatically on the face, hands and the crowned skull in accordance with tenebrist formulae but the interest in foreshortening, in the psychology of the expression, and in the verticality of the composition testify to a certain mannerist tendency common to all Cano's oeuvre. The only colour accents are provided by the red of the hats and the red and gold of the monogram.

REFERENCES

M. Gómez-Imaz, *Inventario de los cuadros sustraidos por el Gobierno intruso en Sevilla (año 1810)*, Seville, 1896, no.9.

M. E. Gómez-Moreno, 'Pinturas inéditas de Alonso Cano', *Archivo Español de Arte*, 1946, p.257, pl.XIV.

M. Martínez Chumillas, *Alonso Cano*, Madrid, 1948, p.82, figs.25 and 26.

Wethey, 1955, pp.167–8, fig.36.

J. Bernales Ballesteros, *Alonso Cano en Sevilla*, Seville, 1976, pp.82–3, 113, 157–9, pl.9.

Wethey, 1983, pp.45–6, 136–7 and 176, no.69, fig.37.

R. Izquierdo and V. Muñoz, *Museo de Bellas Artes. Inventario de Pinturas*, Seville, 1990, p.82, no.87.

Various authors, *Museo de Bellas Artes de Sevilla*, Vitoria, 1991, vol.II, pp.138–9, no.146.

D. Sánchez-Mesa Martín, *El Arte del Barroco. Escultura, Pintura y Artes Decorativas, Historia del Arte en Andalucía (vol.VII)*, Seville, 1991, p.366, fig.234.

AFTER MICHELANGELO MERISI, CALLED CARAVAGGIO 1571–1610

Martha Reproving Mary Magdalen for her Vanity (The Conversion of the Magdalen)

Oil on canvas · 97.7 × 135.8cm

Christ Church Picture Gallery, Oxford[1]

What is widely – but not unanimously – considered to be Caravaggio's original of this composition was acquired by the Detroit Institute of Arts in 1973.[2] The existence of three replicas of the painting, of which the Christ Church picture is one, had long before led scholars to conclude that they must all derive from a lost composition by Caravaggio.[3] The original probably dates from around 1598, when Caravaggio was living in the household of his most important Roman patron, Cardinal Francesco del Monte. The same model used for Mary Magdalen appears in the *St Catherine* (Museo Thyssen-Bornemisza, Madrid) and in the *Judith and Holofernes* (Galleria Nazionale d'Arte Antica, Rome), both painted at about this date. The first reference to a painting of 'Saints Martha and the Magdalen' by Caravaggio is in the will, dated 6 August 1606, of the Genoese nobleman Ottavio Costa, but this may have been a copy. The Christ Church picture is a good quality – if somewhat abraded – copy of Caravaggio's original and was probably painted in the first quarter of the seventeenth century.[4]

The subject, for which there is no biblical source, is rare in Italian art of the sixteenth century, although Caravaggio's picture appears to have kindled an unprecedented interest in the theme in the early decades of the seventeenth. Martha is shown chiding her sister Mary Magdalen for her worldliness and urging her to follow Christ's example. Mary's elaborate coiffure and richly embroidered costume, and her attributes of ointment jar, comb, and mirror, are all traditional symbols of vanity as well as being associated with her profession as a prostitute. It is probable that Caravaggio intended to represent her at the moment of her conversion from courtesan to repentant sinner. The sprig of orange blossom she holds – sometimes employed as a symbol of purity – and the brilliant light bathing her figure and reflected in the mirror have been interpreted as allusions to this spiritual enlightenment.[5]

None of the extant versions of this composition is known to have been in Spain in the seventeenth century, but with its half-length figures painted from life, exquisite still-life details, shallow pictorial space and strong chiaroscuro it may be taken as representative of the type of composition by Caravaggio that has often been invoked as a possible influence on the young

Velázquez. At least one autograph work by Caravaggio was in Spain by the second decade of the century, together with several copies and a few pictures by his immediate followers, but it is unlikely that Velázquez knew many, if any, of these first-hand.[6] The distinctive character of his early works would support the notion that he was imitating not specific Caravaggesque works, but rather the revolutionary approach that the Lombard artist had practised and popularised, with its commitment to painting directly from life, and its use of controlled and highly contrasted lighting.[7] These were characteristics for which Caravaggio was notorious during his own lifetime (as early as 1604, the artist's biographer Karel van Mander confirmed that 'he will not do a single brushstroke without close study from life which he copies and paints')[8] and Velázquez would surely have heard many reports and discussions of his works from visitors to Rome, Naples and Sicily. Whatever the precise nature and extent of Caravaggio's influence on the young Velázquez (for further discussion of this subject see David Davies's essay, pp.51–65), it is an issue which should be assessed within the broader context of the rise of naturalistic painting in Spain as exemplified by such artists as Sánchez Cotán, Ribalta [cat 13] and Ribera [cats 11 and 12].

---

1   Provenance: General John Guise, by 1760; bequeathed by him to the Gallery, 1765.

2   See the five articles devoted to this discovery in *The Burlington Magazine*, 116, 1974, pp.563-93; *The Age of Caravaggio*, New York 1985, cat. no.73.

3   R. Longhi, 'Ultimi studi su Caravaggio e la sua cerchia' in *Proporzioni*, vol.I, 1943, p.11. It later emerged that one of these three 'replicas', that was allegedly in the Manzella Collection in Rome, is identical with the Detroit painting.

4   For full details of the Christ Church picture, see J. Byam Shaw, *Paintings by Old Masters at Christ Church, Oxford*, London, 1967, pp.85–6, cat. no.137.

5   See F. Cummings, 'The Meaning of Caravaggio's *Conversion of the Magdalen*', in *The Burlington Magazine*, cited in note 2, pp.572–8.

6   On Caravaggio and Spain see Ainaud, 1947, pp.345–413; Pérez Sánchez, 1973; López-Rey, 1979, pp.7–9; M. Burke, *Private Collections of Italian Art in Seventeenth-century Spain*, doctoral dissertation, New York University, 1984, vol.I, pp.18–19, 23.

7   See Jordan and Cherry, 1995, pp.37–9.

8   K. van Mander, *Het Schilders-Boek*, 1604, fol.191r (translated in W. Friedlaender, *Caravaggio Studies*, Princeton, 1955, p.260).

❊❊ 11 ❊❊

JUSEPE DE RIBERA 1591–1652

THE SENSE OF SMELL

Oil on canvas · 114 × 88cm
Juan Abello Collection

The Sense of Smell is one of a set of Five Senses painted towards the end of Ribera's stay in Rome (1612/13 to 1616). In his *Considerazioni sulla pittura,* written in Rome around 1620, Giulio Mancini states that Ribera painted them for a Spanish patron whose name is tantalisingly left blank in all the known copies of the manuscript: 'He made many things here in Rome, and in particular for ***, the Spaniard, who has five very beautiful half figures representing the five senses, a Christ Deposed and others, which in truth are things of most exquisite beauty'.[2] Since 1966 four of the original five have been identified. The *Sense of Hearing* is known through the many copies of the whole series which survive, but Ribera's original remains to be found.[3]

Each of Ribera's *Senses* is represented by a single half-length male figure positioned behind a humble wooden table on which rest objects which play the role of attributes. *The Sense of Smell,* exhibited here, is personified by a shabbily-dressed man, perhaps a beggar, who holds an open onion which draws tears from his eyes. On the table are another onion, its papery skin brilliantly painted, a head of garlic and a richly scented orange blossom. The man representing *The Sense of Sight* (Museo Franz Mayer, Mexico City) holds a telescope and on the table before him are a mirror and a pair of spectacles; *Taste* [fig 6.8] is a vulgar and corpulent *buongustaio* who tucks into a plate of pasta while *Touch* (Norton Simon Foundation, Pasadena) is represented by a blind scholar who, having discarded a painted portrait, feels the form of a classical bust.[4] The *Sense of Hearing* is represented by a luteplayer.

The setting for each of the personifications is a shallow and bare interior, with the light falling sharply from above and casting a diagonal shadow on the rear wall, a device adopted from Caravaggio's Roman works of the 1590s and early 1600s. Despite the vigorous naturalism of the paintings, the 'posed' studio character of the compositions is very apparent and is comparable to the Sevillian genre scenes of Velázquez,[5] although it is unlikely that Velázquez knew Ribera's *Senses* at such an early date.

Ribera was born in Játiva, near Valencia, and may have trained with Francisco Ribalta [see cat 13]. As a young man he went to Italy and is recorded in Parma in 1611. He lived in Rome for several years before settling in Naples in 1616 where he became the leading painter in the city. The striking naturalism and dramatic chiaroscuro of his works is strongly influenced by the works of Caravaggio and his closest followers, although from the mid–1630s Ribera painted more open compositions employing a more luminous palette. He was much patronised by the Spanish viceroys of Naples who took many of his works to Spain where they exercised a great influence on Spanish painters. Ribera painted mostly religious subjects and frequently martyrdoms, although he also produced some mythologies and portraits. Ribera and Velázquez would certainly have become acquainted during the latter's two trips to Naples in 1630 and 1650.

The most original aspect of Ribera's treatment of the subject of the *Senses* is that allegorical subject-matter is presented as genre.

This approach contrasts sharply with the traditional imagery of the *Senses* where the personifications are overtly allegorical, almost invariably female, and usually semi-naked.[6] The spareness of the imagery of Ribera's works is also very different from the 'encyclopaedic' allegories of the senses by Jan Breughel and Van Balen (Museo del Prado, Madrid) dating from a few years later, in which the figures are all but swamped by the myriad attributes.

The human types employed by Ribera recall those that appear in the works of the Roman Caravaggesque painters Bartolomeo Manfredi, Cecco del Caravaggio and Valentin. The literalness employed in recording the particular models, the forceful physical presence of the figures in confined surroundings and the diagonal fall of light, which renders the confrontation with the viewer more dramatic, are the defining characteristics of Ribera's early Caravaggism. From his earliest known works Ribera was committed to the imitation of natural appearances and accurate visual reportage. His handling of paint, often characterised by the use of a thick impasto, conveys in a convincing manner both the mass and texture of the objects represented.[7]

Although Pérez Sánchez has recently remarked that the *Five Senses* could date from any time in Ribera's Roman sojourn,[8] it is likely that they are from the end rather than the beginning. Mancini says that they were commissioned works, and the same author states that when Ribera first came to Rome 'he worked for a daily wage for those who have workshops and sell paintings through the labours of similar young men'.[9]

1 Provenance: Possibly Prince Youssoupoff collection, Moscow and St Petersburg; (?) Duveen Brothers, New York; Private Collection, New York; Christie's East, New York, 14 March 1985, lot 139; Piero Corsini, Inc., New York; acquired by the present owner in 1989. The history of the series remains unclear. It should be noted that a set of *Five Senses* by Ribera was among a group of mainly Spanish pictures put up for sale in London in 1736/7 by Sir William Chapman. See G. Finaldi, 'Zurbarán's *Jacob and his Twelve Sons*; a family reunion at the National Gallery', *Apollo*, 140, 1994, pp.11, 14, n. 36. A set of *Five Senses* by Ribera (the same pictures?) was auctioned at Christie's, London, 2 February 1920, lot 329: 'Ribera The Senses – a set of five. 45½in × 33½in' They sold for the considerable sum of £180 to the dealer Weekes. Although the dimensions correspond, there is no way of knowing if this set was made up of the autograph pictures or copies.

2 C. Felton, 'Ribera's Early Years in Italy: the *Martyrdom of St Lawrence* and the *Five Senses*', *The Burlington Magazine*, 133, 1991, pp.71–81.

3 Pérez Sánchez and Spinosa, 1991, pp.60–4.

4 The iconography of this painting probably alludes to the story of the ancient philosopher Carneades, who was blind and recognised a bust of the countryside deity Paniscus by feeling it with his hands.

5 Jordan and Cherry, 1995, pp.39–42.

6 See the series of prints by Jacob de Backer (*The Sense of Taste* is reproduced in *Jusepe de Ribera, Lo Spagnoletto, 1591–1652*, Fort Worth, 1982, fig.110, p.92) and Goltzius (see W. L. Strauss (ed.), *The Illustrated Bartsch*, New York, 1980, figs. 116–22).

7 See the comment by Kristeller in Trapier, *Ribera*, New York, 1952, p.15.

8 Pérez Sánchez and Spinosa, 1991, pp.60 and 64.

9 Felton, cited in footnote 2.

❧ 12 ❧

JUSEPE DE RIBERA 1591–1652

STS PETER AND PAUL

Oil on canvas · 126 × 112cm

Signed on the stone block: IOSEPH. RIBERA HISPANVS VALEN | TINVS CIVITATIS SETABIS. ACA | DEMICVS ROMANVS.

Jusepe Ribera, Spaniard, Valencian, from the town of Játiva; Roman Academician

Musée des Beaux-Arts, Strasbourg[1]

The autograph inscription highlights the pride Ribera took both in his Spanish origins and in his membership of the Roman Academy of Painters, the Accademia di San Luca. Ribera was born in Játiva (the Roman *Setabis*) near Valencia and, although throughout his career he signed himself simply *Jusepe de Ribera español*, there is a handful of works up to 1640, including this one, in which he records that he was 'Játivan'. Ribera never returned to Spain after coming to Italy, probably in 1607–8, although he told Jusepe Martínez, an Aragonese painter who visited him in Naples in 1625, that he very much wanted to.[2] Ribera was associated with the Academy in Rome from at least 1613 and clearly enjoyed the prestige which the title of Academician brought with it.[3]

Despite the prominent autograph inscription, the painting has been attributed to several different artists including Gerard Douffet and Pietro Novelli, Il Monrealese.[4] The fraught attributional history of this picture and of the various paintings in the series of the *Five Senses* [cat 11] shows just how recently the early work of Ribera has begun to be understood and reconstructed.

The vigorous, even slightly raw, naturalism of the work, the compressed composition and confined space, the diagonal fall of light and the superb still life of the open book indicate that the painting is very close in date to the *Five Senses* painted in Rome in about 1615. It is very likely, though, that it dates from immediately after the artist's move to Naples in 1616, since the same model for Peter appears in the Girolamini *Peter*, one of a group of works recorded in Naples from an early date and which must have been executed in that city. A fixed point in the chronology of Ribera's early Neapolitan works is offered by the four paintings of Saints and the *Crucifixion* in Osuna, near Seville, which are referred to by the Florentine Cosimo del Sera in letters to the secretary of the Grand Duke Cosimo II in 1618.[5] These were being painted in 1617–18 for the Viceroy and Vicereine of Naples, the Duke and Duchess of Osuna. Those compositions are larger, more spacious in design, and generally more ambitious than *Sts Peter and Paul*, suggesting a greater maturity and confidence. *Sts Peter and Paul* then, like the Girolamini pictures, seems to fit in between the Senses and the Osuna pictures and is therefore datable to 1616–17.

The two saints are engaged in a discussion on a Greek text on the scroll. The same pseudo-Greek characters appear on the spine of the closed book and at the top of the page of the open tome; Ribera frequently used them. The subject of the disputation of the saints is not very common and a celebrated example, which Ribera may have been seeking to emulate, was the picture by Guido Reni of about 1605–6 made for the Sampieri family in Bologna (now Pinacoteca di Brera, Milan). In Ribera's painting Paul holds a sword whose pommel marks the apex of the diamond shaped geometric design of the composition, while at the base of the composition, on the projecting corner of the stone block, are the two keys of Peter, one gold and one silver, in accordance with tradition, signifying his power in heaven and on earth. The powerful colour mass of Peter's yellow robe is balanced by Paul's weighty green and red garments and the whole complex arrangement of colour and forms is forcefully held together and in equilibrium by the sharp fall of light from upper left. Ribera's use of light as a means of unifying and dramatising his compositions is deeply indebted to the example of Caravaggio, although Ribera's handling of paint, which is heavily impasted and physically expressive, contrasts sharply with the flatter and smoother finish of Caravaggio.

Ribera probably moved to Naples in the early summer of 1616 in order to acquire the patronage of the ruthless but cultivated and art-loving Duke of Osuna, Don Pedro Girón, who had been appointed Viceroy but had not yet arrived in the city. He succeeded in achieving his objective fairly rapidly since, in a document of September 1617, he styles himself 'Jusepe de Rivera, Spaniard, painter to His Excellency, the Lord Duke of Osuna'.[6] The pictures painted for the Duke and Duchess of Osuna were brought to Spain in 1620–1 and were donated to the Collegiate Church of Osuna by the Duchess in 1627. Although Jusepe Martínez states that Ribera's works were well known and admired in Spain by 1625, the Osuna pictures are the first works by him to be documented in Spain. The Peter and Paul can in all probability be identified as the 'Painting of Peter and Paul by the hand of Ioseph de Ribera' listed by Padre Francisco de los Santos in 1657 as hanging in the anteroom to the sacristy in the monastery of El Escorial.[7] Several copies of the picture exist in Spain. We may speculate that *Sts Peter and Paul* might also have come to Spain with the cargo of the Duke and Duchess of Osuna and perhaps been given to the monastery, or to its patron, the King, as a gift. It disappeared during the Napoleonic wars and next appeared in Paris in the Rothan collection and was acquired by Strasbourg in 1890.

[1] Provenance: Probably Monastery of San Lorenzo, El Escorial, before 1657; Gustav Rothan collection before 1890; sold Galerie Georges Petit, Paris, 29–31 May 1890, lot 233 (as Ribera); acquired by Wilhelm von Bode for the Musée des Beaux-Arts, Strasbourg, in 1890. See Pérez Sánchez and Spinosa, 1991, no.8, pp.67–8. This includes a full bibliography.

[2] For Jusepe Martínez's fascinating account of his conversation with Ribera in 1625, see Pérez Sánchez and Spinosa, 1991, pp.239–40.

[3] See Pérez Sánchez and Spinosa, 1991, p.232, under 27 October 1613.

[4] See A. E. Pérez Sánchez and N. Spinosa, *L'Opera completa del Ribera*, Milan, 1978, no.13, p.93, and Pérez Sánchez and Spinosa, 1991, no.8, pp.67–8. The attribution to Douffet was due to Herman Voss, and that to Novelli was due to Mayer.

[5] G. Finaldi, 'The patron and date of Ribera's Crucifixion at Osuna', *The Burlington Magazine*, 133, 1991, pp.445–6.

[6] Jusepe de Rivera español pintor de Su Exa el Sr Duque de osuna ... The document in which he describes himself thus is a power of attorney drawn up on 16 September 1617 so that money owed to him in Rome by one David de Leon could be recovered on his behalf by a certain Gaspar Balover, Archivio di Stato, Naples, Notai del Seicento, Andrea Fasano 87/4, ff.334v–335r.

[7] See F. J. Sánchez Cantón, *Fuentes literarias para la Historia del Arte Español*, 5 vols., vol.II, Madrid, 1933, p.233.

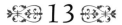
ATTRIBUTED TO FRANCISCO RIBALTA 1565–1628

Ramon Lull (?)

Oil on canvas · 102 × 85cm · Inscribed on the lining canvas: Nº 6 EL BEATO REMON LVLIO and D.G.H. surmounted by a ducal crown, the cipher of Don Gaspar Méndez de Haro y Guzmán, 7th Marqués del Carpio.[1]

Museu Nacional d'Art de Catalunya, Barcelona

The identification of the figure as the medieval Catalan writer, mystic and missionary, Ramon Lull (1232/3–1313/15), is based on the inscription on the reverse. The picture belongs to the genre of 'philosopher' paintings made popular by Jusepe de Ribera (1591–1652), the Valencian painter active in Rome and Naples.[2] Ribera's philosophers are usually old men and hold a book or sheet of paper. They are only rarely identified by original inscriptions and tend to be unspecific ragged scholars of a vaguely Stoic character.

The attribution of this painting remains problematic. The work was first published by Mayer in 1927 as by Ribera. He later changed his mind and declared it to be an early work by Velázquez, a view confirmed by Longhi. The attribution of the painting to Ribalta dates from 1947 when Ainaud de Lasarte identified it, on the basis of the inscriptions on the reverse, with a work listed in the inventory of paintings belonging to Gaspar Méndez de Haro, 7th Marqués del Carpio, one of the greatest Spanish collectors of the seventeenth century: 'A canvas 1 ¼ varas in height (approx. 105cm). Portrait of Ramon Lull. Original by Francisco Ribalta'.[3] Ainaud thought that the influence of Ribera was so marked that Ribalta must have been responding to works by Ribera who, according to Spanish secondary sources, had been his pupil before going to Italy. He therefore dated the picture to the last years of Ribalta's activity, 1625–8. Subsequently the picture has been attributed to Francisco's precocious son, Juan Ribalta (1596–1628), and one author has even considered it to be a collaborative effort between them.[4]

Francisco Ribalta was born in Solsona in Catalonia. The style of his early works is indebted to the Italianate mannerist painters of El Escorial. After 1598 he moved to Valencia where he became the favourite painter of St Juan de Ribera (c.1532–1611), the reforming archbishop who was also a great patron of the arts. After about 1615 his work became more naturalistic and he adopted a tenebrist manner, perhaps under the influence of the Caravaggesque works imported from Italy which could be seen in Valencia.

The tight handling of the paint, the extreme chiaroscuro, and the spareness of the composition, do not correspond very closely with any of Francisco Ribalta's works, despite attempts to relate the style of the painting to such works as his late *St Peter* from the main altarpiece of the Carthusian monastery of Porta Coeli, Bétera (now in the Museo de Bellas Artes, Valencia). Nor do the works of Juan Ribalta provide closer comparisons. There are, on the other hand, interesting parallels with Velázquez's Sevillian works.[5] The execution of the hands and face is comparable with that of the flesh painting in the *The Waterseller* and *Mother Jerónima de la Fuente* [cats 31 and 42], and there are similar profile views of senescent men in several early pictures. The *mise en scène* of this picture, however, would appear to be alien to Velázquez, whose early compositions tend to be much more compact and crowded.

Although he remains uncanonised, Ramon Lull was venerated throughout Spain as a saint. Born in Palma de Mallorca, he dis-

tinguished himself as an Arabic scholar, poet and philosopher. He travelled to Rome, Paris, Naples and Cyprus, suffered imprisonment for his evangelising activities in North Africa, and eventually was martyred at Bougie. Today he is chiefly admired for his literary works in Catalan. The iconography of Lull was established from quite an early date and he is usually shown with a long patriarchal beard and wearing a scholar's gown or religious habit. He sometimes looks up at a crucifix or vision of the crucified Christ and often has a halo.[6] The absence of any of the typical attributes in the picture and the wholly secular character of the representation should at least alert us to the possibility that it may have been intended as a generic representation of a scholar or philosopher and that the Lull identification was imposed at a later date. Although there were a few portraits of scholars and poets listed in the 1688 Carpio inventory, it is difficult to discern that a conscious effort was made by him to form a series of portraits of famous men of which the Ramon Lull might have been a part.[7] For the present then, the questions of the attribution of the work and even the appropriateness of the Lull identification remain open.

[1] The inscription presumably records an older inscription on the reverse of the original canvas; it is reproduced in Ainaud, 1947, p.357. Gaspar Méndez de Haro y Guzmán, 7th Marqués del Carpio y Heliche (1629–87); in the nineteenth century it was in a private collection in Palma de Mallorca; acquired by Leopoldo Gil, Barcelona, in 1916; deposited in the Barcelona Museum in 1922; acquired by the Museum in 1944.

[2] On this topic, see Fitz Darby, 1962, cited in cat.11, footnote 4, and O. Ferrari, 'L'iconografia dei filosofi antichi nella pittura del secolo XVII in Italia', *Storia dell'Arte*, 57, 1986, pp.785–9. For Ribera's series of philosophers painted for the Prince of Liechtenstein. see C. Felton 'Ribera's *Philosophers* for the Prince of Liechtenstein', *The Burlington Magazine*, 128, 1986, pp.785–9.

[3] Ainaud, 1947, pp.345–413; pp.356–9. For the Carpio inventory entry, A. M. Barcia, *Catálogo de la colección de pinturas del Excmo. Sr. Duque de Berwick y de Alba*, Madrid, 1911, p.261: *Un lienzo de cinco cuartas de alto. Retrato de Raimundo Lulio. Original de Francisco Ribalta*. The status of the document in the Alba archive from which Barcía quotes is uncertain. The Ribalta entry appears among a list of paintings drawn up on 29 July 1803 which incorporates the contents of an incomplete copy of the inventory, drawn up in 1661, of paintings belonging to Don Luis Méndez de Haro (1598–1661), father of Gaspar. The 1661 inventory itself, known only from a copy made of it in about 1802, does not list the Ribalta 'Raimon Lull', see Burke, 1984, II, cited in cat.10, footnote 6, pp.196–7 and 205.

[4] *L'Època dels Genís. Renaixement i Barroc*, Museu d'Historia de la Ciutat, Barcelona, 1989. For the picture's attributional history see the long entry by Joan Sureda, no.19, pp.160–8, and the entry by María Margarita Cuyás in *Du maniérisme au baroque; art d'élite et art populaire*, Chambéry, 1995, n.p.

[5] See Professor José Milicua's comments in Pérez Sánchez and Spinosa, 1991, pp.11–12.

[6] For the iconography of Ramon Lull, see Barcelona, 1989, no.19, pp.160–8, cited in footnote 4.

[7] For the 1688 inventory, see Burke, 1984, vol.II, pp.251–71, cited in cat.10, footnote 6. No painting of Ramon Lull and no works by Ribalta appear in this inventory. Juan Ribalta seems to have contributed to a series of portraits of famous Valencians formed by Diego de Vich: see D. M. Kowal, *Ribalta y los Ribaltescos*, Valencia, 1985, pp.289–97. These are portrait busts and several have identifying inscriptions. The portraits accepted as by Juan Ribalta are clearly by a different hand from the Ramon Lull.

14

JUAN ESTEBAN ACTIVE 1597–AFTER 1611

A MARKET STALL

Oil on canvas · 129 × 167.5cm
Signed and dated along edge of table: *Joannes Stephanus faciebat ubete. 1606*
Museo de Bellas Artes, Granada

Acquired by the Museum from a private collection in Úbeda, the painting's early history is unknown.

The painter was from Úbeda (Andalusia) but is first recorded in Madrid in 1597 collaborating with other artists on an altarpiece.[1] Later, he was active in Úbeda in 1611 and in neighbouring Baeza in 1606 as a religious artist.[2] The present painting is the only known *bodegón* by Esteban and seems to derive from Netherlandish and, or, Lombard examples of similar subjects. It has the distinction of being the earliest extant *bodegón* by a Spanish painter.

[1] C. Pérez Pastor, 'Noticias y documentos relativos a la historia y literatura española', *Memorias de la Real Academia Española*, Madrid, vol.XI, 1914, p.73, no.356.

[2] Ponz, 1947, pp.1410, 1419.

❧ 15 ❧

SPANISH SCHOOL, EARLY SEVENTEENTH-CENTURY
STILL LIFE WITH FISH

Oil on canvas · 66 × 84cm
Teresa Heinz Collection

Traditionally said to have been purchased in Seville in 1845 by William Stirling, later Sir William Stirling-Maxwell, Bt. (1818–1878), pioneer British collector of Spanish art, the picture was recorded in his *Annals of the Artists of Spain*, 1848, vol.III, p.1410, as by Velázquez.

The painting was described as 'School of Seville, early seventeenth-century' in the exhibitions *Seventeenth-Century Art in Europe* (Royal Academy, 1938, no.214), and *El Greco to Goya* (National Gallery, London, 1981, no.55). Recently the attribution to the School of Seville has been questioned and the painting has been ascribed to the Toledan artist Alejandro de Loarte (*c.*1600–26) or a follower.[1] According to Jordan and Cherry, the painting is by an unknown artist working in Toledo or Madrid in the first third of the seventeenth century. They rightly point to the influence of the Toledan painter Juan Sánchez Cotán.[2] The stone niche setting, the isolated components strongly lit against the dark background, some hanging, others placed on the ledge, are all derived from the Toledan master.

[1] Cherry, 1991, vol.II, p.300, note 26, and pl.26.

[2] Jordan and Cherry, 1995, no.4.

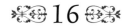

DIEGO VELÁZQUEZ

AN OLD WOMAN COOKING EGGS

Oil on canvas · 100.5 × 119.5cm · Fragmentary date at lower right: *16[1]8*

National Gallery of Scotland, Edinburgh

Purchased with the aid of the National Art Collections Fund, 1955

Joyce Plesters has pointed out that X-rays show that this picture was painted on a canvas of relatively open weave, and has suggested that it was cut from the same roll as other early paintings by Velázquez, including the *Kitchen Scene with Christ in the House of Martha and Mary* [cat 21], *The Waterseller* [cat 31], *The Immaculate Conception* [cat 33] and *St John the Evangelist on Patmos* [cat 34].[1]

It is probably identical with a painting recorded in the 1690 inventory of the collection of Nicolás Omazur, a Flemish merchant and patron of Murillo, and described in detail in that of 1698 (no.126): 'An old woman frying a couple of eggs, and a boy with a melon in his hand'. (*Una vieja friendo un par de huebos, y un muchacho con un melon en la mano*)[2]. It was recorded in England in the John Woollett sale (Christie's 8 May, 1813, no.45: as 'A woman poaching eggs and a servant boy with a melon and a bottle of wine. Various utensils in foreground'). Originally catalogued as Murillo, this is corrected in ink to 'Velasquez – 1st Manner' and there is a further annotation 'from Spain'. Presumably to correspond with an attribution that was then less esteemed, the reserve of £300 was reduced and it went to Samuel Peach for 36 guineas! (letter from Francis Russell). Later it was in the collections of J. C. Robinson and Francis Cook and his descendants, from whom it was acquired by the Gallery in 1955.

This and the *Kitchen Scene with Christ in the House of Martha and Mary* [cat 21] are the earliest dated paintings by Velázquez. In these works, known as *bodegones,* the format is generally horizontal and the scene is set in a kitchen or tavern (thus the name *bodegón*). The figures are humble, placed around or beside a table in the foreground, and are shown half-length and under life-size.

The models for the two figures and nearly all the still-life objects reappear in Velázquez's other paintings of the period. The old woman, with more wrinkles, is seen in the *Kitchen Scene with Christ in the House of Martha and Mary* [cat 21]; the young boy would appear to be the same as that in *The Waterseller* [cat 31], and is perhaps the youth who is described by Pacheco as posing for Velázquez. The glass flask held by the boy resembles that in the *Tavern Scene with Two Men and a Boy* [cat 26]. The mortar and pestle together with the green-glazed jug are among the kitchen utensils in *Christ in the House of Martha and Mary* [cat 21]. The mortar and pestle, now separate, and a similar green-glazed jug are also in the scene of the *Two Young Men at a Table* [cat 24]. The decorated, white-glazed jug and the basket hanging on the wall are similar to those in the *Kitchen Maid with the Supper at Emmaus* [cat 22].

The subject of this painting has been compared with a scene in a novel by Mateo Alemán, where a woman cooks eggs for a young boy; but the roguish element in this and other picaresque novels, to which Velázquez's *bodegones* have sometimes been related, is nowhere evident in this work.

A replica of uncertain date was in a collection in Paris in 1878, attributed to Velázquez, and known only from a photograph.

[1] MacLaren and Braham, 1970, p.124, n.1.

[2] D. Kinkead, 'The Picture Collection of D. Nicolás Omazur', *The Burlington Magazine*, 128, 1986, pp.132–144.

REFERENCES

López-Rey, 1963, no.108; 1979, no.6.

Brigstocke, 1993, pp.191–3.

JACOB MATHAM 1571–1631

FOUR ENGRAVINGS AFTER PAINTINGS BY PIETER AERTSEN

The highly innovative secular works of the Netherlandish painter Pieter Aertsen (1508/9–1575), who worked in Amsterdam and Antwerp, and of his pupil Joachim Beuckelaer (c.1533–1573/4), have long been recognised as important compositional models for Velázquez's *bodegones*.[1] Specifically, the type of double composition which Aertsen invented in the early 1550s, consisting of a prominent foreground market or kitchen scene with a small-scale biblical episode represented in the background, provides a direct precedent for two surviving works by the young Sevillian, the *Kitchen Scene with Christ in the House of Martha and Mary* [cat 21] and the *Kitchen Maid with the Supper at Emmaus* [cat 22].

Paintings by Aertsen and his followers are recorded in Seville in Velázquez's day. A fish piece by Aertsen, for example, is listed in the 1637 posthumous inventory of the 3rd Duke of Alcalá, one of the most powerful noblemen in the city (who had probably acquired it considerably earlier). Another, a kitchen scene by an unidentified imitator of Aertsen, was inserted shortly after 1600 into a ceiling in the Archbishop's Palace, where it remains today [fig 4.13].[2] (For the decoration of which this latter picture formed part see Juan Miguel Serrera's essay, pp.37–43). However, Velázquez's most direct access to Aertsen's compositions would have been through the reproductive engravings by Matham exhibited here, impressions of which he may have owned, or could have studied in the studio of his master Pacheco. To judge from the numerous examples of borrowings and adaptations from Northern engravings in Sevillian painting of the seventeenth century, the trade in such prints must have been brisk, although it is not well documented.[3] Reproductive prints were evidently imported in large numbers by Flemish merchants resident in the city, and distributed primarily through booksellers.

Three of the exhibited prints [cats 18, 19 and 20], one of them dated 1603, belong to a series of four thematically related scenes which, notwithstanding the religious episode present in each, may have been intended as a cryptic representation of the four elements. No such painted series by Aertsen is known, but a comparable series by Beuckelaer came to light recently and is now in the Museum voor Schone Kunsten in Ghent.[4] The three foreground figures and the foodstuffs in the *Vegetable Stall with the Rest on the Flight into Egypt* [cat 20] correspond closely, in reverse, to a picture by Aertsen in the Nationalmuseum in Stockholm.[5] In the background of the latter, however, is an architectural view with 'Christ and the Woman Taken in Adultery'. The Stockholm picture may nevertheless have served as the principal model for Matham's engraving, for the landscape, rustic buildings and figures substituted in the background of the print are so reminiscent of the style of the Utrecht artist Abraham Bloemart (comparable works by whom Matham was engraving at just this time), that they are likely to have been designed by him, or poached from him by Matham. The *Market Scene with the Parable of the Labourers in the Vineyard* [cat 17], issued as an independent print and distinguished from the others by its calligraphic Latin inscription, also reproduces faithfully a painting by Aertsen in Frankfurt, but again a portrayal of Christ and the Adultress was suppressed.[6] In this case, however, the stylistic discrepancy between the two sections of the print is not obtrusive. It is a testament to the enduring fascination of Aertsen's compositions that Matham

should have deemed it commercially viable to publish these reproductive engravings – the first after Aertsen's kitchen and market scenes to be issued – several decades after the pictures which they record were painted.

In adapting the Netherlandish example, Velázquez opted for far greater simplicity. He reduced the almost obscene profusion of foodstuffs to a few simple ingredients and utensils of the kind that could be found in any Sevillian kitchen, their varied textures masterfully captured and differentiated. The spatial continuum created by the inclusion of the middle ground in the prints is eliminated and the scene subjected to a simple but fairly rigorous compositional geometry. This is especially apparent in the *Kitchen Scene with Christ in the House of Martha and Mary*, where Christ's seated figure is framed – and given prominence – by an additional doorway leading to a dark room beyond.

Velázquez's reductive approach to the Aertsen prototype brings into focus the most intractable problem presented by such double compositions, namely the question of how contemporaries might have interpreted the relationship between their secular and religious components. In the case of Aertsen's pictures, a bewildering range of theories has been advanced to explain this curious juxtaposition, involving as it does an inversion of the nominal importance of the two elements: for example, that they are essentially moralising, didactic images contrasting the spirituality and simplicity of Christ's example with the materialism of a foreground scene loaded with symbolism and sexual innuendo; or that they were a compromise response to the Calvinist censure of religious images; or that the biblical narrative was included to justify what would otherwise have been viewed as trivial and unworthy subject-matter; and so on.[7]

Fortunately, in borrowing a compositional device Velázquez seems to have taken a characteristically independent approach *vis-à-vis* content. Although the precise meaning of his 'religious *bodegones*' remains elusive, there is an implicit harmony rather than contrast between their secular and religious elements. His pensive kitchen maids seem to betray an awareness, however elliptic, of the event illustrated in the subsidiary scene, to offer a contemporary, domestic gloss, as it were, on the biblical lesson. The relationship is an extremely subtle one, and that the biblical narrative was not necessarily indispensable to an appreciation of such pictures is suggested by the existence, on the one hand, of a possibly autograph replica of the *Kitchen Maid with the Supper at Emmaus* which omits the biblical scene [cat 23] and, on the other, of *bodegones* [eg. cat 24] closely related in theme and mood, but which have no religious component.

Although Velázquez appears to have abandoned the painting of *bodegones* completely when he moved to the Court in Madrid in 1623, he never forgot the organisational principle he had first learnt from Aertsen's works. Indeed, he applied it in modified and much more sophisticated form in his two most celebrated late works, both now in the Prado: *Las Hilanderas*, where the ostensible subject, the *Fable of Arachne*, is relegated to a back room and dominated by a genre scene of women preparing and spinning wool; and *Las Meninas*, in which the most important protagonists – Philip IV and his Queen Mariana of Austria – appear only as a framed reflection in a distant mirror.[8]

17: MARKET SCENE WITH THE PARABLE OF THE LABOURERS IN THE VINEYARD

Engraving (Hollstein, XI, 319; Bartsch, III, 164)
23.5 × 34cm · Inscribed at upper centre: *Lange Pier Pinx.*
Maetham Sculp. et excud.; with a legend in lower margin [9]

Trustees of The British Museum, London

18: KITCHEN SCENE WITH THE SUPPER AT EMMAUS

Engraving (Hollstein, XI, 320; Bartsch, III, 165)
24.5 × 32.7cm · Inscribed in the lower margin: *Cum privil. Sa. Ca. M. IESUS*
in fractione panis agnoscitur. Jacobus Maetham fecit.

Trustees of The British Museum, London

19: KITCHEN SCENE WITH THE PARABLE OF DIVES AND LAZARUS

Engraving (Hollstein, XI, 321; Bartsch, III, 166)
23.2 × 32.9cm · Inscribed in the lower margin: *Cum privil. Sa. Ca. M.*
Maetham fecit et excud.

Trustees of The British Museum, London

20: VEGETABLE STALL WITH THE REST ON THE FLIGHT INTO EGYPT

Engraving (Hollstein, XI, 322; Bartsch, III, 167)
23.7 × 34cm · Inscribed in the lower margin: *Cum privil. Sa. Ca. M.*
Langepier pinxit I. Maetham Sculp. et excud. 1603. [10]

National Gallery of Scotland, Edinburgh

---

[1] For Aertsen see K. Moxey, *Pieter Aertsen, Joachim Beuckelaer, and the Rise of Secular Painting in the Context of the Reformation*, New York and London, 1977; *Art before the Iconoclasm: Northern Netherlandish Art 1525–1580*, Amsterdam, 1986, vol.I, pp.119–24; *Nederlands Kunsthistorisch Jaarboek*, vol.40, 1989 (volume devoted to Aertsen).

[2] For these works see Jordan and Cherry, 1995, pp.16, 19, 37.

[3] On the use of Northern prints by Sevillian painters, see most recently B. Navarrete Prieto, 'Otras fuentes grabadas utilizadas por Francisco de Zurbarán', in *Archivo Español de Arte*, 67, no.268, pp.359–76 (with further references at notes 1 and 3); *idem*, 'Génesis y descendencia de *Las doce tribus de Israel* y otras series Zurbaranescas', in *Zurbarán: Las doce tribus de Israel*, Madrid 1995, pp.45–99.

[4] See *Joachim Beuckelaer: Het markt- en keukenstuk in de Nederlanden 1550–1650*, Museum voor Schone Kunsten, Ghent, 1986–87, cat. nos.8–11. The above-mentioned *Kitchen Scene* in the Archbishop's Palace in Seville represents 'Earth' in a series of the Four Elements.

[5] See Moxey, cited in note 1, fig.10.

[6] See Moxey, cited in note 1, fig.9.

[7] For a survey of these various interpretations, see K. Moxey, in *Nederlands Kunsthistorisch Jaarboek*, cited in note 1, pp.29–39.

[8] Harris, 1982, pp.159–62.

[9] *Non nisi per duros iter est super astra labores, | Et nisi certanti nulla corona datur. | Omnibus in medio posita est victoria: quisque | Hoc agat, ut palma pramia summa serat. | Hinc est, ad vites cur nos Pater ille colendas | Usque vocet, resides nec velit esse manus. | Molliet inde brevem merces. aterna laborem. | Hac si delectet, nec minus ille iuvet.* (with the anonymous author's monogram SHS).[There is no way to the heavens above but by hard work, | And no crown is given without striving. | Victory is within the grasp of everyone; and whosoever | Follows this path will merit the supreme victor's palm. | Thus it is that Our Father bids us cultivate the vine | Nor need there be strength in our hand. | Eternity will softly repay this brief exertion. | If this path is chosen you will surely benefit.]

[10] Lange Pier ('Lanky Peter') was Aertsen's nickname; he was known in Italy as Pietro Lungo and in Spain as Pedro Longo. The privilege referred to in the inscription of this and the preceding two prints was granted to Matham in 1601 by the Holy Roman Emperor Rudolf II; its absence from cat.17 above would suggest that this print predates 1601, although probably not by very long.

DIEGO VELÁZQUEZ

KITCHEN SCENE WITH CHRIST IN THE HOUSE OF MARTHA AND MARY

Oil on canvas · 60 × 103.5cm · Fragmentary date: 1618
Trustees of the National Gallery, London

The small scene in the background illustrates the episode described in *Luke* X, 38–42:

> Now it came to pass, as they went, that he entered into a certain village: and a certain woman named Martha received them into her house.
> And she had a sister called Mary, which also sat at Jesus' feet, and heard his word.
> But Martha was cumbered about much serving, and came to him, and said, Lord, dost thou not care that my sister hath left me to serve alone? Bid her therefore that she help me.
> And Jesus answered and said unto her: Martha, Martha, thou art careful and troubled about many things:
> But one thing is needful: and Mary hath chosen that good part which shall not be taken away from her.

Here and in the *Kitchen Maid with the Supper at Emmaus* [cat 22], the religious subject is represented on a smaller scale than the foreground scene. In the present painting their relationship has been much disputed. Is the religious scene a picture on the wall, a reflection in a mirror of a scene at which the two women are looking, or a view through a hatch? Since the viewpoint is to the left of the table, clearly indicated by the angle and visible edge of the table, the scene of Christ with Martha and Mary must be seen from the left. From that angle it would be optically impossible to see the recessed left side of a hatch in the wall. Therefore what is visible must be the side of a frame of the hatch. Reflected light along its left edge, as seen in old photographs, confirms this.[1] It is not a frame of a mirror, since the reflection is not sharply defined and the direction and intensity of light are different from the foreground scene. Furthermore, a mirror would seem inappropriate on a kitchen wall. It is unlikely to be the frame of a painting since it abuts on to the top and sides of the picture. As such it would not be read as an independent picture on the wall, as it is in *The Musical Trio* illustrated on p.140. It is

undoubtedly the frame of a hatch as in Dieric Bouts's *Last Supper* (St Peter's, Louvain), Pacheco's *St Sebastian Attended by St Irene* (destroyed 1936) and Velázquez's later *Kitchen Maid with the Supper at Emmaus*.

The special combination of kitchen or tavern and religious scene is derived from northern examples, notably those of Pieter Aertsen and Joachim Beuckelaer [cats 17–20] that were disseminated in 'modern', that is, early seventeenth-century engravings. This tradition supports the interpretation of Velázquez's religious scene taking place in an adjoining room. The composition may also owe something to the tradition of Venetian portraiture, as exemplified in El Greco's portrait of *Giulio Clovio* (Museo di Capodimonte, Naples).

To a greater degree than his predecessors, Velázquez compels the viewer to read the picture on more than a literal level. By means of the gestures and expressions of the kitchen maid and her companion, he gives it a moralising meaning. The subject of Martha and Mary traditionally signified the active and contemplative lifes. In this painting, the old woman could be seen as giving the message of Christ to the modern Martha, who is preparing, significantly, a meal of abstinence. In this kitchen scene as in the *Kitchen Maid with the Supper at Emmaus* there my also be an allusion to the idea of Christ among the lowly. In this connection, the words of St Teresa of Avila are relevant: 'The Lord walks even among the kitchen pots, helping you in matters spiritual and material.'[2]

[1] We are grateful to Philip Troutman for convincingly demonstrating this point.

[2] M. Soria, 'An unknown early painting by Velázquez' *The Burlington Magazine,* 91, 1949, pp.125–8.

REFERENCES

López-Rey, 1963, no.8.

MacLaren and Braham, 1970, pp.121–5.

❊❦ 22 ❦❊

DIEGO VELÁZQUEZ

KITCHEN MAID WITH THE SUPPER AT EMMAUS

Oil on canvas · 55 × 118cm
National Gallery of Ireland, Dublin

The canvas has been cut on both sides. At the left, only the hand and forearm of the disciple are visible. The paint layer is thin all over, which may explain the lack of definition of the angle of the walls behind the maid.

The early history of the painting is not known. According to a label on the back it was, at some time, in the collection of the Reverend Swiney. Reportedly it was in the possession of Sir Hugh Lane, *c.*1909. By 1913 it was in the collection of Sir Otto Beit, London. Inherited by his son, Sir Alfred Beit, who moved to Ireland in 1953, it was presented by Sir Alfred and Lady Beit to the Gallery in 1987. The painting was first exhibited and recorded as by Velázquez when it was exhibited at the Grafton Galleries, 1913–14 (no. 41).

The composition is similar in character to that of the *Kitchen Scene with Christ in the House of Martha and Mary* [cat 21] with the religious subject seen through a hatch in the background. This had been painted over at some time and was only revealed after cleaning in 1933.

The basket hanging on the wall and the jug on the table are like those in *An Old Woman Cooking Eggs* [cat 16]. The pile of plates upside down is repeated in the *Two Young Men at a Table* [cat 24].

The absorbed air and half-lit face of the mulatto kitchen maid suggest an inner experience, a dawning realisation of the significance of the miracle taking place behind her:

And it came to pass, as he sat at meat with them, he took bread, and blessed it, and brake, and gave to them.
And their eyes were opened, and they knew him: and he vanished out of their sight (Luke XXIV, 30–31)

In this kitchen scene, as in *Christ in the House of Martha and Mary*, there may also be an allusion to the idea of the presence of Christ among the lowly. In this context it is surely significant that the kitchen maid is of negroid origin and probably one of the many slaves in Seville. Salvation is possible, therefore, for all those who love Christ, irrespective of their social status or ethnic origin. Representations of the Supper at Emmaus were one of the subjects considered as suitable decorations in guest rooms of convents and monasteries.[1]

[1] W. Friedlaender, *Caravaggio Studies*, Princeton, 1955, p.164.

REFERENCES

López-Rey, 1963, no.18; 1979, no.17.
Mulcahy, 1988, pp.79–82.

❧ 23 ❧

DIEGO VELÁZQUEZ

THE KITCHEN MAID

Oil on canvas · 55 × 104cm

The Art Institute of Chicago
Robert Waller Memorial Fund, 1935.380

The painting is in a poor state of preservation having suffered extensive cleaning and lining damage. Its early history is unrecorded. It was first noted in a private collection in Zurich and first published by Mayer in 1927, when it was with Goudstikker in Amsterdam.[1] It was acquired by the Art Institute in the mid-1930s.

This painting appears to be a replica of that in Dublin [cat 22] with slight variations and without the religious scene in the background. Its replica status is supported by the facial expression of the kitchen maid which is meaningful in a religious context but anomalous in this genre scene. This leaves unanswered the question whether this is an autograph or studio production. The elimination of the religious scene, the reduction of the canvas at the left and the simplification of the patterns of light and dark give formal coherence to the composition and prominence to the kitchen maid. Seen from a slightly closer viewpoint and complemented by the round forms of the pot, pan, jug and plates, her physical presence now dominates the scene. In spite of its poor condition this *bodegón* would seem to be worthy of the hand of the young master.

[1] A. L. Mayer, *Velázquez*, 1936, no.105.

REFERENCE

López-Rey, 1963, no.99; 1979, no.18.

24

DIEGO VELÁZQUEZ

TWO YOUNG MEN AT A TABLE

Oil on canvas · 65.3 × 104cm

Trustees of the Victoria and Albert Museum, London

Wellington Museum, Apsley House

The painting is first recorded in 1768 when it was purchased by the Spanish King Charles III from the collection of the Marqués de la Enseñada and valued by Mengs at 1,000 *reales*. This and *The Waterseller* [cat 31] were among the baggage of Joseph Bonaparte captured by the Duke of Wellington on the battlefield of Vitoria in 1813. It is almost certainly one of the *bodegones* described by Antonio Palomino (1724), somewhat inaccurately: 'Velázquez made another painting of two poor men eating at a small and humble table, on which are some earthenware vessels, oranges, bread, and other things, all observed with extraordinary meticulousness'[1] Palomino does not say where he saw it.

The pile of plates is similar to that in the *Kitchen Maid with the Supper at Emmaus* [cat 22]; the up-turned mortar appears in *An Old Woman Cooking Eggs* [cat 16] and in the *Kitchen Scene with Christ in the House of Martha and Mary* [cat 21]. The attitudes of the two men and the setting are reminiscent of representations of Jacob and Esau, for instance by Jacopo Bassano.

[1] Palomino, 1947, p.893; Harris, 1982, p.197, (for translation).

REFERENCES

López-Rey, 1963, no.105; 1979, no.24. Two copies are known (López-Rey, 1963, nos.106–7).

Kauffmann, 1982, pp.139–40.

25

AFTER DIEGO VELÁZQUEZ
THE MUSICAL TRIO

Oil on canvas · 87.6 × 117cm

Art Hispania, s.a. (Carlos Ferrer), Barcelona

One of four versions of the painting in Berlin (López-Rey, 1963, no.109,), which is considered by most critics to be the autograph original, despite darkening and apparent restoration. None of the paintings has a known early history. The Berlin original, first recorded in Ireland, was published in 1906, when it was acquired by the Berlin Museum. The earliest recorded version is the painting exhibited at the Grafton Galleries, London, 1913–14, no.39, where it was said to have been mentioned in the catalogue of Mr John Skippe's collection, 1793, 'purchased in London' (López-Rey no.111). This *Musical Trio* was sold at Sotheby's, 19 October 1966, no.19. Its present whereabouts is unknown. The version formerly with Wildenstein & Co., Paris (López-Rey no.112) was said to have been acquired at the Bamberger sale, Paris, 17 March, 1923 (no.83). Though it is said to have been in the Salamanca collection this provenance is now disproved. Its present whereabouts is not known. The only version with a Sevillian provenance – the collection of José Cañaveral (early nineteenth century) – was later in Geneva and Zurich (1936) and is now in a private collection, Barcelona (López-Rey no.110).

The provenance of the painting in this exhibition has hitherto been incorrectly described. It is first recorded in Paris in 1952 in the collection of Tenaud de Leygonie (National Gallery, London, Archive). It was later in the Marcos collection from which it was acquired by the present owner (Christie's, New York, 11 January 1991, no.81). López-Rey's identification of this painting with his no.112, pl.179 is wrong as there is no picture on the wall, whereas there is in the painting he illustrates. The painting in the Tenaud de Leygonie collection was first published by J. Gudiol.[1] He then considered it to be an earlier autograph version of the Berlin painting, but made no mention of it in his monograph on Velázquez published in 1973. Although its history prior to 1952 is not known, it is this picture (and not López-Rey's no.112) that can be identified by the seal on the stretcher with the item catalogued in the Salamanca Sale, Paris, 1875 (no.34) under the name of Velázquez: *Aveugles jouant du violon et de la guitare. Première manière du maître. Galerie de Don Celestino.* Canvas, 88 × 118cm. Santiago Alcolea has pointed out that Don Celestino is probably Don Celestino García de Luz, the source of two other items in the sale (nos.45, 48). No other mention of him has come to light.

The composition of the present painting corresponds fairly closely to that of all the other versions. The main difference between this and the Berlin painting and two of the other versions (López-Rey nos.110, 112, pls. 178, 179) is the absence of a picture on the wall or a landscape seen through an aperture. In addition, there are chromatic and tonal differences. Most striking is the much lighter costume of the central figure and the table covering. In another version, also without picture or aperture (López-Rey no.111), the central figure is also light in tone, the colour of his costume light green (see the catalogue of the Grafton Galleries exhibition mentioned above). In this connection, the light underpaint revealed in radiographs of the Berlin painting does not necessarily imply, as has been suggested, that

these details were originally lighter in the finished picture. Their darkening could be due to either chemical change or repainting by the artist or restorer. Nevertheless, that they were originally lighter is supported by the present painting and the version just mentioned. Only scientific investigation can settle the problem.

For the relationship between the head of the central figure and that revealed in a radiograph of the *Head of a Young Man* in the Hermitage, [see cat 27]

The subject of *The Musical Trio* is rare, if not unique, in Seville, even in Spain, in Velázquez's time. Elsewhere in Europe paintings of musicians and musical gatherings gained in popularity in the wake of the 'Caravaggesque Movement'.[2] The components of Velázquez's composition – the tavern setting, the humble musicians, the table set with a simple repast – are in the Caravaggesque tradition. But the general effect is less artificial and theatrical than in most other examples of the genre. These components, the placing of the three figures at a table, and the naturalistic treatment, also relate *The Musical Trio* to Velázquez's other *bodegones*, in particular to the tavern scenes. Yet, though the types of the sitters are similar, the musicians do not seem to appear elsewhere in his early oeuvre.

The presence of the monkey with its various connotations – Taste, Lust, Folly, etc – has raised the question whether this is more than a genre scene.[3] Yet the evidence, pictorial and literary, is too limited for it to be seen as other than a group of strolling musicians with their traditional companion, the monkey. The claim in the Salamanca sale catalogue that the musicians are blind is clearly inaccurate, though from the expression on the face of the central figure, he might well be sightless.

[1] *Varia Velazqueña*, 1960, vol.I, p.415; vol.II, pls.5b, 6b.

[2] B. Nicolson, *The International Caravaggesque Movement*, Oxford, 1979, pp.217–18.

[3] H. W. Janson, *Apes and Ape Lore in the Middle Ages and the Renaissance*, London, 1952, p.255, n.14.

Velázquez *The Musical Trio* (Staatliche Museen, Gemäldegalerie, Berlin)

❧ 26 ❧

DIEGO VELÁZQUEZ
TAVERN SCENE WITH TWO MEN AND A BOY

Oil on canvas · 108.5 × 102cm
Hermitage Museum, St Petersburg

This picture was first recorded in the Hermitage in 1773 as by an unknown Flemish painter. The identification of the artist as Velázquez was made by W. Bode in 1895.

A tavern with people eating and drinking was the type of subject to which the *bodegón* gave its name. The combination of humble setting and lowly protagonists was a commonplace in the picaresque novel. But whether the facial expressions and gestures of the men in the picture signify the *pícaro's* roguish intent or merely convivial mood is not clear.

It was no doubt the striking realism of Velázquez's portrayal of this relatively novel subject that gave rise to many copies and variants, especially in Seville. The only one of these that has any claim to autograph status is the painting in Budapest [cat 28]. In some copies of the present picture the head of the figure on the right has been replaced by that in the Budapest variant [see cat 29]. The boy in the centre bears some resemblance to the boy in *An Old Woman Cooking Eggs* [cat 16] and *The Waterseller* [cat 31]. He may also have been the model for the boy in the *bodegón* by Francisco López Caro [fig 8.1]. The old man is repeated in the *Tavern Scene* [cat 29] and recalls *The Waterseller* and one of the Kings in *The Adoration of the Magi* [cat 36].

REFERENCES

C. Pemán, 'Acerca de los llamados "Almuerzos" Velazqueños', *Archivo Español de Arte*, 34, 1961, pp.303–11.

López-Rey, 1963, no.113, 1979, no.3.

V. Kemenov, *Velázquez in Soviet Museums*, Leningrad, 1977, p.29 ff.

Tesoros del Ermitage, Madrid, 1981, pp.26–8.

L. Kaganė, *Spain in The Hermitage, Leningrad. Western European Painting of the 13th to 18th centuries*, Leningrad, 1989, pp.378–9.

27

DIEGO VELÁZQUEZ [?]

HEAD OF A YOUNG MAN IN PROFILE

Oil on canvas · 39.5 × 35.5cm
Hermitage Museum, St Petersburg

Purchased in 1814 with other Spanish paintings for Czar Alexander I from the gallery of W. G. Coeswelt, an English banker in Amsterdam, as by Velázquez. Catalogued in the Hermitage in 1863 as by Zurbarán but restored to Velázquez in the 1912 catalogue, an attribution accepted by Allende Salazar (1925) and Mayer (1936). In the 1958 catalogue it was given to an unknown seventeenth-century Spanish painter but reinstated as a Velázquez by López-Rey in the following year. The attribution has been disputed by Haraszti-Takácz (1966) and Brown (1986).

López-Rey considered this to be a sketch for the young man in the Budapest *Tavern Scene* [cat 28]. However, technical examination has shown that the canvas has been cut on the left and at the bottom. X-ray examination has revealed that the picture was painted over the head of a man seen at right angles, illustrated below. This head must have been part of a larger composition and one of a different format. It resembles (in the opposite direction) that of the central figure in *The Musical Trio* [see cat 25]. The visible head is related to that of the young man in the Budapest picture and even more closely to the head in some of the later variants.

The hard outlines, sharp tonal contrasts and the weak modelling of the head raise once again the question as to whether or not the fragment is autograph.

REFERENCES

López-Rey, 1963, no.121; 1979, no.8.

V. Kemenov, *Velázquez in Soviet Museums,* Leningrad, 1977, pp.49–51.

L. Kagané, *The Golden Age of Spanish Art*, Wäino Aaltonen Museum of Art, Finland, 1994, pp.73–75.

X-radiograph of Velázquez *Head of a Young Man in Profile* turned through 90° (Hermitage Museum, St Petersburg)

4145

28

DIEGO VELÁZQUEZ AND ASSISTANT
TAVERN SCENE WITH TWO MEN AND A GIRL

Oil on canvas · 96 × 112cm

Szépmüvészeti Múzeum, Budapest

Harászti-Takács has suggested that this was the painting recorded in the collection of Pedro Alonso O'Crouley in Cadiz in 1795: *Un lienzo apaisado con una serrana y dos zagales. Es una de sus mejores obras* ('A horizontal canvas with a country girl and two shepherds. It is one of his best works').[1] By 1897 the painting was in Scotland in the Edinburgh collection of Arthur Sanderson[2] and in 1908 it was acquired by the Budapest Museum.

The painting is essentially a variant of that in the Hermitage [cat 26], but horizontal in format and without the trappings on the wall. The old man is in most respects a repetition. The young woman who pours wine from an earthenware jug into a glass has replaced the grinning boy; she wears a white cap similar to that worn by the servant girl in the *Kitchen Scene with Christ in the House of Martha and Mary* [cat 21]. The young man on the right is in the same pose and dress but his head is shown in profile and may be based on a different model. It is interesting to note that this same figure appears in several variants of the Hermitage composition [cat 29] and in the fragment [cat 27]. The motif of the white table cloth here and in the Hermitage picture appears inappropriate for a tavern table. Even more inappropriate is the silver gilt standing salt, more fitting to the table of an aristocrat as in J. B. de Espinosa's *Still Life*.[3]

Attempts to give symbolic meaning to the objects on the table have not been convincing. Velázquez's authorship of the painting has been questioned by some critics, such as Mayer (1936), Pemán (1961) and Brown (1986). Recent cleaning has revealed inconsistencies in the handling, suggesting that the painting is only partially autograph. The modelling of the head, hands and clothing of the figure on the left, in particular, the modelling of the woman's hands and the awkward way in which she holds the jug are weaknesses that point to studio participation. On the other hand, the free and subtle modelling of the woman's head, the firm, assured painting of the young man and the sensitive rendering of the strictly ordered still life are characteristic and worthy of the young master. This appears to be the only example of Velázquez's collaboration with an assistant in his work in Seville. There is only one known repetition of the composition, a pastiche (López-Rey, 1963, no.122)

[1] Haraszti-Takács, 1983, pp.220–1, no.209. *Catalogue of the O'Crouley Collection*, Madrid, 1795, p.567.

[2] C. Monkhouse, 'A Northern Home', *The Art Journal*, 1897, p.272. J. L. Williams, *Dutch Art and Scotland*, National Gallery of Scotland, Edinburgh, 1992, p.170.

[3] See Jordan and Cherry, 1995, pl.9. For a similar piece, see A. M. Johnson, *Gold and Silver Work; The Hispanic Society of America Handbook*, New York, 1938, pp.199–200.

REFERENCE

López-Rey, 1963, no.120; 1979, no.9.

29

AFTER DIEGO VELÁZQUEZ

TAVERN SCENE WITH TWO MEN AND A BOY AT A TABLE

Oil on canvas · 86.4 × 109.2cm

Private Collection

First recorded in the La Touche collection, Bellevue, County Wicklow, Ireland, where it was paired with *The Musical Trio* now in Berlin, illustrated on p.138, this was in the La Touche Sale, May 1906, and subsequently in the collection of Lord Iveagh, London. It was later acquired by Lord Moyne.

The composition is derived from two autograph paintings by Velázquez in St Petersburg and Budapest [cats 26 and 28]. The format and measurements are similar to the latter. The figures of the old man and the boy are copied from the Hermitage painting, the young man from the painting in Budapest. Most of the still-life objects come from one or other original. This combination of figures with the same still life occurs in four other paintings.[1] The number of repetitions suggests that they may be based on a lost original by Velázquez.

[1] López-Rey, 1963, nos.114, 115, 116, 118.

REFERENCE

López-Rey, 1963, no.117.

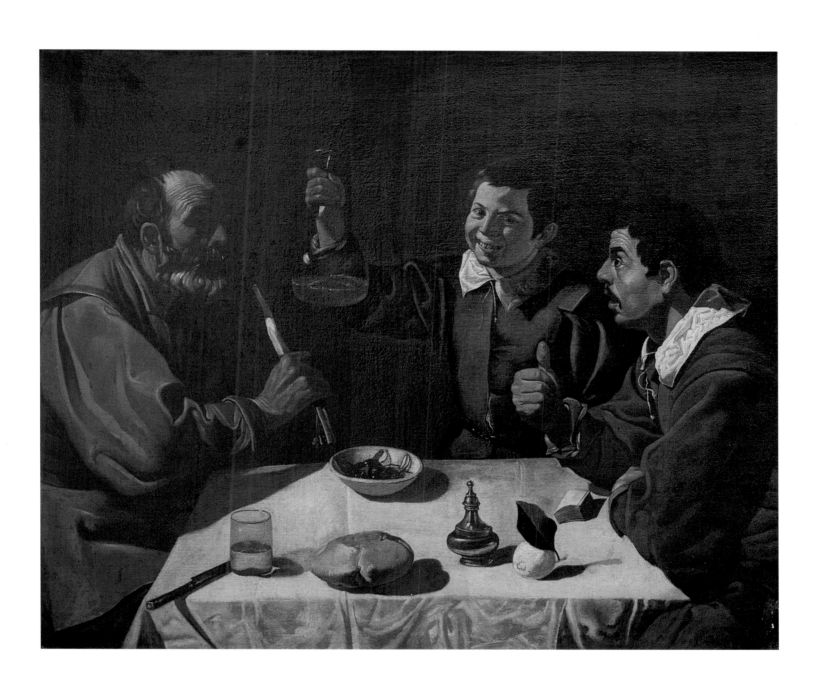

❦ 30 ❦

FOLLOWER OF DIEGO VELÁZQUEZ
TAVERN SCENE WITH FOUR MEN AT A TABLE

Oil on canvas · 119 × 142cm
Viscount Windsor

Presumably this is the painting recorded by Ponz in the collection of Sebastián Martínez in Cadiz in the late eighteenth century.[1] Said to have been acquired in Spain 1812–14 by an ancestor of Lord Plymouth, the picture was exhibited at Burlington House (1902, no.169) and the Grafton Galleries, London (1913–14, no.35) as by Velázquez.

The composition of figures around a table recalls Velázquez's early *Tavern Scenes* [cats 26 and 28]. The figure on the left appears in a *Tavern Scene with Two Men and a Woman* also recorded by Ponz in the Martínez collection.[2] The central figures are copied from Velázquez's *Topers* (Prado, Madrid), which means that the painting must date from after *c.*1628. It is this feature that identifies it with the painting described by Ponz.

The unknown painter must have had access to Velázquez's studio or the royal collection.

[1] Ponz, 1947, p.1587, describes in detail three *bodegones* in the Martínez Collection and admires their verisimilitude. For this collection, see M. Pemán, 'La Colección Artística de Don Sebastián Martínez', *Archivo Español de Arte*, 51, 1978, pp.53–62.

[2] Sotheby's, 4 July 1990, no.81, as North Italian first half of seventeenth century (reproduced).

REFERENCE

López-Rey, 1963, no.130.

31

DIEGO VELÁZQUEZ

THE WATERSELLER OF SEVILLE

Oil on canvas · 106.7 × 81cm (including a 4cm strip added at the top).

Trustees of the Victoria and Albert Museum, London

Wellington Museum, Apsley House

This is the only work painted in Seville of which there is a record in Velázquez's lifetime. The artist himself must have been proud of it when he chose to take it to Madrid in 1622 or 1623. He apparently gave it or sold it to his friend and patron, Juan de Fonseca y Figueroa, the King's chaplain, whose portrait he painted. At Fonseca's death in January 1627, Velázquez was appointed to appraise his collection and valued *The Waterseller*, described in the inventory as *Un quadro de un aguador, de mano de Diego Velazquez*, at 400 reales. This was higher than his valuation of any other picture in the collection, reflecting his confidence in his own ability. Velázquez's *Waterseller* was recorded in the inventory of the Buen Retiro Palace (1701) as 'a portrait of a Waterseller by Velázquez called *el corzo* [the Corsican] of Seville'. It is described there by Velázquez's biographer, Antonio Palomino (1724), in fanciful terms: 'an old man very badly dressed in a shabby coat, torn so as to show his chest and stomach with its scabs and thick, hard callouses. Beside him is a boy to whom he is giving a drink. So celebrated was this painting that it has been kept to this day in the Buen Retiro Palace'.[1]

A waterseller was a common sight in Spain until modern times, especially in the south. In picaresque literature he figures as a low-life character, for example in Estebanillo González's, *Vida y hechos*, published in Antwerp in 1646.[2]

There are pentiments at the collar of the waterseller's jacket, his right sleeve and the fingers of both hands. The dark object at the bottom of the glass, long thought to be a fig, is more probably a blue glass bubble.[3] Three painted copies of Velázquez's painting are known, in all of which the waterseller wears a cap. There is also a red chalk drawing by Goya preparatory to an etching (Kunsthalle, Hamburg) but no print is known. *The Waterseller* and the *Two Young Men at a Table* [cat 24] were among the paintings removed from the Royal Palace, Madrid, by Joseph Bonaparte and captured at Vitoria by the Duke of Wellington (1813), to whom they were later presented by the Spanish King Ferdinand VII.

[1] Palomino, 1947, pp.892–3; Harris, 1982, p.197 (for translation).

[2] A. Valbuena Prat, *La novela picaresca española*, Madrid, 1968, p.1756.

[3] E. Ramírez-Montesinos, 'Objetos de vidrio en los bodegones de Velázquez', *Velázquez y el Arte de su tiempo, V. Jornadas de Arte*, Madrid, 1991, pp.397–404.

REFERENCES

López-Rey, 1963, no.124; 1979, no.16.

Kauffman, 1982, pp.140–1.

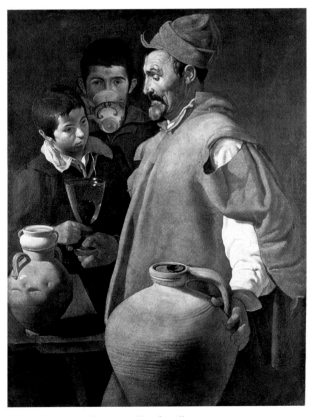

After Velázquez *The Waterseller of Seville*
(Contini-Bonacossi Collection, Pitti Palace, Florence)

❋❋❋ 32 ❋❋❋

JUAN MARTÍNEZ MONTAÑÉS 1568–1649

THE VIRGIN OF THE IMMACULATE CONCEPTION

Polychromed wood · 155cm high

Arzobispado de Sevilla

Parroquia de Nuestra Señora de Consolación, El Pedroso

This is the central figure from the altarpiece in the Chapel of St Catherine (Santa Catalina) in the church at El Pedroso. The altarpiece was commissioned from Montañés in collaboration with Francisco Pacheco in a contract dated 9 May 1606.[1] According to the agreement the sculptor undertook to supply the wood and direct the installation in person, and to finish the architectural framework and decoration of the whole altarpiece within eight months. In fact, the inscription on the base of the retable notes that the work was not completed until 1608, and the last payment was made on 19 April, 1609.[2] Montañés was probably chosen by Bartolomé de Morales, the chaplain of the Chapel and prebendary of Osuna Cathedral (Osuna is about 70 km. east of Seville). Morales had been appointed by Diego Pérez, a cleric resident in the Indies, who had founded the chaplaincy of the Chapel of St Catherine with the request that Morales erect a retable. Gonzalo de Morales, Bartolomé's uncle, paid for the work, which cost 580 ducats. On the altarpiece the figure of the Virgin is flanked by figures in high relief of St James the Great and St Bartholomew respectively, while above was set a figure of St Catherine that already existed, but which was restored by Montañés.

The Virgin stands looking downwards to her right, her hands clasped together, and her right leg bent. She is placed on a crescent moon, with a cherub's head at the centre. Her cloak and robe are decorated by *estofado* designs in blue, gold and pink.[3] The figure is based on traditional images of the Virgin represented as the Woman of the Apocalypse (for example that of the early sixteenth-century Castilian sculptor Felipe Vigarny), but invested with a new meaning.[4] The subject of the Immaculate Conception (the Virgin conceived without sin) was widely represented in Spanish painting and sculpture of the seventeenth and eighteen centuries, notably in the works of Bartolomé Esteban Murillo (1617–1682) and Alonso Cano (1601–1667), as well as in the paintings by Pacheco and Velázquez in the present exhibition [cats 5 and 33]. The painter and theorist Francisco Pacheco was to recommend that the Virgin should be represented as a young girl of twelve or thirteen, and dressed in a blue cloak over a white dress, although Montañés clearly did not follow these precepts in his interpretations of the subject. He produced at least three versions of the *Immaculate Conception*, the finest of which is the figure known as *La Purísma* in Seville Cathedral, dating from 1628–31; the figure from El Pedroso seems to have been the first.[5]

[1] C. López Martínez, 'Montañés y Pacheco en El Pedroso', *El Liberal*, 15.1.1935, quoted in Hernández Díaz, 1987, p.124.

[2] The inscription on the base reads: ACABOSE ESTE RETABLO AÑO | DE 1608 SIENDO CAPELLAN PERPETVO DE LA CAPELLANIA BARTOLOME | DE MORALES RACIONERO DE LA SANTA IGLESIA | DE OSUNA FUNDOLA DIEGO PEREZ CLERIGO. (Proske, 1967, p.151, note 178.)

[3] *Estofado* polychromy was used to produce patterns imitating embroidered stuffs (*estofa*) and brocades: a layer of gold leaf was applied to the prepared surface of the wood and overpainted with coloured pigments; these are then scratched away to reveal the gold.

[4] Stratton, cited below, p.78, p.85, fig.53.

[5] For the figure in Seville Cathedral, see Proske, 1967, figs.175–6. He also made a figure for the church of Santa Clara, Seville (*c*.1621–6); Hernández Díaz, 1987, fig.239. An attributed variant of *c*.1630 is in the church of the Annunciation at the University of Seville, Hernández Díaz: 1987, fig.308.

REFERENCES

Proske, 1967, pp.47–9, p.151 and figs.9, 27 and 28.

W. Braunfels (ed.), *Lexikon der Christlichen Ikonographie*, vol.2, Freiburg im Breisgau, 1974, pp. 338–44 (for the iconography of the Immaculate Conception).

Sevilla en el Siglo XVII, Seville, 1983–4, p.181, no.E.14, (with detailed bibliography).

Hernández Díaz, 1987, pp.124–5 and figs.95 and 96.

Pacheco, 1990, pp.575–7 (for the iconography of the Immaculate Conception).

S. L. Stratton, *The Immaculate Conception in Spanish Art*, Cambridge, 1994 (for the iconography of the Immaculate Conception).

33

DIEGO VELÁZQUEZ

THE VIRGIN OF THE IMMACULATE CONCEPTION

Oil on canvas · 135 × 101.6cm

Trustees of the National Gallery, London

Purchased with the aid of the National Art Collections Fund, 1974

First recorded, together with the *St John the Evangelist* [cat 34], in 1800 in the Chapter House of the now destroyed Convent of Shod Carmelites, Nuestra Señora del Carmen, in Seville, for which they were probably painted.[1]

Both paintings were bought by Bartholomew Frere, Minister Plenipotentiary in Seville from November 1809 to January 1810. According to Frere, he acquired them from Manuel López Cepero, Canon (later Dean) of the Cathedral, who had bought them from the convent on condition that he furnished copies. The originals, Frere adds, were 'at the painters when I bought them'. They were acquired by the National Gallery from his heirs, the *St John* in 1956, *The Immaculate Conception* in 1974.

The Mystery of the Immaculate Conception, the belief that the Virgin Mary was conceived without the stain of Original Sin, did not become dogma until 1854. Much disputed in the Catholic Church since the Middle Ages, it aroused increasing controversy culminating in a papal bull prohibiting public censure of the doctrine (1617). This was greeted with fervent enthusiasm, especially in Spain and particularly in Seville, renowned for its devotion to the Virgin Mary. By then the doctrine was ardently supported by King, Church and populace alike.

The pictorial representation of this abstract, theological concept was codified by Francisco Pacheco, Velázquez's master and father-in-law, in his treatise *Arte de la pintura*:

In this most lovely mystery the Lady should be painted in the flower of her youth, twelve or thirteen years old, as a most beautiful young girl, with fine and serious eyes, a most perfect nose and mouth and pink cheeks, wearing Her most beautiful golden hair loose, in short with as much perfection as a human brush could achieve ... She should be painted with a white tunic and a blue mantle, as she appeared to Doña Beatriz de Silva, ... She is clothed in the sun, an oval sun of whites and ochres which must surround the whole image, sweetly fusing it with the sky. She is crowned by stars, twelve stars arranged in a light circle between rays parting from Her sacred forehead. The stars are painted as very light spots of dry pure white excelling all rays in brightness ... An imperial crown should adorn Her head which should not hide the stars. Under Her feet is the moon. Although it is a solid planet, I took the liberty to make it light and transparent above the landscape as a half-moon with the points turned downward ... In the upper part of the painting one usually arranges God the Father or the Holy Ghost, or both, together with the words spoken by the Heavenly Spouse: Tota pulchra es amica mea et macula non est in te: [Thou art all fair, my love; there is no spot in thee: Song of Songs, IV, 7]. The attributes of the earth will be suitably distributed in the landscape and those of heaven will be arranged, if desired, among the clouds. Seraphim or entire angels holding some of the attributes may be introduced.[2]

Velázquez's image closely corresponds to Pacheco's prescriptions – even to the unconventional transparent moon – except for the colour of the Virgin's robe and the exclusion of the Virgin's crown and the heavenly figures. In addition to the attributes of the Virgin cited by Pacheco and derived from the *Book of Revelation* to St John on Mount Patmos) and the *Song of Songs*, Velázquez has included other traditional Marian emblems. These are mostly taken from the *Song of Songs* and *Ecclesiasticus*. All are included in the Office of the Blessed Virgin Mary:

Mountains, *Psalms* LXXXVI, 1; Cloud, *Ecclesiasticus* XXIV, 6–7; Temple, *Ecclesiasticus* XXIV, 12; Palm, *Songs* VII, 7, *Ecclesiasticus* XXIV, 18; Dawn, *Songs* VI, 9, *Ecclesiasticus* XXIV, 24; City, *Ecclesiasticus* XXIV, 15, *Revelation* XXI, 2; Ship, *Proverbs* XXXI, 14; Sea, *Ecclesiasticus* XXIV, 43; Fountain, *Songs* IV, 12,15; Cedar, *Ecclesiasticus* XXIV, 17; Cyprus, *Ecclesiasticus* XXIV, 17; Enclosed Garden, *Songs* IV, 12.

Since the painting was probably made for a Carmelite convent dedicated to the Virgin, the emphasis on the clouds that billow out at either side of the Virgin as she stands on the crescent moon, suspended above the sea, may also allude to the vision of Elias on Mount Carmel of 'a little cloud arising out of the sea' (*Kings* III, 18, 44). This has long been interpreted by Carmelites as a prefiguration of the Virgin and, in particular, the Virgin of the Immaculate Conception.[3]

The circular temple adopted by Velázquez was traditionally associated with the Virgin and it has a specifically Roman source in one of the temples dedicated to the virgin goddess Vesta, at Tivoli and Rome, illustrated in both Serlio and Palladio.[4]

Radiographs show the lower part of the drapery to have been originally more elaborate, with sweeping folds across the Virgin's legs [see fig 9.14]. The eventual simplification enhances the sculptural qualities of the figure, which must have been still more striking before the darkening of the folds of the outer garment. In fact, the three-dimensional form of the Virgin and the fold structure of her drapery come closer to the polychrome wood sculptures of Montañés than paintings by contemporary artists [cat 32]. Although the composition is traditional, Velázquez's portrayal of the Virgin creates the impression of a living model – possibly his sister Juana (born 1609) – a young girl at the age of puberty, with loose hair and downcast eyes. She is very different from the conventional hieratic, poised and regal model in other versions of the subject. In her person, Velázquez has wondrously evoked the qualities of innocence, humility and piety befitting the *Purísima*.

[1] *Sevilla. Carmen Calzado. Una Concepción y un S Juan Evangelista escribiendo el Apocalipsis, colocados en la sala de capítulo: pertenecen al primer tiempo de Velázquez.* (Seville. Shod Carmelites. A Conception and a St John the Evangelist writing the Apocalypse, located in the chapter house: they belong to Velázquez's first period.) Ceán Bermúdez, 1800, vol.5, p.179.

[2] Pacheco, 1990, pp.576–7; E. G. Holt, *A Documentary History of Art*, 2 vols., New York, 1957, vol.II, pp.222–4 (for translation). See also cat.35.

[3] Cueto, 1991, pp.87, 103 (n.65). For the specific and ancient association of the cloud and the Virgin of the Immaculate Conception, see J. Smet, O. Carm., *Los Carmelitas*, (B.A.C.) Madrid, 1991, vol.III, pp.344–347.

[4] Serlio, *The Five Books of Architecture*, vol.III, chapter 4 and Palladio, *The Four Books of Architecture*, vol.IV, chapters 14, 23.

REFERENCES

López-Rey, 1963, no.21; 1979, no.11.

Curtis, 1883, no.4.

34

DIEGO VELÁZQUEZ
ST JOHN THE EVANGELIST ON PATMOS

Oil on canvas · 135.5 × 102.2cm

Trustees of the National Gallery, London
Purchased with the aid of the Pilgrim Trust and the National Art Collections Fund, 1956

This painting was undoubtedly intended as a pendant to *The Virgin of the Immaculate Conception* [cat 33]. It has the same provenance and virtually the same measurements. This representation of the vision and the visionary as companion pieces would seem to be exceptional. As one of two paintings made for a Carmelite convent, the depiction of St John as a separate image probably reflects the importance attached by the Order to the traditional association of his vision on Patmos with the vision of Elias (Elijah) on Mount Carmel.[1]

Saint John's description of the vision provided the source for the representation of the *Inmaculada*: 'And a great sign appeared in heaven: a woman clothed with the sun, and the moon under her feet, and on her head a crown of twelve stars' (*Revelation* XII, 1). In his depiction of St John's vision, Velázquez has represented the woman winged and threatened by the dragon, in conformity with the Scriptural texts (*Revelation* XII, 3, 4, 14) and conventional illustrations. His pictorial source for the woman was Juan de Jáuregui's engraved illustration to Luis del Alcázar's *Vestigatio arcani sensus Apocalypsi* (Antwerp, 1614)[2] and, for the dragon, Jan Sadeler's engraving of *c*.1580 after Marten de Vos's *St John on Patmos*.[3]

Velázquez's portrayal of St John on Patmos as a young man, not 'old and venerable', does not accord with the view of Pacheco and many commentators, but it does conform to Dürer's interpretation in his celebrated woodcut illustrations of the Apocalypse. Velázquez's model was obviously taken from the life and has features that suggest a mulatto origin.[4] A drawing of St John by Pacheco, dated 1632, [cat 35] appears to have been inspired by Velázquez's painting.

Velázquez has pictorially harmonised the pendants by adopting the same range of colours and tones, and by placing the figures centrally, outlining them simply and clearly, and lighting them both from the top left. With distinct contours and strong contrasts of light and shade, they are equally sculpturally modelled. In each case the focus of attention is on the facial features, carefully painted in contrast to the relatively free brushwork of the draperies. The random brush-strokes visible in the background and foreground are due to the artist wiping excess paint from his brush, probably at the stage when he was blocking in the broad outlines of the composition. This feature recurs in many of Velázquez's works (see ZahiraVeliz's essay pp.79–84).

Velázquez has chosen to represent the scene on Patmos in a nocturnal setting and thereby heightened the visionary effect. Indeed, in the setting of a chapter house which, according to convention, was to be dimly lit,[5] St John and the Virgin would have stood out with dramatic intensity.

[1] B. Borchert, O. Carm., 'L'Immaculée dans l'iconographie du Carmel' in *Carmelus*, vol.2 (1955), fasc. 1, p.108.

[2] Trapier, 1948, p.38.

[3] Justi, 1889, p.78.

[4] Justi, 1889, p.78.

[5] *Charles Borromeo's Instructions Fabricae et Supellectilis Ecclesiasticae 1577*, transl. with commentary and analysis by E. C. Voelker, Syracuse, 1977.

REFERENCES

López-Rey, 1963, no.29; 1979, no.12.

MacLaren and Braham, 1970, pp.129–133.

A. Martínez Ripoll, 'El *San Juan Evangelista en la isla de Patmos*, de Velázquez, y las fuentes e inspiración iconográfica', *Arias*, 1983, pp.201–8.

FRANCISCO PACHECO 1564–1644
St John the Evangelist on Patmos

Pen and ink with greyish wash and touches of lead white on buff paper · 33 × 22.1cm
Inscribed in Pacheco's hand: *6 de setiembre de 1632*. The inscription *Fco Pacheco* at lower right is modern.
Trustees of The British Museum, London

St John is shown as a young man, seated and raising his eyes heavenward seeking inspiration to write his Gospel or the Apocalypse. The eagle on his right is St John's attribute, since his vision of God is, like the bird, the one that flies closest to heaven. It has been suggested that the similarity of the composition to Velázquez's painting of the same subject in the National Gallery [cat 34] indicates that Pacheco based his design on his son-in-law's picture. It is more likely that both artists drew on a common source.

REFERENCES

E. de Gué Trapier, 'Notes on Spanish Drawings', *Notes Hispanic*, New York, 1941, p.15.

Trapier, 1942, p.36.

Angulo Iñiguez, 1944, p.2.

Muller, 1960, cited in cat.5, p.42.

Angulo and Pérez Sánchez, 1985, no.107.

6 de setiembre de 1632   f.co Pacheco

DIEGO VELÁZQUEZ

THE ADORATION OF THE MAGI

Oil on canvas · 203 × 125cm · Dated 1619 on the stone ledge beneath the Virgin's foot.
Museo del Prado, Madrid

A technical examination of the canvas shows that it was not originally extended at the sides as is indicated in the lithograph by Cayetano Palmaroli (1832).[1] It does, however, appear to have been cut at the bottom. Radiographs clarify still further and more accurately than the lithograph the architectural background.[2] The central arch behind the Virgin and Child is seen to be not flat but projecting at an angle thereby giving depth to the setting of the Holy Family.

This was almost certainly painted for the Jesuit Novitiate of San Luis, Seville, where it was first recorded by Francisco de Bruna c.1764: *Noviziado de San Luis. – De Diego Velázquez: Una Adoración de Reyes, lienzo grande en la capilla de los novicios.*[3] Some time after the expulsion of the Jesuits from Spain (1767), the painting was acquired by Bruna, in whose collection it was seen and described by Richard Twiss in 1773.[4] At some time after Bruna's death in 1807, the painting entered the Spanish Royal Collection and was among the exhibits in the newly founded Real Museo del Prado, first catalogued in 1819.

The original location of Velázquez's painting was probably the Chapel of the Novices in the Novitiate, founded in 1609. According to Ortiz de Zúñiga (1677), the Chapel, independent of the church, was the place where the novices practised their spiritual exercises.[5] From the subject, format and size of the painting, it is likely that it was an altarpiece. It is one of the few traditional religious subjects treated by Velázquez in Seville. The Gospel account of the scene occurs only in *Matthew* (II, 11):

And entering into the house, they found the child with Mary his mother, and falling down they adored him: and opening their treasures, they offered him gifts; gold, frankincense and myrrh.

Velázquez's master, Pacheco, devotes several pages of his *Arte de la pintura* to the orthodox treatment of the subject:

The painting will be composed in this manner: The Holy Virgin seated at the mouth of a cave, as described by Nadal, very happy and beautiful, dressed as has been said (in tunic and cloak), and similarly St Joseph standing at her side, rejoicing and marvelling and the Infant Jesus very beautiful and smiling in his Mother's arms; and, contrary to common practice, wrapped in his swaddling-clothes and shawls, as St Bernard has said and Fray Luis de Granada muses: "Oh I wonder at the Child whose swaddling clothes are watched over by angels, attended by the stars and are bowed down to by the followers of wisdom!" The holy Kings, all three prostrate on the ground or kneeling, dressed with elegance and authority; the first one kissing the Child's right foot, which is uncovered, the wrappings removed: but no one should be standing, not even the nearby servants. The old King who is the first to adore should be bare-headed and his head-dress with crown and his offering or gift beside him on the ground; the others should hold their gifts in their hands and wear their head-dresses and crowns; the two animals should appear in the darkness inside the cave. The star should be low and radiating light on the Child.[6]

Velázquez's painting corresponds closely to Pacheco's prescription. The representation of St Joseph as a much younger man than was traditional follows the views of contemporary post-Tridentine writers, including Pacheco. He describes him as 'little more than thirty' when he married the Virgin. The architectural background, *all' antica*, is traditional and signified the old law.

However, Velázquez has introduced some variations on Pacheco's directives. The star is not visible although its presence directly above is implied by the strong light radiating on the figures, especially the Infant Christ. The light of the dawn is perhaps an allusion to His role as Saviour, in accord with the Epistle for the Feast of Epiphany:

> *Arise, be enlightened, O Jerusalem:*
> *For thy light is come, and the glory of the*
> *Lord is risen upon Thee*

The branches of thorn in the foreground relate to the Passion.[7] They may also refer to St Louis, who built the Sainte Chapelle to house a relic of the Crown of Thorns – an attribute of the Saint – and who was the titular saint of the Novitiate. This would lend support to the proposed provenance of Velázquez's painting. The ox and ass are absent, and there is only one servant. It is not the old King who kneels before the Child nor is His foot being kissed. Furthermore, there is no sign of the rich attire, head-dresses and crowns of the Magi in their traditional guise as Kings. In this respect, Velázquez's treatment is unusual. It is conceivable that he was underlining their role as wise men rather than royal as would have been befitting to a chapel of a Jesuit Novitiate.

In this context, the real-life protagonists, sometimes identified as portraits, the details of contemporary costume and the nocturnal setting are painted in a style that is strikingly naturalistic and novel. Both in conception and execution, Velázquez's painting would have been eminently suited to the place where Jesuit novices heard mass and practised their spiritual exercises. In their meditations, the novices would have been inspired to identify with the scene by the realism of Velázquez's imagery with its powerful appeal to the senses. The scene itself would have served to encourage the novices to follow the example of the Magi and propagate the Faith, the fourth vow of their profession. As soldiers of Jesus, they would have found another rolemodel in St Louis, King and crusader, to whom the Novitiate in Seville was dedicated.

[1] Trapier, 1948, p.49, and fig.21.

[2] Garrido Pérez, 1992, pp.67–77.

[3] J. de M. Carriazo, 'Correspondencia de don Antonio Ponz con el Conde del Aguila, *Archivo Español de Arte*, 1929, 5, p.176.

[4] R. Twiss, *Travels through Portugal and Spain, in 1772 and 1773*, London, 1775, p.308.

[5] D. Ortiz de Zúñiga, *Anales Eclesiásticos y Seculares de la muy noble y muy leal ciudad de Sevilla*, Madrid, 1677, pp.607–8, 732. See J. Ainaud, 'Pinturas de procedencia sevillana', *Archivo Español de Arte*, 19, 1946, p.55.

[6] Pacheco, 1990, p.616.

[7] Brown, 1986, p.286, n.49.

REFERENCE

López-Rey, 1963, no.6; 1979, no.13.

37

DIEGO VELÁZQUEZ

ST THOMAS

Oil on canvas · 94 × 73cm · Inscribed at the upper left: S·THOMAS·
Musée des Beaux-Arts, Orléans

According to López-Rey, the painting has been extensively restored around the eye.

First recorded in the Museum in 1843, when it was catalogued as by Murillo. There is no mention of it in the first catalogue of the Museum (1828) and nothing is known of its earlier history. It was identified as a painting by Velázquez by M. Gómez Moreno.[1] R. Longhi noted a similarity to the *St Paul* [cat 38].[2]

Since the Apostles, except for Sts Peter and Paul, are not usually represented as individual figures the *St Thomas* must surely have been intended to form part of a series of twelve. The *St Paul* has been identified as belonging to this series. The measurements are very similar and the inscriptions, which may or may not be original, are so alike in form as to indicate that the paintings must have hung together at some time. They have been identified with paintings believed to by Velázquez, which Ponz records in an unspecified room in the Carthusian Monastery of Nuestra Señora de las Cuevas in Seville: *varias pinturas que representan apóstoles, que, si son de Velázquez como allí quieren, puede ser que las hiciese en sus principos.*[3] However, if they were painted for this Monastery, it is strange that Pacheco, who visited it in 1632,[4] makes no mention of them.

In the period of the Counter-Reformation there was a revival of interest in representations of the twelve apostles as affirmation of the importance of the priesthood (the Sacrament of Ordination), proselytising and martyrdom (Faith and Good Works). Earlier series in Spain had been painted by El Greco and Rubens.

In Velázquez's painting, St Thomas's attributes, the book and lance, which signify his evangelising and martyrdom in India, are prominently displayed. Unusually he is portrayed as a dark-haired young man rather than an aged, bearded figure. This is, perhaps, the most Caravaggesque of Velázquez's paintings. The figure is seen from close to, a pictorial device employed by Caravaggio to engage the viewer and intensify the illusion of reality. With dramatic contrasts of light and shade, the saint, enveloped in a brightly lit yellow-ochre cloak, stands out from the dark background. The three-quarter-length figure is solidly modelled and fills the frame. His powerful presence is enhanced by the emphatic diagonal of the weapon of his martyrdom. The physical impact of Velázquez's image vividly evokes the spiritual fervour of the Apostle as he declaims the Word of God. For the spectator, this would have meant the words of the Creed, traditionally associated with St Thomas: 'And he shall come again with glory, to judge both the living and the dead.'

[1] 'Un Velázquez en la Museo de Orleans', *Archivo Español de Arte y de Arqueología*, 1925, pp.230–1.

[2] R. Longhi, 'Un Tomaso del Velázquez', *Vita Artistica*, 1927, pp.4–12.

[3] Ponz, 1947, p.742.

[4] Pacheco, 1990, p.456.

REFERENCE

López-Rey, 1963, no.37; 1979, no.10.

✠38✠

DIEGO VELÁZQUEZ
St Paul

Oil on canvas · 99.5 × 78cm · Inscribed top left: : S·PAULUS·
Museu Nacional d'Art de Catalunya, Barcelona

This picture was first published by Mayer in 1921 when it was in the collection of Leopoldo Gil, Barcelona.[1]

The subject is identified as St Paul by the inscription, which may or may not be original, and the book. The sword, St Paul's other customary attribute, is missing. His physical type, together with his thick hair and large beard conform to some earlier representations of the saint, which are notably varied.

Together with the *St Thomas* [cat 37], this painting probably formed part of an *Apostolado* (a series of paintings of the twelve Apostles, sometimes including an additional image of Christ). If such a series by Velázquez was ever completed, these appear to be the only surviving paintings that can be seriously considered to have belonged to it. It should be noted, however, that there are significant differences in both the presentation and the painting of the two Apostles, which raise the questions of whether they originally belonged together and whether the *St Paul* is entirely autograph. St Paul appears to be seated rather than standing, though the lower part of the figure is difficult to read. He is placed against a uniform background, the light on his face is less harsh and the modelling of his drapery less sculptural than in the case of St Thomas. The instrument of his martyrdom (the sword) is missing; the book (the *Epistles*) is his only attribute. St Paul's spiritual strength and fervour are here suggested by the radiance of his countenance and the animated lines of his hair and beard. The mood is not dramatic and declamatory, but calm and pensive, anticipating that of Ribera's ancient philosophers.

[1] A. L. Mayer 'Einige unbekannte Arbeiten des Velázquez' *Zeitschrift für bildende Kunst*, vol.56, 1921, pp.35–9.

REFERENCE

López-Rey, 1963, no.34; 1979, no.14.

39

DIEGO VELÁZQUEZ

St Ildefonso Receiving the Chasuble from the Virgin

Oil on canvas · 165 × 115cm

Excmo. Ayuntamiento de Sevilla

Probably painted for the Franciscan convent of San Antonio in Seville, where it was first recorded *c.*1764 by Francisco de Bruna: *San Antonio – De Diego Velazques: San Ildefonso, reciviendo la casulla de manos de la Virgen (esta pintura se halla ya mui maltratada de las injurias del tiempo, por estar en el compás).*[1] Despite its poor condition, the attribution to Velázquez was repeated by Beruete (1898) and has been upheld ever since.[2]

The painting has suffered from severe loss of paint, due especially to exposure to the weather when it was displayed in the atrium (*compás*) of the convent. There was even a large hole in the canvas immediately to the left of the Virgin's head.[3] The provenance and subject of the painting point to a Sevillian origin. The mature qualities of composition and execution – the clear disposition of the figures in space, their modelling in light and the fluent brushwork – place it in the last years of the artist's sojourn in his native city, 1622–3.

The painting represents a vision of St Ildefonso, the seventh-century Benedictine Archbishop of Toledo. As a reward for his treatise on the defence of the perpetual virginity of Mary (*De Virginitate Perpetua Sanctae Mariae*), the Virgin appeared to him in the Cathedral of Toledo during a nocturnal procession to recite the office of Matins. She sat on the episcopal throne in the company of angels and Virgin Saints and presented a chasuble to Ildefonso as a token of gratitude. The cult of St Ildefonso was almost exclusive to Spain and Spanish territories. He was specially revered in Toledo as patron saint and in Seville he was honoured as a pupil of Archbishop Isidore, canonised in 1622, and for his Marian treatise. Seville's devotion to the Virgin was famous. In the words of a contemporary historian: 'Throughout the centuries God has wished that Seville should produce sons to defend the honour and purity of his most holy Mother and our Lady'.[4]

Ildefonso's treatise on the virginity of Mary, first published in Valencia in 1556 by the Carmelite Miguel Alfonso Carranza, was an obvious weapon in the defence of the cult of the Virgin and saints against Protestant attack. It was also perceived as an early defence of the doctrine of the Immaculate Conception.

The vision of the Virgin bestowing the chasuble as a reward for good works was celebrated in many paintings and sculptures in Spain. Velázquez represents the subject in his characteristic manner, a supernatural event in wholly natural terms. The Virgin without her halo and her attendants, who are angels without wings and virgin saints, are unidealised and amazingly life-like. Even their hair-style is modish. The kneeling Saint is a striking figure. His individual features, ascetic countenance and absorbed expression give the impression of a contemporary ecclesiastic. This is strengthened by the fact that he is dressed neither in the regalia of an archbishop nor the habit of a Benedictine, which would have been conventional, but as a cleric.

[1] J. de M. Carriazo, *Correspondencia de don Antonio Ponz con el Conde del Aguila, Archivo Español de Arte*, 5, 1929, p.179.

[2] A. de Beruete, *Velázquez*, Paris, 1898, p.24.

[3] For details of the condition of the painting before and after recent examination and restoration in the Prado, see Garrido Pérez, 1992, pp.103–11.

[4] P. de Espinosa de Monteros, *Historia, Antiguedades y grandezas ... de Sevilla*, Seville, 1627–30, vol.II, f.103r.

REFERENCE

López-Rey, 1963, no.47; 1979, no.22.

40

JUAN MARTÍNEZ MONTAÑÉS 1568–1649

ST HERMENEGILD

Polychromed wood · 209 × 96 × 95cm

Arzobispado de Sevilla

Hermandad de San Hermenegildo

St Hermenegild (550–585), the son of the Visigothic King of Spain, Leovigild, was converted from Arianism to Catholicism by his wife Ingund in Seville [see also cat 4]. At about the same time Hermenegild rebelled against Leovigild, but was defeated and captured in about March 584. He was imprisoned in Tarragona by his father, where he was subsequently beheaded, having refused Communion from an Arian Bishop. At the instigation of Philip II, Pope Sixtus V authorised the cult of Hermenegild in Spain in 1585, where it was cultivated by the Jesuits. The saint is well represented, above all in Spanish art of the seventeenth and eighteenth centuries and particularly in Seville.

The present figure shows Hermenegild in Roman armour, meditating on the martyr's palm and crucifix held in his upraised right hand. It has been convincingly ascribed to Montañés on stylistic grounds. In addition, in 1671 Torre Farfán mentioned a life-size statue of the saint by Montañés, which could well be a reference to this piece. Stylistically, the figure corresponds to the sculptor's early works.[1] The classical poise and grace of the figure would seem to be based in reverse on the *Apollo Belvedere*, and to have inspired Herrera the Elder's rendition in *The Apotheosis of St Hermenegild*, of c.1620 (Museo de Bellas Artes, Seville).[2] The muscular body, and thickly-carved curly hair recall similar features on an early work by Montañés, the *St Christopher* of 1597–8, now in the church of El Salvador, Seville. Additionally, the glossy polychromy of the flesh of the *St Hermenegild* suggests that it pre-dates Pacheco's practice of applying matt colours for the skin.[3] Although the figure now forms part of an altarpiece which was in progress in 1635, it is likely to have been made before this, around 1616. The Chapel of San Hermenegildo was built from 1606 to 1616 by Cristóbal Suárez de Ribera, a priest and patron of the arts, who was especially devoted to the cult of St Hermenegild. The portrait of Suárez by Velázquez, signed in monogram and dated 1620 [see cat 41], hangs in the chapel, so positioned that he appears to be praying before the statue of the saint. Suárez was instrumental in the transfer of the Brotherhood of St Hermenegild from their former church to the newly-erected Chapel of St Hermenegildo in 1616. On 26 April of that year, the procession to the Chapel was accompanied by a statue of the patron saint, which could have been the present figure. Suárez is known to have commissioned a wood crucifix (now lost) from Montañés in 1592, and may well have ordered the statue of St Hermenegild from an artist with whom he was already familiar.[4]

1 F. de la Torre Farfán, *Fiestas de la s. iglesia metropolitana, y patriarcal de Sevilla*, Seville, 1671 (cited in Proske, 1967, p.142, note 57).

2 A. Martínez Ripoll, *Francisco de Herrera 'El Viejo'*, Seville, 1978, p.144, p.14, fig.26. I am grateful to David Davies for pointing out this comparison.

3 See Proske, 1967, p.16 and p.142, note 56.

4 See Hernández Díaz, 1987, p.100.

REFERENCES

Proske, 1967, p.16 and fig 2.

New Catholic Encyclopaedia, vol.VI, New York, 1967, pp.1074–5 (for the life of the saint).

W. Braunfels (ed.), *Lexikon der Christlichen Iconographie*, vol.6, Freiburg im Breisgau, 1974, pp.507–10 (for the iconography of the saint).

Hernández Díaz, 1987, p.269.

41

DIEGO VELÁZQUEZ

CRISTÓBAL SUÁREZ DE RIBERA 1550–1618

Oil on canvas · 207 × 148cm · Signed with monogram and dated: ·DVZ·1620

Museo de Bellas Artes, Seville

On loan from the Confraternity of San Hermenegildo, Seville, since 1970

Much of the surface of the painting has suffered from rubbing. It was cleaned in 1910, following its appearance in that year in the exhibition, *Retratos Antiguos* in Seville (attributed to the School of Seville). The cleaning revealed the monogram and date, located to the right of the sitter. Though the form of the monogram is unique, the painting has been generally accepted as a work by Velázquez since it was first identified by V. von Loga in 1913.[1]

The portrait of this cleric was painted to hang above his tomb in the chapel of San Hermenegildo, which he had founded (1606–16), adjacent to the cell where the saint was imprisoned. It was also at the instigation of Suárez de Ribera that the Confraternity was transferred after 1607 from the church of San Julián to this chapel. He is depicted in the attitude of a donor and shown pointing towards the high altar which is thought to have held a statue of San Hermenegildo by Moñtanés [cat 40].[2] Above his head there is a cartouche with the emblems of the martyred saint (hatchet, palm and cross hung with a crown of roses). The room in which Suárez de Ribera kneels, with its large opening, would seem incongruous as a setting for a funerary portrait. However, the view of cedars and cypresses may well be an allusion to the sepulchral context; a visual conceit on death and resurrection.

Since Suárez de Ribera died on 13 October 1618, the portrait was painted posthumously if the date on the canvas is correct. As he died at the age of sixty-eight but appears younger in the painting it was presumably based on an earlier likeness.

The cleric's connection with Pacheco probably explains how the young artist was commissioned to paint this portrait. When he commissioned Montañés to carve a Crucifixion (now lost) in 1592, Pacheco pledged security for the sculptor.[3] Suárez had also acted as godparent at the baptism in 1602 of Pacheco's daughter, Juana, whom Velázquez married in 1618.[4] The date 1620 on this portrait makes it one of the earliest, if not the earliest, extant portrait by Velázquez. It was in that same year that he received the commission for the famous portrait of the nun, *Mother Jerónima de la Fuente* [cat 42]. Together they make an auspicious beginning to his career as a portraitist.

[1] V. von Loga, 'Zur Zeitbestimmung Einiger Werke des Velázquez', *Jahrbuch der Koeniglich Preuszischen Kunstsammlungen*, 1913, pp.281–91.

[2] Proske, 1967, p.16, fig.2.

[3] Hernández Díaz, 1987, p.100.

[4] *Varia Velazqueña*, vol.II, p.214, doc.4.

REFERENCE

López-Rey, 1963, no.475; 1979, no.19.

✺❀42 & 43❀✺

DIEGO VELÁZQUEZ

MOTHER JERÓNIMA DE LA FUENTE

Oil on canvas · 160 × 107.5cm · Inscribed above inscription on the left: *Diego Velazquez, f.1620*

Museo del Prado, Madrid

MOTHER JERÓNIMA DE LA FUENTE

Oil on canvas · 162.5 × 105cm

Private Collection, Madrid

Mother Jerónima de la Fuente or de la Asunción (1555–1630) was a nun in the Convent of Poor Clares in Toledo, Santa Isabel de los Reyes. Revered for her piety and asceticism, she was chosen to go as a missionary to the Philippines, where she founded the first convent of nuns. On her way to embark from Cadiz, she stopped in Seville, where she was lodged in the Convent of Santa Clara from 1–20 June 1620. After a journey lasting one year, three months and nine days since her departure from Toledo, having spent six months in Mexico, she eventually arrived in Manila. There she founded the Convent of Santa Clara, the first cloistered convent in the Far East, where she spent the rest of her life.[1]

Velázquez must have painted these portraits of the Franciscan nun during her stay in Seville. Despite the importance of the sitter, no record has come to light of the commission or the early history of the two extant autograph versions of the portrait. At some time both paintings must have been sent to Mother Jerónima's convent in Toledo, Santa Isabel de los Reyes, where they were first 'discovered'. It was there that the Spanish inscriptions were no doubt added.

The Prado portrait was first identified as by Velázquez when it appeared in the *Exposición Franciscana* in Madrid in 1927.[2] It was lent by the Convent, where it had been attributed to Luis Tristán. Cleaning revealed the signature of Velázquez and the date 1620. The privately owned painting (known as the Araoz version) was discovered in the same convent in 1931 by the restorer Jerónimo Seisdedos. It was acquired in 1944 for the collection where it is preserved today. A half-length copy of the portrait by a different hand which may originally have been full-length, is in an English private collection.[3] There is a modern copy by Julio Barrera in the Convent today.

The Araoz portrait is generally considered to be an autograph replica, with slight variations and without the pentiments and wipings of the brush that are visible in the Prado painting. The signature and date which appeared on the Araoz painting after it was cleaned in 1942 were proved to be false and have been removed.[4] The Latin inscription at the top of the canvas repeats that of the Prado painting. The scroll with a Latin inscription, regrettably removed from the Prado version because it was thought to be apocryphal, has fortunately been preserved in the Araoz version. The Spanish inscription below, the same on both canvases, though muted in the Prado version, is a later addition. In the replica it appears to replace an earlier inscription in Roman capitals:

Este es verdadero Retrato de la Madre Doña Jeronima de la fuẽte Relixiosa del Couento de Sancta ysabel de los Reyes de T. fundadora y primera Abadesa del Conuento de S. Clara de la Concepcion de la primera regla de la Ciu-

BONVM EST PRESTOLARI CVM SILENTIO SALVTARE DEI·

Este es verdadero ... ...to de la Madr...
Doña Ieronima de la fuete... ... Relixiosa del Cõ...
uente de Sancta ysabel de ... ... los Reyes de T...
fundadora y primera Ab... ... badesa del Conuento de S...
Clara dela Concepcion ... dela primera regla de la Cl...
dad de Manila en filipin ... nas. salio aesta fundacion d...
edad de 66años martes ... veinte y ocho de Abril de...
1620 años. salieron de ... este conuento en su compa...
mia la madre Ana de... ... Chrifto y la madre Leo...
nor de sanct francisco... ... Relixiosas y la herma...
na Iuana de sanct Antonio ... nouicia. Toda personas...
de mucha importancia ... Para tan alta obra...

cat 42

dad de Manila en filipinas. salio a esta fundacion de edad de 66 años martes veinte y ocho de Abril de 1620 años. salieron de este conuento en su compañia la madre Ana de Christo y la madre Leonor de sanct francisco Relixiosas y la hermana Juana de sanct Antonio nouicia Todas personas de mucha importancia Para tan alta obra. (This is the true portrait of Mother Jerónima de la Fuente, a nun of the Convent of Santa Isabel de los Reyes in Toledo, foundress and first Abbess of the Convent of Santa Clara de la Concepción of the first rule in the city of Manila in the Philippines. She set out for this foundation at the age of 66 on Tuesday 28 April 1620. Mother Ana de Christo and Mother Leonor de San Francisco, nuns, and Sister Juana de San Antonio, novice, departed from this Convent in her company: all persons of great importance for such a superior task.)

The Latin inscription at the top of the canvas, in large capitals, is the same in both versions: BONVM EST PRESTOLARI CVM SILENTIO SALVTARE DEI (It is good to wait with silence for the salvation of God: *Lamentations* III, 26).

In the Araoz version, the Latin inscription on the banderole, was removed from the Prado canvas in 1944 because it was thought to be a later addition, has fortunately been preserved: SATIABOR DVM GLORIFICATUS FVERIT (I shall be satisfied when thy glory shall appear: *Psalms* XVI, 15).

These inscriptions may well have been chosen by Mother Jerónima herself. It is recorded that when she took the habit, she committed herself to preserve the silence ordained by the Order; she preferred to speak to God than to speak about God to others.[5]

Velázquez has portrayed this indomitable nun in full-length and in outdoor habit, with cloak and black veil. Following tradition she holds a crucifix in her right hand, in her left a book, probably the Rule of her Order. The position of the crucifix which she firmly grips is the only notable difference between the two pictures. In the Araoz version, Christ's legs are crossed and transfixed with one nail. In the Prado version, the two metal studs at the back of the crucifix indicate that His feet are nailed separately, thus conforming to the representation of Christ crucified with four nails, as promoted by Pacheco (Book III, chapter XV) and followed by Velázquez in his later painting of the subject, now in the Prado. The crucifix in the Araoz version is half turned towards the beholder, making more explicit the nun's missionary role. The attitude and attributes of Mother Jerónima are conventional for representations of saints and other holy persons and it has been suggested that Velázquez may have known the engraving by Miguel Lasne of Father Simón, a priest of Valencia renowned for his holiness but never canonised [see fig 5.6].[6] The process for Mother Jerómina's beatification is still pending.

Mother Jerónima's physical traits are described briefly by Mother Ana de Cristo, who accompanied her from Toledo to Manila and was her first biographer (her biography is preserved in manuscript): *era muy blanca y de linda color ojos garzos, buen encaje de rostro, el cabello era como bronceado muy fino, pequeña de cuerpo, pero bien hecho con aire y gracia.* (She was very pale-skinned with fine colouring, blue eyes, a good countenance and very fine brownish hair; small in stature but well-formed and with a graceful air.)[7]

These words conjure up a very different and more intimate image of a younger person than the sixty-six year old Mother Jerónima portrayed by the twenty-one year old artist. Velázquez has presented an awesome figure, whose rugged features are uncompromisingly represented. In this acclaimed 'true portrait', he has evoked the spirit of this Poor Clare, famed for her piety and missionary zeal.

1   P. Ruano Santa Teresa, O.F.M., *La V.M. Sor Jerónima de la Asunción*, Madrid, 1993, is an up-to-date biography based mainly on contemporary sources.

2   *Sociedad Española de Amigos del Arte*, Madrid, 1927, no.18.

3   J. López-Rey, *Velázquez' Work and World*, London, 1968, p.122, note 1: 'Now that I have seen it I would catalogue it as a copy of good quality'.

4   C. Garrido Pérez, 1992, pp.78–95.

5   Ruano Santa Teresa, cited in note 1, p.26.

6   J. Ainaud de Lasarte, 'Francisco Ribalta', *Goya*, 20, 1957, pp.86–9.

7   Ruano Santa Teresa, cited in note 1, p.82.

REFERENCES

López-Rey, 1963, nos.577, 578; 1979, nos.20, 21.

BONVM EST PRESTOLARI CVM SILENTIO SALVTARE DEI

Este es verdadero   Re
Doña Jeronima de la fuét e.
vento de Sancta ysabel de
fundadora y primera Al
Ciara dela Concepcion
dad de Manila en filipin
edad de 66 años martes
16 20 años salieron de
ma la madre Ana de
nor de sanct francifco
na luana de sanct Antonio
de mucha importancia

trato de la Mad
Relixiofa del Cô
los Reyes de T.
badefa del Conuento deS.
de la primera reg la de la Cru
nas. falio aefta fundaciond
veinte y ocho de Abril de
efte conuento en fu comp
Christo y la madre Leo
Relixiofas y la herma
nouicia Toda'perfon
Para tan alta obra

✳❀ 44 ❀✳

DIEGO VELÁZQUEZ

PORTRAIT OF A MAN WITH A RUFF

Oil on canvas · 40 × 36cm
Museo del Prado, Madrid

It is possible that this portrait was acquired in Seville by Queen Isabel Farnese, wife of Philip V, during the court's stay there from 1729 to 1733. It was then that the Queen bought a large number of paintings by Murillo, the first of his works to enter the royal collection.

The portrait is first recorded in 1746 (on the death of King Philip V) in the inventory of the palace of San Ildefonso, La Granja, where it was attributed to Tintoretto (43; the number is still visible on the canvas). It was still there with the same attribution in the inventory of 1818. In 1819 it came to the newly established Real Museo del Prado, where it is described in the first catalogue by Luis Eusebi as by Velázquez (Salon Segundo, no.113): *Un Retrato desconocido: por Velazquez en su primer tiempo* (A portrait of an unknown man by Velázquez in his first period).

The sitter, with his moustache and goatee, has been identified as Francisco Pacheco ever since Allende-Salazar drew attention to a resemblance to Pacheco's self-portrait in his *Last Judgement* 1610–11 (Private Collection), then known only in a nineteenth-century engraving.[1] Pacheco records that, at lower left, 'between a beautiful youth and a woman I put my portrait, front view and bust length (for I was certainly present that day)'.[2] On the evidence of the engraving (the painting has not been reproduced) the identification is plausible. It is feasible that the painting represents a man of Pacheco's age, the mid-fifties. The sitter also bears some resemblance to St Joseph in *The Adoration of the Magi* [cat 36], which may include family portraits.

The dating of the portrait is not necessarily determined by the ruff worn by the sitter. Although the ruff was proscribed by a royal decree published in January 1623, the ban was not immediately observed.[3] Nevertheless, the painting is datable to before the ban. Stylistically, it unquestionably belongs to the end of Velázquez's Seville period, that is between the portraits of Mother Jerónima de la Fuente [cats 42 and 43] and Luis de Góngora [cat 45]. This striking work is the earliest known bust-length portrait by the young master, foreshadowing his great achievements in this genre as court painter.

[1] J. Allende-Salazar, *Velazquez: des Meisters Gemäldes*, Berlin and Leipzig, 1925, pp.12, 273. For Pacheco's *Last Judgement*, see Valdivieso and Serrera, 1985, p.79, no.143, pl.25 (engraving). Engraving by E. Bocourt in Charles Blanc, *Histoire des Peintres de toutes les écoles. Ecole Espagnole*, Paris, 1869.

[2] Pacheco, 1990, p.313; illustr. p.308, fig.18.

[3] See R. M. Anderson, 'The Golilla; a Spanish Collar of the Seventeenth Century', *Waffen und Kostümkunde*, 1969, pp.5–8.

REFERENCE

López-Rey, 1963, no.549; 1979, no.23.

45

DIEGO VELÁZQUEZ
LUIS DE GÓNGORA Y ARGOTE

Oil on canvas · 51 × 41cm

Museum of Fine Arts, Boston

Maria Antoinette Evans Fund

Luis de Góngora y Argote (1561–1627), celebrated poet from Cordoba, prebendary of the Cathedral and chaplain to the King, was painted by Velázquez during the artist's visit to Madrid in the spring of 1622. The sixty-year-old poet, wearing a clerical collar, was originally represented crowned with a wreath of bay (visible in the x-radiograph below), which the artist painted over. The portrait was painted at the request of Pacheco, who probably knew the poet. He no doubt wanted a likeness of his famous fellow Andalusian as a model for a drawing for his *Libro de retratos*.[1] It is not, however, among the surviving drawings.

The portrait of Góngora was apparently the only painting that Velázquez made on his first visit to the court. Although he tried to portray the new young King and Queen, there was, according to Pacheco, no opportunity. The portrait, Pacheco says, was much admired in Madrid. It is probable that this likeness of a famous sitter greatly contributed to Velázquez's reputation, and won him the invitation to return to the court in the following year. Several painted copies of Velázquez's portrait were made.[2] It also served as a model for engraved portraits. The earliest, by Juan de Courbes, appeared in a work on Góngora dated 1630 [cat 46], and in the poet's collected works published in 1633. The portrait of Góngora is the earliest painting by Velázquez to be recorded in an engraving. The painter's name, however, is not on the prints. The present painting has no recorded early history. Although Pacheco asked Velázquez to paint the portrait, it is not known whether or not Velázquez took it back with him to Seville. This or a copy must have been in Madrid where it served as a model for the engraving by Juan de Courbes.

A portrait of Góngora is listed in the inventory of the artist's possessions at his death, without the artist's name. A portrait of Góngora attributed to Velázquez is recorded in 1677 and later inventories of the Madrid palace of his patron, the Marqués del Carpio.[3] Velázquez's painting is not the only portrait of Góngora made from the life. In 1620 Góngora dedicated a sonnet to a Flemish artist who had painted his portrait.[4] The painter is not identified and the portrait is known only in an engraving illustrated on p.182, that was inserted in the front of a manuscript containing this and other sonnets.[5] The engraving gives his age as sixty and the features are similar to those in Velázquez's painting. However, Góngora looks more frail and gaunt and even timid. The engraver has not been identified but the engraving bears some resemblance to the style of Courbes. The coat-of-arms and the inscription below are the same in both prints. There is no doubt that it is Velázquez's portrait that has made memorable the image of the poet for posterity. In spite of Góngora's ill-health in 1622 – he continually complained of catarrh and failing eyesight[6] – Velázquez has imbued his sitter with energy and vitality by means of incisive draughtsmanship and dramatic play of light and shade. The powerfully modelled head with ascetic countenance, high brow, fixed look, beaked nose and down-turned mouth, evokes the strong character of the sitter, renowned for his learning, acuity and caustic wit.

The poet himself has left this description of his appearance in earlier years:

He is not large in stature, but he could pluck you figs from any fig tree. A normal head, with features well distributed, his nape being at the back, his crown on top. A broad forehead, neat and clean, although, like any town square, it has its nooks. The eyebrows arched like little bows for drawing blood from those creatures recognised by their footprints. His eyes are large, and his eyesight even more impressive, for he can spot a single hound amidst a hundred chickens. His nose is curved to such an extent that it could serve as an apothecary's retort. His mouth is nothing special, but at lunchtime it affords him more pleasure than that of his fair nymph. His beard is neither very short, nor very long, thereby economising on shirt collars. Its colour once was brown, but now is pepper and salt.[7]

Regrettably, the poet who had dedicated sonnets to El Greco and to the unknown Flemish painter has left no record of his response to this arresting likeness or to its author.

1. Pacheco, 1990, pp.203–4; Pacheco, 1983.

2. For copies known today, López-Rey, 1963, nos.497–9.

3. E. Harris, 'Las Meninas at Kingston Lacy', *The Burlington Magazine*, 132, 1990, p.125; López-Rey, 1979, p.325.

4. Luis de Góngora, *Sonetos Completos*, B. Cipljauskaité (ed.), Madrid, 1969, p.100, no.45.

5. Known as the 'Chacón' manuscript, Biblioteca Nacional, Madrid. See R. Foulché-Delbosc, 'Notes sur trois manuscrits des oeuvres potiques de Góngora', *Revue Hispanique*, vol.VII, 1900, p.457. Here and elsewhere the engraving has been incorrectly described as a drawing.

6. M. Artigas, *Don Luis de Góngora y Argote*, Madrid, 1925, pp.327ff.

7. Extract from his *romancillo*: Góngora, *Obras Completas*, J. and I. Millé (ed.), Madrid, 1956, p.88. Translation kindly provided by Michael Woods.

REFERENCE

López-Rey, 1963, no.496; 1979, no.25.

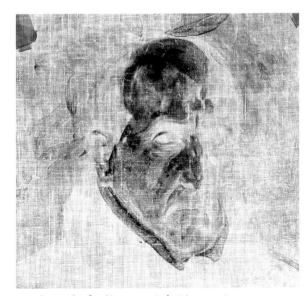

X-radiograph of Velázquez *Luis de Góngora y Argote* (Museum of Fine Arts, Boston)

46

JUAN DE COURBES 1592–c.1641
Luis de Góngora y Argote

Engraving · 13.7 × 13.4cm · Signed: *I de Courbes F.*
Biblioteca Nacional, Madrid

The engraving by the French-born artist Courbes reproduces
Velázquez's portrait of Góngora [cat 45] and is from José Pellicer
de Salas y Tovar, *Lecciones solemnes a las obras de Don Luis de Góngora
y Argote*, Madrid, 1630. It is re-used in *Todas las obras de Luis de
Góngora en varios poemas*, Madrid, 1633.

The portrait is in an oval surround with an architectural frame
bearing the arms of the Cardinal Infante Don Fernando, to whom
the book is dedicated. The engraving, as is usual, shows
Velázquez's painting in reverse. There are minor alterations and
the bust is embellished with the allegorical figure of Fame blow-
ing a trumpet and crowning the poet with a bay wreath, recall-
ing the crown that Velázquez had originally intended. Inscriptions record Góngora's birth, death and status and proclaim his
fame.

REFERENCES

R. Foulché-Delbosc, 'Bibliographie de Góngora', *Revue Hispanique*, vol.XVIII,
1908, pp.105–6, pl.1.

E. Páez Ríos, *Iconografía Hispana*, Madrid, 1966–70, vol.II, no.3885–1.

E. Páez Ríos, *Repertorio de Grabados Españoles*, Madrid, 1981, vol.I, p.251, no.527–
36.

J. M. Matilla, *La estampa en el libro barocco. Juan de Courbes*, Madrid, 1991, pp.3, 23,
104, no.74.

Engraving after the lost portrait of Luis de Góngora y
Argote by an unknown Flemish painter

PRINCIPE DE LOS POETAS LYRICOS DE ESPAÑA ✠ DON LVIS DE GONGORA Y ARGOTE CAPELLAN DE SV MAG.ᵈ

Tu nombre oyran los terminos del mundo

Y PRINCIPE DE CORDOVA Y RACIONERO DE LA S.ᵗᵃ IGLESIA DE CORDOVA

Viuio Don Luis de Gongora LXV. Años. X. Meses y XIII. Dias.

De amiga Idea de valiente mano   Bien assi o Huesped doctamente humano
Molestado el metal, viuio en mi vulto   Copias perdona de mi Genio culto
Emulo tibio; y el intento vano   (Quando aun la Fama del pincel presuma)
Si vida se vsurpo, merindio culto   Que no ai de mi mas copia que mi pluma.

A.   A.   M.   L.   L.   P.

I. de Courbes F.

❧ 47 ❧

FRANCISCO PACHECO 1564–1644
PORTRAIT OF A POET

Black and red chalk over wash · 18.6 × 15cm
Biblioteca Nacional, Madrid

This drawing comes from the *Libro de retratos* which Pacheco worked on throughout his life. At some point it was cut out and separated from the book. The identity of the sitter, whose laurel wreath signifies he is a poet, has been the subject of much speculation. He has been identified variously as Francisco Rojas y Zorrilla (1607–1648), Agustín Moreto (1618–1669), Luis Belmonte Bermúdez (1587–1650), and Gaspar de Aguilar (1551–1623). There is a portrait of the last-named, Gaspar de Aguilar, in the Museum in Valencia and he bears no resemblance to the sitter in Pacheco's drawing.

The most probable candidate is Luis Belmonte Bermúdez, who was an acquaintance of Pacheco whom he would have met in the literary gatherings held in Seville. He was a native of the city and twenty years younger than Pacheco. Both men were friends of the poet Juan de Arguijo.

REFERENCES

J. M. Asensio, *Francisco Pacheco; Sus obras artísticas y literarias*, Seville, 1886, p.74.

A. L. Mayer, *Die Sevillaner Malerschule*, Leipzig, 1911, p.97.

A. Barcia, *Catálogo de la colección de dibujos originales de la Biblioteca Nacional de Madrid*, Madrid, 1906, no.414.

A. L. Mayer, *Dibujos originales de maestros españoles*, New York, 1920, pl.14.

E. de Gué Trapier, 'Notes on Spanish Drawings', *Notes Hispanic*, New York, 1941, p.14.

A. L. Mayer, *Historia de la pintura española*, Madrid, 1947, p.228.

A. E. Pérez Sánchez, *El dibujo español de los Siglos de Oro*, Madrid, 1980, no.198.

Angulo and Pérez Sánchez, 1985, no.195.

Piñero and Reyes, 1985, p.421.

D.ᵗ Albᵉⁿ dᵉ Pacheco.

48

FRANCISCO PACHECO 1564–1644
ANTONIO VERA BUSTOS

Black and red chalk over wash · 29 × 19cm
Patrimonio Nacional, Biblioteca de Palacio Real, Madrid

This drawing comes from Francisco Pacheco's *Libro de retratos*.[1]
It is one of seven portraits which were cut out of the book and
are now in the Royal Library in Madrid. This drawing is accompanied by a literary description which praises the sitter's virtues,
highlighting his gifts as a musician and poet. It also describes
him as a person skilled in making 'objects in ivory and crystal'.
An inscription on the reverse states that the drawing was made
by Velázquez when he was living in Pacheco's house. This is not
credible, however, and the drawing has always been considered
to be by Pacheco himself.

[1] See Angulo and Pérez Sánchez, 1985, pp.40–2.

REFERENCES

Cossens, *The Atheneum*, 25 July 1874, p.59.

Angulo and Pérez Sánchez, 1985, no.192.

Piñero and Reyes, 1985, pp.399–401.

Devida mente sele deve este lugar a Antonio de Vera Bustos, por su buen in=
genio, por su valor de animo, por su Musica i Poesia, sin las demas partes=
de Virtud de que fue a dornado, i por ecelençia mereçio toda alabança en ha=
zer cosas de marfil, i cristal, con que suplia los defetos i faltas de mayor impor=
tancia alos Ombres. cassi queriendo con la propiedad dellas contender con las=
mismas dela Naturaleza que onrrando el Siglo en que floreçio, hizo tan feliçe=
esta insigne Ciudad en hazerlo natural della. i el mismo hizo asu Retrato este Son=

Son

49

SPANISH, C.1550

ESCRITORIO (WRITING DESK)

Walnut, chestnut, boxwood and bone, iron handles: 63 × 103 × 46cm

Trustees of the Victoria and Albert Museum, London

This quality of furniture would have graced the noble interiors of the residences of Velázquez's Sevillian patrons in the residences in which his *bodegones* would have been displayed. The carcass of the writing desk is walnut, and decorated with boxwood, chestnut and bone, the inside is composed of five tiers of drawers, adorned with grotesques and scroll patterns, and two recesses, the doors of which are decorated with medallions. The inside of the lid features a rosette in the centre, flanked by vases, from which emanate scrolls, foliage and pomegranates. The outside of the lid is decorated with the story of Noah's ark, vases with foliate scrolls and pomegranates, with a townscape in the background. Immediately below the lock, a replacement of about 1650, there is an unidentified coat of arms. The edges are inlaid with oblique strips of walnut and chestnut. The sides, to which iron handles are attached, feature vases, flowers and pomegranates, underneath an arch supported by slender balustrades. The top has two rosettes, separated by a series of symmetrically arranged 's' scrolls. The stand consists of a series of three columns at each end, linked by an arcaded stretcher, to which long iron hooks are attached, the function of which is unclear. The stand was probably made in the nineteenth century, not long before it was sold to the Museum in 1870, by Juan Riaño, the leading authority on Spanish decorative arts at the time.

From about 1870, such pieces of furniture were known as *vargueños,* named after the town of Vargas in Castile, from whence they were supposed to have originated. During the sixteenth century, they were known as *escritorios* (writing desks). Examples of Spanish inlay and bone decoration, mostly associated with the regions of Catalonia and Aragon, are remarkably similar to the 'Certosina' work of Carthusian monks of Italy from about 1450. It has been suggested that Spanish work of this type was referred to in contemporary inventories as 'obra de Nápoles' or 'obra de Sicilia', both ruled by Spain during this century. By about 1550 – the time that this piece was made – Islamic decoration, known in Spain as *mudéjar,* was being replaced by the *plateresca,* a form of local mannerism, very much associated with extravagant embellishments on silver. After the appearance of Francisco de Villalpando's translation of Sebastiano Serlio's treatise *L'Architettura* (1552), classical decoration became more widespead in architecture and the applied arts, throughout Spain.

REFERENCES

Victoria & Albert Museum, *50 Masterpieces of Woodwork,* London, 1955, no.20 (no pagination).

W. H. Pollen, *Ancient & Modern Furniture and Woodwork in the South Kensington Museum,* London, 1974, pp.74–6.

María Paz Aguilo Alonso, *El Mueble clásico en España,* Madrid, 1987, pp.139–47.

María Paz Aguilo Alonso, *El Mueble clásico en España – Siglos XVI-XVII,* Madrid, 1993, p.274.

SELECT BIBLIOGRAPHY
AND FREQUENTLY CITED SOURCES

AINAUD 1947
J. Ainaud de Lasarte, 'Ribalta y Caravaggio', *Anales y Boletín de los Museos de Arte de Barcelona* 5, 1947, pp.345–410

ALLENDE-SALAZAR 1925
J. Allende-Salazar, *Velázquez; Klassiker der Kunst*, Berlin and Leipzig, 1925 (4th ed.)

ANGULO IÑIGUEZ 1944
D. Angulo Iñiguez, 'Cinco nuevos cuadros de Zurbarán', *Archivo Español de Arte*, 1944, pp.1–9

ANGULO AND PÉREZ SÁNCHEZ 1975
D. Angulo and A. E. Pérez Sánchez, *A Corpus of Spanish Drawings; Spanish Drawings 1400–1600*, vol.I, London, 1975

ANGULO AND PÉREZ SÁNCHEZ 1977
D. Angulo and A. E. Pérez Sánchez, *A Corpus of Spanish Drawings; Madrid 1600–1650,* vol.II, London, 1977

ANGULO AND PÉREZ SÁNCHEZ 1985
D. Angulo and A. E. Pérez Sánchez, *A Corpus of Spanish Drawings; Seville 1600–1650,* vol.III, London, 1985

BRAHAM 1981
A. Braham, *El Greco to Goya; The Taste for Spanish Paintings in Britain and Ireland*, The National Gallery, London, 1981

BRIGSTOCKE 1993
H. Brigstocke, *Italian and Spanish Paintings in the National Gallery of Scotland*, Edinburgh, 1993 (2nd ed.)

BROWN 1978
J. Brown, *Images and Ideas in Seventeenth-Century Spanish Painting*, Princeton, 1978

BROWN 1986
J. Brown, *Velázquez; Painter and Courtier*, New Haven and London, 1986

BROWN AND KAGAN 1987
J. Brown and R. L. Kagan, 'The Duke of Alcalá; His Collection and its Evolution', *Art Bulletin*, 69, 1987, pp.231–55

CEÁN BERMÚDEZ 1800
J. A. Ceán Bermúdez, *Diccionario histórico de los más ilustres profesores de las Bellas Artes en España*, 6 vols., Madrid, 1800

CHERRY 1991
P. Cherry, *Still Life and Genre Painting in Spain in the First Half of the Seventeenth Century*, doctoral thesis, The Courtauld Institute of Art, University of London, 1991

CUETO 1991
R. Cueto, 'The Wilder Shores of Carmelite Spirituality; Ravens, Deserts, Clouds and Prophecies in the Discalced Reform' in Margaret A. Rees (ed.), *Leeds Papers on St John of the Cross*, 1991, pp.63–104

CURTIS 1883
C. B. Curtis, *Velázquez and Murillo*, London, 1883

DELENDA 1993
O. Delenda, preface by J. Baticle, *Velázquez peintre religieux*, Paris, 1993.

DOCUMENTOS 1927–46
Documentos para la historia del arte en andalucía, Facultad de Filosofiá y Letras, Universidad, Seville, 1927–46

DOMÍNGUEZ ORTIZ, PÉREZ SÁNCHEZ AND GÁLLEGO 1990
A. Domínguez Ortiz, A. E. Pérez Sánchez and J. Gállego, *Velázquez*, The Metropolitan Museum, New York, and Museo del Prado, Madrid, 1989–90

ELLIOTT 1986
J. H. Elliott, *The Count-Duke of Olivares*, New Haven and London, 1986

ELLIOTT 1989
J. H. Elliott, *Spain and its World 1500–1700*, New Haven and London, 1989

GARRIDO PÉREZ 1992
M. C. Garrido Pérez, *Velázquez; Técnica y Evolución*, Madrid, 1992

GONZÁLEZ MORENO 1969
J. González Moreno, *Don Fernando Enríquez de Ribera, tercer duque de Alcalá de los Gazules, 1583–1637*, Seville, 1969

GREENHAM 1969
P. Greenham, 'On Velasquez's *Portrait of a Buffoon of Philip IV*', in C.Weight (ed.), *Painters on Painting*, London, 1969

GRIFFIN 1988
C. Griffin, *The Crombergers of Seville*, Oxford, 1988

HARASZTI-TAKÁCS 1973
M. Haraszti-Takács, 'Quelques problèmes des bodegones de Velasquez', *Bulletin Musée Hongrois*, 1973–4, pp. 21–48

HARASZTI-TAKÁCS 1983
M. Haraszti-Takács, *Spanish Genre Painting in the Seventeenth-Century*, Budapest, 1983

HARRIS 1982
E. Harris, *Velázquez*, London and Oxford, 1982

HERNÁNDEZ DÍAZ 1987
J. Hernández Díaz, *Juan Martínez Montañés*, Seville, 1987

JORDAN 1985
W. B. Jordan, *Spanish Still Life in the Golden Age 1600–1650*, Kimbell Art Museum, Fort Worth, 1985

JORDAN AND CHERRY 1995
W. B. Jordan and P. Cherry, *Spanish Still Life from Velázquez to Goya*, The National Gallery, London, 1995

JUSTI 1888
C. Justi, *Diego Velazquez und sein Jahrhundert*, Bonn, 1888, (English edition, *Velázquez and his Times*, London, 1889)

KAUFFMANN 1982
C. M. Kauffmann, *Catalogue of Paintings in the Wellington Museum*, London, 1982

LLEÓ CAÑAL 1979
V. Lleó Cañal, *Nueva Roma; mitología y humanismo en el renacimiento sevillano*, Seville, 1979

LÓPEZ MARTÍNEZ 1929
C. López Martínez, *Desde Jerónimo Hernández hasta Martínez Montañés*, Seville, 1929

LÓPEZ-REY 1963
J. López-Rey, *Velázquez; A Catalogue Raisonné of his Oeuvre*, London, 1963

LÓPEZ-REY 1979
J. López-Rey, *Velázquez; The Artist as a Maker, with a Catalogue Raisonné of his Extant Works*, Lausanne-Paris, 1979

MACLAREN AND BRAHAM 1970
N. MacLaren and A. Braham, *National Gallery Catalogues; The Spanish School*, London, 1970 (revised ed.)

MALE 1951
E. Mâle, *L'Art Religieux de la fin du XVIe siècle, du XVIIe siècle et du XVIIIe siècle. Etude sur l'Iconographie après le Concile de Trente*, Paris, 1951

MAYER 1936
A. L. Mayer, *Velázquez; A Catalogue Raisonné of the Pictures and Drawings*, London, 1936

MORALES PADRÓN 1977
F. Morales Padrón, *Historia de Sevilla,* vol.3, *La ciudad del quienientos*, Seville, 1977

MULCAHY 1988
R. Mulcahy, *Spanish Paintings in the National Gallery of Ireland*, Dublin, 1988

MURPHY 1992
M. Murphy, *St Gregory's College Seville, 1592–1767*, The Catholic Record Society, Southampton, 1992

NICOLSON 1990
B. Nicolson, *Caravaggism in Europe*, L. Vertova (ed.), 3 vols., Turin, 1990

OKADA 1991
H. Okada, 'La forma de trabajo de los pintores sevillanos en la época de Velázquez', *Velázquez y el arte de su tiempo, V Jornadas de Arte*, Departamento de Historia del Arte, 'Diego Velázquez', Madrid, 1991

PACHECO 1956
F. Pacheco, *Arte de la pintura*, 1638, F. J. Sánchez Cantón (ed.), Madrid, 1956

PACHECO 1983
F. Pacheco, *Libro de descripción de verdaderos Retratos de Ilustres y Memorables varones*, 1599, Diego Angulo (ed.), Seville, 1983

PACHECO 1990
F. Pacheco, *Arte de la pintura*, 1638, B. Bassegoda i Hugas (ed.), Madrid, 1990

PALOMINO 1947
A. Palomino de Castro y Velasco, *El Museo Pictórico y Escala Óptica*, Madrid, 1715–24, M. Aguilar (ed.), Madrid, 1947

PÉREZ SÁNCHEZ 1973
A. E. Pérez Sánchez, *Caravaggio y el Naturalismo Español*, Seville, 1973

PÉREZ SÁNCHEZ 1983
A. E. Pérez Sánchez, *Pintura española de bodegones y floreros de 1600 a Goya*, Museo del Prado, Madrid, 1983

PÉREZ SÁNCHEZ AND SPINOSA 1991
A. E. Pérez Sánchez and N. Spinosa, *Ribera 1591–1652*, Museo del Prado, Madrid and The Metropolitan Museum of Art, New York, 1991–2

PÉREZ SÁNCHEZ 1995
A. E. Pérez Sánchez, *Tres siglos de dibujo sevillano*, Hospital de los Venerables, Seville, 1995–96

PIKE 1966
R. Pike, *Enterprise and Adventure; The Genoese in Seville and the Opening of the New World*, Ithaca, 1966

PIKE 1972
R. Pike, *Aristocrats and Traders; Sevillian Society in the Sixteenth-Century*, Ithaca, 1972

PIÑERO AND REYES 1985
P. Piñero and R. Reyes, *Edición de 'El libro de descripción de retratos de ilustres y memorables varones de Francisco Pacheco'*, Seville, 1985

PONZ 1947
A. Ponz, *Viaje de España*, 18 vols., Madrid, 1772–94, Casto María del Rivero (ed.), Madrid, 1947

PRADO 1985
Museo del Prado, Catálogo de las Pinturas, Madrid, 1985

PROSKE 1967
B. G. Proske, *Juan Martínez Montañés, Sevillian Sculptor*, New York, 1967

REES 1994
M. A. Rees (ed.), *Leeds Papers on Symbol and Image in Iberian Arts*, Leeds, 1994

DE SALAS, GLENDINNING AND PÉREZ SÁNCHEZ 1976
X. de Salas, N. Glendinning and A. E. Pérez Sánchez, *The Golden Age of Spanish Painting*, The Royal Academy, London, 1976

SERRERA 1987
J. M. Serrera, 'Vasco Pereira, un pintor portugués de la Sevilla del último tercio del siglo XVI', *Archivo Hispalense*, LXX (213), Seville, 1987

SEVILLE 1983–84
Sevilla en el Siglo XVII, Museo de Artes y Costumbres Populares, Seville, 1983–84

STIRLING-MAXWELL 1848
W. Stirling-Maxwell, *Annals of the Artists of Spain*, 4 vols., London, 1848

TRAPIER 1948
E. du Gué Trapier, *Velázquez*, New York, 1948

VALDIVIESO 1978
E. Valdivieso, *Juan de Roelas*, Seville, 1978

VALDIVIESO 1990
E. Valdivieso, *Francisco Pacheco*, Seville, 1990

VALDIVIESO AND SERRERA 1979
E. Valdivieso and J. M. Serrera, *Catálogo de las pinturas del Palacio Arzobispal de Sevilla*, Seville, 1979

VALDIVIESO AND SERRERA 1985
E. Valdivieso and J. M. Serrera, *Historia de la pintura española; Pintura sevillana del primer tercio del siglo XVII*, Madrid, 1985

VARIA VELAZQUEÑA 1960
Varia Velazqueña; Homenaje a Velázquez en el III centenario de su muerte, 1660–1960, 2 vols., Madrid, 1960

VELÁZQUEZ. HOMENAJE EN EL TERCER CENTENARIO 1960
Velázquez; Homenaje en el tercer centenario de su muerte, Instituto Diego Velázquez, Madrid, 1960

VELÁZQUEZ Y LO VELAZQUEÑO 1960
Velázquez y lo Velazqueño, Casa del Buen Retiro, Madrid, 1960

VELIZ 1986
Z. Veliz, *Artists' Techniques in Golden Age Spain; Six Treatises in Translation*, Cambridge, 1986

WETHEY 1955
H. E. Wethey, *Alonso Cano, Painter, Sculptor, Architect,* Princeton, 1955

WETHEY 1983
H. E. Wethey, *Alonso Cano; Pintor, escultor y arquitecto*, Madrid, 1983